MAKING THE WHITE MAN'S WEST

MAKING THE WHITE MAN'S WEST

WHITENESS AND THE CREATION OF THE AMERICAN WEST | Jason E. Pierce

UNIVERSITY PRESS OF COLORADO
Boulder

Published by University Press of Colorado
5589 Arapahoe Avenue, Suite 206C
Boulder, Colorado 80303

 The University Press of Colorado is a proud member of
The Association of American University Presses.

The University Press of Colorado is a cooperative publishing enterprise supported, in part,
by Adams State University, Colorado State University, Fort Lewis College, Metropolitan State
University of Denver, Regis University, University of Colorado, University of Northern Colorado,
Utah State University, and Western State Colorado University.

∞ This paper meets the requirements of the ANSI/NISO Z39.48–1992 (Permanence of Paper).

ISBN: 978-1-60732-395-2 (cloth)
ISBN: 978-1-60732-396-9 (ebook)
ISBN: 978-1-60732-906-0 (paperback)

Library of Congress Cataloging-in-Publication Data
Pierce, Jason (Jason Eric)
  Making the white man's West : whiteness and the creation of the American West / by Jason E.
Pierce.
     pages cm
  Includes bibliographical references.
  ISBN 978-1-60732-395-2 (cloth : alkaline paper) — ISBN: 978-1-60732-906-0 (pbk : alk. paper) —
ISBN 978-1-60732-396-9 (ebook)
  1. West (U.S.)—Race relations—History. 2. Whites—West (U.S.)—History. 3. Whites—Race
identity—West (U.S.)—History. 4. British Americans—West (U.S.)—History. 5. Racism—West
(U.S.)—History. 6. Cultural pluralism—West (U.S.)—History. 7. Frontier and pioneer life—West
(U.S.) 8. West (U.S.)—History—19th century. 9. West (U.S.)—History—20th century. I. Title.
  F596.2.P54 2016
  305.800978—dc23

                              2015005246

For my loving and patient Mondie,
my ebullient boys,
and my teachers

for whom this is a small payment on a large debt.

CONTENTS

The trans-Mississippi West seemed destined to foster and shelter the white race. Concretions of myth and reality built up a society in which whites occupied the pinnacle, exercising power and control over non-white peoples. Myth and reality became inseparable, each supporting the other. The resulting society appeared as a refuge where Anglo-Americans could exist apart from a changing nation, a nation increasingly inhabited by non-Anglo and potentially incompatible immigrants. The overwhelmingly white population in certain areas of the West (the Great Plains and the Rocky Mountains) reified the ideology of a white-dominated West, while the mythology obscured the presence of Indians, Hispanics, and Asians in California and the Southwest. The resulting society appeared, therefore, as a homogeneous population of Anglo-American whites, and this became the white man's West. The purpose of this work, then, is to look at how the idea of the West as a white racial refuge and the settlement of the region by Anglo-Americans interacted to create a region dominated by white Americans. Together, the continuing settlement of supposedly desirable Anglo-Americans and intellectual justifications underlying and supporting this settlement formed something of a feedback loop. The myth supported the reality, and reality supported the myth.

Beginning in the 1840s, white Americans increasingly saw opportunity in the West, finding a sense of mission in expansion to the ocean, a belief encapsulated in the term *Manifest Destiny* (and the bane of students in introductory courses in US history). Accomplishing this conquest fell to the rugged, individualistic white settler, the homespun hero of a new American nation. In *The Winning of the West*, Theodore Roosevelt, for example, celebrated white frontiersmen, "the restless and reckless hunters, the hard, dogged frontier farmers [who] by dint of grim tenacity overcame and displaced Indians, French, and Spaniards alike, exactly as, fourteen hundred years before Saxon and Angle had overcome and displaced Cymric and Gaelic Celts." Driven by instinct and desire, these intrepid settlers fought to claim a new continent. "They warred and settled," he continued, "from the high hill-valleys of the French Broad and the Upper Cumberland to the half-tropical basin of the Rio Grande, and to where the Golden Gate lets through the long-heaving waters of the Pacific."[1] Roosevelt argued that these men, while inheritors of a Germanic-English ancestry, stood as representatives of a new people. "It is well," he warned, "always to remember that at the day when we began our career as a nation we already differed from our kinsmen of Britain in blood as well as name; the word American already had more than a merely geographic signification."[2] A continent tamed, the native population defeated, and American institutions rooted in new soil— all marked the legacy of the white man's West. Roosevelt saw in this process a clear demonstration of the continuing march of Anglo civilization. Just as the Saxons and Angles had conquered the ancient Celts, their descendants wrested control of North America from inferior Indians, Spaniards, and Frenchmen.

These lesser groups, in particular American Indians, played merely the foil to the heroic frontiersman. Indeed, Roosevelt's use of racialized terms like *blood* signified his view that race played the key role in determining the success of these new "Americans," a group he saw as having a very narrow racial and ethnic composition. Roosevelt's ideas on race and American superiority were remarkable only in their conformity to the common view of the day: the West had been settled by tough, individualistic, freedom-loving Anglo-Americans. This mythology, and the society it helped create and justify, soon came to seem natural and self-evident. Had not these brave whites tamed and settled the Wild West after all?

While historians and novelists could celebrate a white man's West, the reality proved more problematic. Non-whites had played important roles in the settlement of the region, roles that largely went unnoticed for decades. The West in the nineteenth and twentieth centuries included the largest populations of Hispanics, American Indians, and Asians in the nation—hardly the racial monolith celebrated in the imagination. Yet there nevertheless existed kernels of truth in the idea of a white man's West. The presence of those racial and ethnic groups had indeed been obscured and their positions in society marginalized. In various ways, religion, political values, economic motives, and violence helped carve out areas of the West where whites composed the vast majority of the population (as in the Dakotas) or presided over non-white groups through political control and intimidation, as in California. Through these mechanisms, whites came to control the West, fashioning it into something that approximated the white man's West of the imagination.

In the twentieth-first-century West, the legacy of a society dominated by whites remains powerful, an insistent echo that somehow refuses to die. At issue is the question of who controls the region. As the historian Patricia Nelson Limerick asked, "Who [is] a legitimate Westerner, and who [has] a right to share in the benefits of the region?"[3] When white Americans conquered the West, they instituted a process of control based around racial identity that forced the region's many minority groups to cling to the peripheries of power, society, and even space, as in the case of Indian reservations.[4] Despite its long history of racial diversity, many promoters, developers, and dreamers touted the West as the ideal location for a society of Anglo-Saxon whites. Blessedly free of undesirable immigrants—those Eastern and Southern European hordes, descending upon the Eastern Seaboard in the thousands—the Anglo-American could find refuge and respect in the West. This dream of a white refuge never fully died.

Indeed, the controversy surrounding Arizona's new immigration bill serves as one recent example of the battle over control of the West. Senate Bill 1070, signed into law by Arizona governor Jan Brewer in April 2010, was seen as the strictest immigration law in the country.[5] It mandated that immigrants carry documentation showing their status and allowed police officers to detain and arrest people suspected of being in the country illegally. Governor Brewer and other supporters of the bill argued it would not be used to single out Hispanics. Critics, including President Barack Obama, denounced the law as targeting not only illegal aliens but also legal residents of Hispanic descent. From Los Angeles, Roger M. Mahoney, a cardinal in the Catholic Church, compared the bill's requirements for people to show papers to "Nazism." The Mexican-American Legal Defense and Educational Fund called the act an effort in "racial demagoguery," "cowardly," and "tantamount to a declaration of secession."[6]

Clearly, legislators designed the law to target Hispanics, and some legal residents will likely be detained, if only briefly, by law enforcement officials. The law, however, raises deeper questions and exposes underlying racial tensions in the American West. Mexicans had long lived in Arizona and the rest of the Southwest. They did not come to the United States; the United States came to them with the signing of the Treaty of Guadalupe Hidalgo in 1848. In the decades following the acquisition of the Southwest, the border remained permeable, crossed and re-crossed by those in search of opportunity. Nevertheless, many white Americans have never been completely at peace with the Hispanic presence in the United States. Part of the reason for this uneasiness, beyond simple racism, is that Anglo-Americans never envisioned the West as an ordinary place. In thousands of novels, movies, and cigarette advertisements, the West had long been the crucible of American desires and dreams, and its swaggering heroes had always been white.

As whites began their settlement of the West in the 1840s and 1850s, they saw the region as the nation's last chance to create a white racial utopia. Such a dream seemed tangible, even in the racially diverse West, since American Indians and Asians were denied citizenship and power, and even Hispanics, though technically citizens, often found themselves marginalized. The East, in contrast, witnessed an influx of Southern and Eastern European immigrants in the late nineteenth century, immigrants whose ethnicity, culture, and language made them suspect but who, nevertheless, could be naturalized as citizens since, as Europeans, they belonged to the white races— although such categorization had long been contested. To be sure, practical economic considerations—such basic things as the location of valuable minerals or access to fertile farmland—provided a strong motivation for settlement, but when envisioning their new cities and towns, westerners imagined them filled with desirable citizens. In the minds of nineteenth-century white Americans, a desirable citizen was, like themselves, white.

Racial schizophrenia, therefore, characterized the West, in reality diverse but in mythology a white refuge. The region's wide open spaces, attitudes toward privacy, and supposed status as white man's country attracted extremist groups like the Aryan Nations, anti-government right-wing groups like the Freemen, and extremists like the Unabomber Ted Kaczynski, a left-wing terrorist.[7] Richard G. Butler founded the Aryan Nations in 1974, purchasing a 21-acre "compound" in Hayden Lake, Idaho, that would become the headquarters for the avowedly racist organization.[8] He envisioned the creation of a "Northwest Territorial Imperative," a whites' only homeland to include the states of Idaho, Washington, Oregon, Montana, and Wyoming. Drawing—consciously or not—from the old racial Aryanism and Social Darwinism of the nineteenth century, Butler declared, "Aryans are Nordic in their blood . . . North Idaho is a natural place for the white man to live."[9] Indeed, when the allegedly racist Los Angeles homicide detective Mark Furhman, at the center of the O. J. Simpson trial, relocated from Los Angeles to Sandpoint, Idaho, his choice of destination seemed appropriate.[10]

While contemporary extremist groups sought out the region for its alleged fitness for their ideals, another powerful institution grappled with the legacy of its own exclusionary past. The Church of Jesus Christ of Latter-day Saints, from the time of its founding until 1978, denied the priesthood to black men (all white men in good standing could be priests) on the basis of blacks having been saddled with "the Mark of Cain." As the Civil Rights movement advanced and Americans became more accepting of African American equality, the doctrines of the Mormon church seemed increasingly anachronistic. The doctrine also proved problematic in efforts to win converts in the Third World, regions of the world where the church saw tremendous growth. Thus, on June 9, 1978, Spencer Kimball, the head of the church, announced that he had received revelation from God opening the priesthood to all males "without regard for race or color."[11] Kimball also promised the opening of missions in predominately black areas of the United States as well as Africa.[12]

Millions of people from all over the world received the message and converted. Addressing the church's past perhaps, the official website states, "There are estimated to be between 350,000 and 500,000 members of the Church with African heritage."[13] The church, however, has struggled to change its image as predominately white. In response to the misconception that all Mormons are white, the church's website, for example, assures viewers of their inclusiveness on its "Frequently Asked Questions" section, noting, "There are no race or color restrictions as to who can join The Church of Jesus Christ of Latter-day Saints. There are also no race or color restrictions as to who can have the priesthood in The Church of Jesus Christ of Latter-day Saints."[14] In perhaps the final arbiter of relevance, Google's search engine ranks "Are All Mormons White" behind only "Are All Mormons Rich" and ahead of polygamists and Republicans—despite their best efforts, therefore, Mormons still have some work to do in addressing their past.

Arizona's immigration law, the presence of white supremacist groups in the Pacific Northwest, and the Mormon church's genuine efforts to wrestle with its past are just some of the echoes of an older vision of the Anglo-American West as a domain for whites. Behind these recent events are older ideas and beliefs that shaped, in ways both successful and unsuccessful, the white man's West.

Before launching into the overall discussion of the role whiteness played in defining the West, it is important to wrestle with a few definitions of some major issues. The first is determining the "West" for the purpose of this study. Scholars have long debated the difference between the West and the "frontier" as a process, the former a physical location and the latter an ever-moving process of change. Just as important and no less confusing, scholars have pointed out the myriad differences in environment, ethnic composition, and culture. No less a historian than Frederick Jackson Turner argued that there were four subregions of the West: the Prairie states, the Rocky Mountain states, the Pacific Slope, and the Southwest. Each of these represented very distinctive natural and human environments. More recently, David M. Wrobel, Michael C. Steiner, and their contributors to *Many Wests: Place, Culture, and Regional Identity* struggled to divine the boundaries of the West. Unable to effectively locate the region, they decided to "present the West in all its regional diversity by focusing on many of the Wests that constitute the larger whole."[15]

This study takes a broad view of the role whiteness played in the intellectual and physical creation of the trans-Mississippi West, including chapters on railroad settlement programs in Minnesota and the Dakotas, efforts to define whiteness among the Mormons in Utah, and attempts to square the beneficent climate of the Southwest with the racial history of Anglos, Aryans, and other descendants of Northern European settlers. Each of these places, to be sure, showcased different environmental and cultural characteristics, but each played a smaller role in a larger story of the Anglo-American set-tlement and transformation of the trans-Mississippi West in the nineteenth century. Interestingly, the various promoters and creators of whiteness in the West ignored the larger issues and focused more on issues closer to their subregion. Promoters in California, for example, spent a great deal of time explaining how climate would allow whites to develop a level of culture and innovation unprecedented in world history. Promoters in colder climates, like the Dakotas, instead focused on the similarities between the ancestral climates of newcomers—Norwegians, Germans, and Swedes—and the land they offered for sale. Comparatively few, therefore, focused on the West as a larger region, and none seemed to view the West as homogeneous. From our perspective, however, viewing the larger trans-Mississippi West through the lens of whiteness reveals fascinating patterns. In places like North Dakota, for example, where Northern European whites formed the vast majority of the population, whiteness came to be celebrated as self-evident. In eth-nically diverse places like the Southwest, promoters, in the view of scholars like William Deverell, literally whitewashed the non-Anglo past, creating a white-dominated society with just enough of a non-white presence to lend a sense of exoticism.

Finally, despite the environmental differences, the trans-Mississippi West as a whole came to be settled by Anglo-Americans in the decades between the 1840s and 1890s. This meant that the cultural influences shaping this set-tlement, including the promotion of whiteness as the standard of belonging, were extended throughout the region at roughly the same time. Whiteness provided the basis for meting out privilege and control; falling on the wrong side of the line meant falling into a secondary status. These subregional dif-ferences certainly influenced both the perception and reification of white-ness, but only by studying the West as a larger region can we ascertain the full scope of the process of making the white man's West.

Like defining the West, defining whiteness at first seems an easy task. A white person is, most obviously, a person who appears to be white. Indeed, this seemingly obvious fact informed legal decisions. In cases about racial identity and therefore fitness for citizenship, the courts often deferred to the "man on the street" definition of whiteness. In other words, if an average man walking down the street saw an individual as white, then that person could legally claim membership in the white race. If this sounds subjective, it was. Peoples of mixed parentage fell between categories like black and white, as did various other ethnic groups. At times some ethnic groups, like the Irish in the nineteenth century and Italians at the end of that century, found their whiteness contested. Living in a nation that separated peoples into either white or non-white categories, these newcomers struggled with being in-between. Not surprisingly, immigrants quickly realized the benefits whiteness conferred and tried hard to claim it for themselves. In time, most European ethnic groups succeeded and soon came to be considered as white as their Anglo-American neighbors.[16]

Racial identity, therefore, remained largely a social construction, shaped, defined, and contested by those claiming whiteness and those arbitrating it. As such, it could also be contradictory. A group could be seen as non-white in one locale and then be perceived as white in another, as Linda Gordon's interesting study of Irish-Catholic orphans in *The Great Arizona Orphan Abduction* has demonstrated. The historian Ariela J. Gross, meanwhile, has argued that defining "race" meant hitting a constantly moving target. Americans could use the term to describe the supposedly "grand divisions of mankind" (the Caucasian race or the African race) but also to describe smaller groupings like the "Italian" races or "Celtic" races.[17]

This work, building off of previous whiteness studies, looks at the role whiteness played in setting the West apart as the most desirable region of the country and in defining who controlled what was truly the country's most diverse region. Most westerners, certainly the boosters and opinion shapers featured here, used a narrow definition of whiteness to exclude others. They focused their efforts on appealing to a supposedly declining Anglo-American, a person whose ancestry could be traced to England or the Germanic tribes of Northern Europe. This left other groups, like the Irish, Italians, and other, more recent immigrants, beyond whiteness; but, of course, this proved to be the easiest boundary to cross and more and more European ethnic groups crossed it, at least in part. These groups, nevertheless, could be seen as threatening the domination of Anglo-Americans, and thus it was with no small measure of relief for whiteness promoters like Frank Bird Linderman that comparatively few of these groups lived in the West, excepting perhaps in the mining districts of the Rockies. Indeed, for Linderman, those polluted, immigrant-ridden mining towns stood for everything he despised in modern America and were in marked contrast to the idyllic world of Anglo-American settlers and friendly Indians. Similarly, Hispanics in the Southwest, although legally classified as whites, generally found themselves excluded as beyond the limits of whiteness. African Americans, American Indians, and Asians, of course, could not aspire to whiteness. Promoters of whiteness could then proclaim the region as a refuge from a changing population in the late nineteenth century. The East, filled with suspect recent immigrants, represented a fallen civilization, but the West remained the true white man's homeland— white, of course, in this most limited sense. Barred from contesting their whiteness (unlike those eastern immigrants), American Indians, Asians, and Hispanics lent the region a veneer of exoticism that masked the reality of Anglo domination.

Notes

1. Theodore Roosevelt, *The Winning of the West: The Spread of the English-Speaking Peoples* (New York: G. P. Putnam's Sons, 1889), 41.

2. Ibid., 34.

3. Patricia Nelson Limerick, *The Legacy of Conquest: The Unbroken Past of the American West* (New York: W. W. Norton, 1987), 349.

4. Indeed, sometimes marginalizing Indians was not enough, as promoters often left reservations completely off of maps in an effort not to alarm potential settlers. See David M. Wrobel, *Promised Lands: Promotion, Memory, and the Creation of the American West* (Lawrence: University Press of Kansas, 2002), 34.

5. Randal C. Archibold, "Arizona Enacts Stringent Law on Immigration," *New York Times*, April 24, 2010.

6. "MALDEF Condemns Arizona Governor," Mexican-American Legal Defense and Education Fund, http://maldef.org/news/releases/maldef_condemns_az_governor_042310/ (accessed May 17, 2010).

7. The deep causes of these disparate movements are examined in Richard White, "The Current Weirdness in the West," *Western Historical Quarterly* 28, no. 1 (Spring 1997): 4–16. While the violence White discusses has declined in the last twenty years, the underlining tension, if anything, has become more palpable.

8. The Aryan Nations, "The History of the Aryan Nations," http://aryan-nations .org/?q=node/5 (accessed December 20, 2011).

9. Evelyn A. Schlatter, *Aryan Cowboys: White Supremacists and the Search for a New Frontier, 1970–2000* (Austin: University of Texas Press, 2006), 64–68.

10. See Fox Butterfield, "Behind the Badge," *New York Times*, March 2, 1996, http://www.nytimes.com/books/97/03/23/reviews/fuhrman-profile.html (accessed December 20, 2011).

11. Limerick, *Legacy of Conquest*, 325.

12. Newell G. Bringhurst, *Saints, Slaves, and Blacks: The Changing Place of Black People within Mormonism* (Westport, CT: Greenwood, 1981), 196–97.

13. Church of Jesus Christ of Latter-day Saints, "Mormon Church Demographics," http://www.mormonbeliefs.org/mormon_beliefs/mormon-beliefs-culture/mormon-church-demographics (accessed December 20, 2011).

14. Church of Jesus Christ of Latter-day Saints, "Frequently Asked Questions," http://mormon.org/faq/#Race (accessed December 15, 2011).

15. David M. Wrobel and Michael C. Steiner, eds., *Many Wests: Place, Culture, and Regional Identity* (Lawrence: University Press of Kansas, 1997), 9, 14.

16. Matthew Frye Jacobson, *Whiteness of a Different Color: European Immigrants and the Alchemy of Race* (Cambridge, MA: Harvard University Press, 1998), shows the racialization of the "new immigrants" to America and how they gradually were able to claim whiteness and its benefits.

17. Ariela J. Gross, *What Blood Won't Tell: A History of Race on Trial in America* (Cambridge, MA: Harvard University Press, 2008), ix.

ACKNOWLEDGMENTS

A book project produces a litany of debts, most of which I can never repay, but the many people who provided assistance deserve at least a note of thanks. This project began as a dissertation at the University of Arkansas under Elliott West. Dr. West's advice, encouragement, and insight helped make this a better book. I had long admired his work from afar, but now that I know him, I have grown to admire his compassion for his students, his high standards, as well as his dedication to his craft, patience, and good humor. He embodies, I think, all the great qualities an educator and intellectual should possess, and it was a great pleasure to work with him.

The University of Arkansas was a great place to study for five years, and I would like to express my deep gratitude for being the first Distinguished Doctoral Fellow in the history department. I hope I can repay the investment. Doctors Charles Robinson, Patrick Williams, and Jeannie Whayne served on my committee and provided insightful comments that strengthened the final version of my dissertation. Dr. Whayne in particular has been a tremendous mentor.

Here at Angelo State University, I benefited tremendously from the support of the history department. In particular, I would like to single out the nearly legendary Dr. Arnoldo de León for graciously reading the complete draft of my manuscript and for suggesting many more active verbs. Angelo State also awarded me a Summer Research Fellowship that enabled me to spend two weeks studying at the L. Tom Perry Special Collections at the Harold B. Lee Library, Brigham Young University.

I thank Kim Walters of the Braun Research Library, at the Southwest Museum and Autry National Center, for assistance on Charles Fletcher Lummis. I am grateful for the research grant the Autry National Center provided me as the Visiting Summer Scholar in 2006.

I would also like to thank the staffs at the Denver Public Library's Western History Collection and History Colorado for help with the Denver and Rio Grande Western Railway. Other archivists who gave generously of their time and expertise include Greg Ames at the Saint Louis Mercantile Library, Peter Blodgett at the Huntington Library, and David Whittaker and the staff at the L. Tom Perry Special Collections, Brigham Young University.

Mark Carroll and James Leiker provided excellent comments at the Mid-America Conference on History and the Western History Association Conference, respectively. In addition, several eminent historians kindly answered emails that suddenly appeared in their in-boxes; among them were Sherry L. Smith, Jan Shipps, Quintard Taylor, Carlos Schwantes, and Elizabeth Schlatter. For assistance with photographs, I thank Scott Rook at the Oregon Historical Society, Marilyn Van Sickle at the Southwest Museum, Autry National Center, Kellyn Younggren at the Mansfield Library, University of Montana, and Sarah Hatfield for permission to use photographs of her fascinating ancestor Frank Bird Linderman.

My thanks also to Darrin Pratt, director of the University Press of Colorado, who believed in this project very early on and was willing to offer me an advanced contract based solely on its potential. Thanks to his enthusiasm, I knew I had something worthwhile on my hands. Jessica d'Arbonne, the press's acquiring editor, has also been a friendly and helpful voice of advice and support throughout the development and production of this work. Cheryl Carnahan did a terrific job of editing the manuscript and correcting some of my more awkward literary efforts.

I would like to thank my parents, Marilyn Owings and Mark Pierce, for help-ing me in various ways (not just financially) over the years. My dad's work ethic is an inspiration to me, and my mother has long taught me to explore the world as only a mother can. Both allowed their children to chart their own course in the world. My mother and my sister, Claire Bloodsworth, also put their English degrees to good use by agreeing to read a draft of this man-uscript, and they both provided useful insight.

My wife, Mondie, has found herself hopping around the nation like an "army wife," but she has stayed with me and helped me follow my dream. Meeting her has been one of the greatest joys of my life, and I cannot imag-ine my life without her. My sons, Cyrus and Darius, have shown me that the world is always fascinating to those who stop to see it. Together they make sure I stay away from my work enough to remain grounded.

A NOTE ON TERMINOLOGY

Throughout this work I employ the terms *Anglo-Saxon, Anglo,* and *white.* These terms are somewhat imprecise because they describe arbitrary and contested categories. Anglo-Saxon referred to Germanic tribes that migrated to the British Isles in the first millennia AD and drove out occupying Celtic tribes. Americans, however, used the term to refer to people of English ancestry. This helped differentiate early white-skinned Americans, who migrated from England, from later groups including the Germans and Irish, the first immigrant groups to come in large numbers in the decades after the revolution. The term endured throughout the nineteenth century and into the twentieth century as a way to separate "real" white Americans from the supposedly inferior immigrants from Southern and Eastern Europe who were coming to America in great numbers. Claiming Anglo-Saxon ancestry, therefore, provided a shorthand definition for "real" American citizenship. Out West, however, the Saxon often disappeared, and the term *Anglo* came into wide use to separate Hispanics from non-Hispanics. Following this tradition, I try to employ *Anglo-American* to describe white-skinned Americans of Northern European ancestry, even if the term is imperfect. In general, Anglo-Americans over the course of the nineteenth century came to see a close affinity with other Northern Europeans, Germans, and so on, and often *Anglo* came to mean any non-Hispanic white person.

The most contested and troublesome category is *white*. White is a racial category, an amalgam of European ethnicities into a generic and arbitrary single "race." White or Caucasian differs from black or African, Asian, and American Indian. It also, as used by the US Census Bureau today, includes Hispanics who claim a European ancestry. The inclusion of Hispanics, many of whom have at least some American Indian ancestry, came about with the 1848 Treaty of Guadalupe Hidalgo, which offered citizenship to former citizens of Mexico. Since citizenship at the time required that one be white, Hispanics came to be considered white by the fact that they allegedly had Spanish ancestors. As in the case of the new Americans created with the 1848 treaty, claiming whiteness also proved advantageous since it conveyed citizenship and thus the full protection of law, but, despite the letter of the law, the bulk of Hispanic peoples were treated as inferior, second-class citizens and were informally segregated, especially in Texas. The nation's first immigration law in 1792 formally codified whiteness as a condition of citizenship. Not until the ratification of the Fourteenth Amendment in 1868 did the definition of citizenship expand beyond the category of white.

Yet, and here is where the issue of racial and ethnic identity becomes confusing but also very interesting, white Americans, especially in the West, could use all of these terms interchangeably. When it suited them, writers like Charles Fletcher Lummis and Frank Bird Linderman could embrace Anglo-Saxonism to attempt to build a wall between old-stock Americans and new immigrants from Southern and Eastern Europe whose values and beliefs, they argued, did not fit with those of people already living here. Anglo, meanwhile, endured as a handy way to distinguish between Hispanics and non-Hispanics in the Southwest. The generic category of white, further, effectively locked out American Indians, Asians, and African Americans from inclusion in society. European ethnic groups, however, pushed to be included in this category, as scholars like David Roediger, Matthew Frye Jacobsen, and Noel Ignatiev have argued. In the West (as elsewhere in the country), Greeks, Armenians, and other borderline groups fought, often in court, to be included in the category. While I endeavor to define my terms as precisely as possible, the terms themselves are ambiguous. It also goes without saying that I employ *white American* or *Anglo-American* to discuss the views of the dominant racial group (even though the formulation can be a bit clunky and repetitive). Using white and American interchangeably, as Toni Morrison and others have shown, makes everyone else invisible and makes *white* universal and ubiquitous but also invisible.[1] This is not my intention, but there can be little doubt that Anglo-Americans viewed themselves as the standard by which others were to be judged, and therefore describing them in these terms has utility.

Finally, I use *American Indian* to describe all Indian peoples in a generic sense (since they often were lumped together as such by whites) when they are described as such, but I prefer to use tribal or group names as much as possible. Similarly, while I use *Asian*, I endeavor to differentiate between Chinese and Japanese. For Hispanics, when possible, I employ the narrower terms *Californio* for Hispanic Californians and *Tejano* for Hispanic Texans. These terms appear to be commonly used, especially the latter, although the most common term appears to have been *Mexican* or *Mexican American*. The latter I use as a synonym for Tejano to vary the writing and also because it does seem to have been used; the former, since it refers to a citizen of the nation of Mexico, I try to employ only in that narrower sense.

All these terms can be a bit confusing, but the confusion again comes from the imprecise and constructed nature of these categories since race and ethnicity really have no biological basis. Yet copious amounts of ink and blood were spilled to make these amorphous notions tangible. In the end, the power inside these definitions enabled Anglo-Americans to claim and possess a continent. Whiteness and the closely related concept of white supremacy (the latter essentially an applied form of whiteness) proved tools more powerful than guns in the conquest of the West and the creation of the white man's West.

NOTE

1. See Toni Morrison, *Playing in the Dark: Whiteness and the Literary Imagination* (New York: Vintage, 1992).

MAKING THE WHITE MAN'S WEST

INTRODUCTION

Whiteness and the Making of the American West

In Los Angeles, the pugnacious editor Charles Fletcher Lummis declared, "Our 'foreign element' is . . . a few thousand industrious Chinamen and perhaps 500 native Californians who do not speak English. The ignorant, hopelessly un-American type of foreigners, which infests and largely controls Eastern cities, is almost unknown here. Poverty and illiteracy do not exist as classes."[1] California and the West, Lummis argued, offered Americans a last chance to create a perfect society. Lummis's utopian vision of the West imagined small, orderly cities, productive mines and farms, and a population dominated by Anglo-Americans with enough Hispanic, American Indian, and Asian elements to be exotic. At the same time, eastern residents—old-stock Americans like Lummis himself—feared losing control of eastern cities to Southern and Eastern European immigrants who, unlike Asians and most Indian peoples, could vote and therefore wield power. Lummis intentionally used the term *infestation* to link these immigrants to vermin. Thankfully, he believed, the threat of un-American immigrants existed back East and far from his bucolic land of sunshine (the title, incidentally, of the magazine he edited).

DOI: 10.5876/9781607323969.c000

FIGURE 0.1. Settler's Day Parade, San Angelo, Texas. Parades like this celebrated the Anglo conquest of Texas. Former Texas Ranger and Confederate soldier John W. Long observed the 1910 version of this parade. Sharing his thoughts with the *San Angelo Standard Times* correspondent, he reflected, "I glory in the knowledge that West Texas will always be what we fought for and what the Lord intended it to be—a white man's country." *Courtesy,* Tom Green County Historical Society Collection, West Texas Collection, Angelo State University, San Angelo, TX.

In 1910, a decade and a half after Lummis's pronouncement, residents of San Angelo, Texas, gathered to celebrate and lament the receding of Texas's heroic age. The parade of aged settlers marching down crowd-lined streets moved a correspondent for the *San Angelo Standard Times* to a paroxysm of nostalgia: "The old boys, a surviving remnant of the Old Guard, lined up today and with stride as nimble as that of youth and with step as elastic as that of boyhood's halcyon days, fell in line and proudly marched in grand parade." The paper continued, "The parade was in every way characteristic of the 'Wild and Wooly West.' To make the event all the more typical of early day[s,] pistol shots and cowboy yells rang out as the procession marched down Chadbourne Street." Behind the geriatric pioneers came the police, a military band, assorted ranchers and stockmen, and members of the Ku Klux Klan.[2] It was in every way the epitome of a small-town celebration.

Too infirm to participate, another pioneer, John W. Long, stood off to the side watching the procession. The reporter observed, "Few of the great multitudes who witnessed Monday's parade of Old Timers were cognizant of the fact that there stood in their midst one . . . of the fathers of Texas."[3] Long claimed to have served as a Texas Ranger under Sul Ross at the 1860 "battle" of Pease River, the attack in which Cynthia Ann Parker, the white woman who was the mother of the Comanche leader Quanah Parker, was "redeemed" from a life among the Comanches—an event whose importance to Texas was surpassed in magnitude only by the Alamo and the Civil War.[4] Scarcely a year later Long, like many young Texans, found himself fighting for the Confederacy. Reflecting on his career, Long told the journalist, "I fought for years with the rangers and pioneers to make this a white man's country and fought four years to keep the nigger from being as good as a white man. In the first I won out; in the second I lost, but I glory in the knowledge that West Texas will always be what we fought for and what the Lord intended it to be—a white man's country."[5]

Charles Fletcher Lummis, a relatively egalitarian defender of Indian and Hispanic rights, and John Long, the aged Texas Ranger, had little in common. Both, however, articulated a vision of the West as a white man's country. Long, in his self-mythologizing view of his past, cleared out hostile Indians, thereby bringing civilization to a savage land, and fought against efforts to end slavery and make blacks the equal of whites. He and his fellow Texans had indeed been successful in the elimination of Indian peoples from the state through a campaign of conquest and violence historian Gary Clayton Anderson has described as "ethnic cleansing."[6] His melancholy over the status of African Americans at first seems unwarranted; after all, in 1910 African Americans occupied subservient roles in the Jim Crow South, as any of the dozens of segregated buildings in San Angelo illustrated. Perhaps his lamentation came from the fact that without slavery, the boundary between the races could no longer be drawn with so fine a hand. Texas, however, had certainly become a white man's country. Lummis meanwhile sought a more racially diverse and colorful West, but even in his vision Anglo-Saxon whites (rather than native peoples or non-Anglo immigrants) would control the region.

This book examines how people like Lummis and Long projected a vision onto the trans-Mississippi West in the nineteenth and early twentieth centuries as a white racial utopia and how to varying degrees that vision became a reality. This process entailed several steps. In part one, "From Dumping

Ground to Refuge: Imagining the White Man's West," I argue that early visitors struggled to understand the region, much of which seemed so different from anything in the American experience. Some visitors feared that Anglo-Americans would degenerate into savages in the region or, alternatively, that the temperate climate of the Southwest would lead them into torpidity and sloth, similar to the supposed state of American Indian peoples and Hispanics. Yet as expansion continued, visitors and settlers concluded that, in fact, the climate of the Southwest in particular would free Anglo-Americans from the centuries-old struggle with nature, enabling them to turn their efforts toward more productive enterprises. This intellectual transformation of the West from savage and inhospitable to a seeming paradise marked an important, if somewhat intangible, aspect of the creation of the white man's West.

Yet the West remained the most racially diverse section of the country as large populations of American Indians, Hispanics, and Asian peoples made their home in the region. This diversity seemed in marked contradiction to the idea of a region reserved for Anglo-Americans, but whiteness advocates in the last third of the nineteenth century came to a much different conclusion. These groups wielded little political power. Asians could not claim citizenship and thus could not challenge Anglo-American control, and Hispanics and Indian peoples mostly saw their influence marginalized, the latter segregated on reservations and the former, though citizens, unable to assert political influence in most areas. Posing little threat to Anglo control, they could be celebrated as part of what made the West unique. As the historian Elliott West has observed, these groups went from being people of color to being "people of local color."[7] Romanticized versions of their cultures helped forge a unique regional identity and came to be held up as models by those who feared the encroachment of an alienating industrial society. In particular, writers like Lummis and Frank Bird Linderman and artists like Linderman's friend Charles M. Russell and Frederic Remington celebrated American Indian culture and lamented the conquest of the West and the loss of the authentic "first" Americans who inhabited it.[8] Even Hispanics and Asians could sometimes celebrated for adding variety to the western cultural landscape—San Francisco's Chinatown, for example, became a popular tourist destination. This fetishistic fascination with non-Anglos but simultaneous denial of their political and often economic power enabled these writers and intellectuals to hold the West up as superior to the East, a place supposedly in the grips of an immigrant invasion of largely inferior peoples. Thus Linderman, for example, championed the preservation of American Indian culture while denigrating recent immigrants to the United States, and together Lummis and Linderman could argue that Anglo-Americans retained far greater control in the West than in the immigrant-infested East.

From the acquisition of Louisiana in 1803 to the Progressive Era of the early twentieth century, visitors, boosters, and intellectuals had successfully reinvented the West, transforming it from an alien and dangerous world of possible racial degeneration into a homeland for powerful but increasingly alarmed Anglo-Americans. The land itself did not change markedly, its mountains, plains, and deserts still remained, but it underwent an intellectual reinvention that remade inhospitable into idyllic.

Part 2, "Creating and Defending the White Man's West," looks at efforts to apply the emerging belief in the West as having a special destiny for Anglo-Americans into reality. Developers and promoters consciously worked to organize and fashion a society composed of and dominated by Anglo-Americans and desirable immigrants from Northern Europe, who, though not Anglo, were nevertheless "white" and compatible. In the turbulent 1850s, this meant restricting the extension of slavery but also limiting the number of free blacks in new states like Oregon and California. Both of these far western states successfully prevented slavery, but they also attempted, ultimately with less success, to forbid the settlement of free African Americans. These campaigns, however, demonstrate early attempts to create an almost entirely white society and to avoid the nettlesome racial issue of the 1840s and 1850s that slowly pushed the nation toward war. Forbidding slavery would preclude threats to free labor, and preventing the settlement of African Americans would ensure the continued domination of the allegedly superior race.

Promoting whiteness also came about in less overt but more successful ways. Railroads, eager to find settlers for the lands along their lines, advertised heavily to Northern Europeans, ignoring newly freed African Americans in the 1870s and after who seemed interested in relocating to land on the Great Plains. Railroad companies desired these European settlers (most notably the Mennonites) because they considered them to be honest, hard-working, experienced with agriculture, and, perhaps most important, white. Their success in places like Minnesota and the Dakotas transformed these regions, leaving behind orderly farms and an almost completely white population.

Similarly, the Church of Jesus Christ of Latter-day Saints, or the Mormon church, recruited heavily among Northern Europeans. Missionaries spread out across Europe but soon found Catholic-dominated Southern Europe, an area without the tradition of Protestantism, unsuited to their efforts. This meant that Northern Europeans comprised the vast majority of converts making their way to the shores of the Great Salt Lake. At the same time, Pacific Islanders began to convert to Mormonism in large numbers, but these converts would remain in the Pacific rather than make the long, expensive journey to Utah. Northern European whites, therefore, composed the population of the Mormon's new Zion. However, because of their fringe religious beliefs, mainstream white Americans often attacked the Mormons and in some cases attempted to strip them of their whiteness, arguing that any person who submitted to Mormon authority, regardless of national ancestry, could not be truly white. Nevertheless, Mormons would continue to defend both their whiteness and their status as patriotic citizens of the United States, and in time both would no longer be contested.

The trans-Mississippi West, therefore, in many ways did come to reflect the idea of a white man's West, in practice if not in law. Following the period of conquest and settlement, thousands of square miles from Utah to Minnesota fell under the control of Anglo-Americans and Northern Europeans as the former haunts of Lakotas, Cheyennes, and Utes became farms and ranches. Even in the more racially diverse Southwest, white Americans came to dominate virtually all aspects of society.

Yet tens of thousands of non-whites also made their homes in the West. Promoters like Lummis and Linderman could celebrate their continued presence, but presence did not connote power, and controlling these groups and keeping them in a subordinate status became paramount. Should Hispanics, African Americans, American Indians, or Asians push back (and they did) against their consignment to secondary status, Anglo-Americans had one final tool they could use to keep them in their place: violence.

Across the West, Indians made new lives for themselves on often dismal reservations or existed, as in California, in a kind of peripheral twilight, deprived of rights, land, and dignity. Violence had been loosed upon them to wrest control of their territory and would continue to be used as necessary, especially in California, to control them. Hispanic Californios and Tejanos, meanwhile, saw their landholdings stripped from them and their range of opportunities compressed until they dwelled in a subservient and semi-segregated status. Hispanics and African Americans—particularly in Texas—also sometimes became the targets of vigilante violence. Even in New Mexico, where Hispanics remained the majority, their status and influence declined with the arrival of Anglo-Americans. The Chinese faced some of the harshest treatment, becoming targets of mob violence and the subjects of blatantly discriminatory legislation. Violence, therefore, helped ensure that the West remained simultaneously the most diverse section in the nation and yet almost totally controlled by one particular ethnic group: Anglo-Americans and other acceptable whites.

· This book examines how the trans-Mississippi West, in ways both tangible and intangible, came to be seen as the white man's West, a region dedicated to a narrowly defined Anglo-American and Northern European dominance and supposedly free of the allegedly unpleasant characteristics of an emerging, less ethnically homogeneous nation. Why, though, did this particular region of the nation become so closely identified with one racial group, especially given its actual diversity? Several factors influenced this development. First, in the last half of the nineteenth century, Northeast cities like New York and Boston emerged as the primary points of entry for immigrants, and the crowded neighborhoods these newcomers occupied became symbols of the negative consequences of industrialization. Eugenicists and race scientists warned of the dangers these immigrants posed, especially their amazing fecundity. Some old-stock Americans even compared these immigrants to invasive flora and fauna—all bent on aggressively squeezing out "natives" and transforming the nation.[9] Meanwhile, racial issues could not be overlooked in the South; indeed, they were as obvious as black and white. The numbers of African Americans in the South, quite simply, meant that no one could mistake the region as overwhelming white. That, of course, did not prevent whites from enacting Jim Crow legislation in an effort to protect white privilege and supremacy. These characteristics, therefore, precluded the East and the South from consideration as refuges for whites.

The West, however, offered an ideal place. Lacking the obvious racial binary of black and white, the more diverse region, somewhat ironically, made overlooking racial concerns easier.[10] Indeed, the most obvious non-white peoples in the West, American Indians, had been forced onto reservations (literally pushed to the margins of society) at the same time Reconstruction in the South became contested and an ever-growing number of immigrants entered America from Southern and Eastern Europe. With Indian peoples supposedly rapidly disappearing, as artists and race scientists alleged, the West beckoned as an open and largely uninhabited country. As Elliott West has shown, the 1870s became a seminal decade in the formation of American racial ideas, and in many ways the decade marked the limits of citizenship with the imposition of segregation in the South, the defeat of Indian peoples in the West, and the denial of citizenship to the Chinese.[11]

While these efforts effectively circumscribed the position of African Americans, Asians, and Indian peoples in society, they nevertheless left open the question of the compatibility of new stock immigrants. Indeed, by the early 1900s it appeared to some Anglo-Americans that the East might be ethnically and racially irredeemable, leaving only the West as a possible place of refuge. Promoters grasped the significance of these issues, often portraying areas with high populations of Anglo and Northern European whites as "wonderlands of whiteness," places like North Dakota and Wyoming with overwhelming white populations. Meanwhile, according to the historian David Wrobel, boosters in more racially diverse areas, like California, promoted their landscapes as "wonderlands for whiteness . . . where cultural diversity was nothing more than an attractive background to the main stage where a narrative of white economic and social opportunity and dominance played out."[12] Space and time, therefore, conspired to make the West appear perfectly suited to white settlement; "wonderlands of whiteness" tempted with their seeming abundance and "wonderlands for whiteness" promised destiny brought to fruition. A few decades earlier, the West had appeared as anything but ideal for whites, but interpretations had clearly changed as events themselves had changed.

Finally, mythology also played a role. From the moment the Pilgrims landed at Plymouth Rock, the frontier, always just out there to the west, seemed redolent with possibility. To be sure, it could be a scary and dangerous place, but if one possessed strength, intellect, fearlessness, and individualism (all soon considered "American" traits), then one could be successful in this New World.[13] The frontier, historian Frederick Jackson Turner famously argued, brought out the best in the American character. The frontier created American exceptionalism, Turner declared in "The Significance of the Frontier in American History," an essay that was both paean and dirge, both a celebration of the American character and a warning about its future.[14] By 1890 the frontier had vanished into memory, but the West remained, persisting as the place where American desires could find room enough to roam. It should not be a surprise, therefore, that the West came to be identified with such a grandiose vision as the white man's West, for the region had always been as much an idea, a belief, as a physical place; if it fostered the characteristics that forged Englishmen into Americans, then it stood to reason that it offered the best locale for preserving those values in the face of a changing world.

Efforts to somehow cultivate and nurture whiteness, however, were not new. The belief that America had a special destiny as a white nation, in fact, predated the founding of the United States and remained salient in the years after the Revolution. Benjamin Franklin, in 1751, celebrated the ties between England and the colonies but warned of threats to America, both economic and, more important, racial. The British colonies offered an opportunity, he argued, to create a white sister nation to Great Britain, a sister that would in time grow to be larger and more powerful. This would only come to pass, however, if the crown put measures in place to assure the preservation of the Anglo majority. Franklin worried about the proliferation of white Englishmen. He noted, "The Number of purely white People in the World is proportionally very small. All Africa is black or tawny. Asia chiefly tawny. America (exclusive of the new Comers [sic]) wholly so." Though clearly superior to other peoples, whites felt threatened by the much greater numbers of dark peoples. Yet the leaders of Britain and the colonies took no action to address the danger posed by massive immigration of non-white peoples into the colonies. Slavery posed a particularly troubling problem, as it threatened to unleash African peoples upon the allegedly temperate and fertile North American continent, a situation that would invariably lead to a dramatic population increase. "Why," Franklin asked, "increase the Sons of Africa, by Planting them in America, where we have so fair an Opportunity, by excluding all Blacks and Tawneys [sic], of increasing the lovely White and Red?" Slavery, he argued, was artificially importing thousands of inferior blacks into America. This would inevitably "darken its people."[15] Franklin, like Thomas Jefferson, felt ambivalent about the presence of American Indians. While clearly "tawney" and thus inferior, Native Americans could perhaps be redeemed through civilizing efforts. Franklin harbored no such optimism for Africans. The British colonies in North America could be a biracial nation, composed of the "lovely white and red."

Franklin defined the white race, however, in much narrower terms than society does today. He did not even consider most Europeans, with but a few exceptions, white. "In Europe, the Spaniards, Italians, French, Russians and Swedes, are generally of what we call a swarthy Complexion; as are the Germans also, the Saxons only excepted, who with the English, make the principal Body of White People on the Face of the Earth. I could wish their Numbers were increased," he sighed. Thus even Swedish and German immigrants, particularly in Franklin's Pennsylvania, presented a dilemma. Foreshadowing centuries of anti-immigrationist rhetoric, Franklin wrote, "Why should Pennsylvania, founded by the English, become a Colony of *Aliens?*" These immigrants would "shortly be so numerous as to Germanize us instead of our Anglifying them." They would further remain separate and "never adopt our Language or Customs, any more than they can acquire our Complexion."[16] Such alien people, with different customs, language, and features, would undermine the harmony of the colonies.

Franklin's views point to a fundamental and slippery problem when defining racial differences. Put simply, looking white did not always make one white. Franklin's beliefs on race expose some of the fundamental problems with studying the unstable and ever-changing landscape of race. Race is not a biological reality; it is a social construction, and, as such, it can change and be refashioned to suit the needs of an individual or a group.[17]

Franklin, like generations of Americans after him, made distinctions not just in race but also in what we today call "whiteness." For Franklin, the Germans seemed irredeemably foreign and non-white, but later generations considered these newcomers among the most desirable of the immigrant groups. Membership in the white race, therefore, often rested on one's perspective, location, and time. Whiteness scholars have argued that there have been at least three enlargements of whiteness, when previously non-white groups came to be considered white and therefore full members of society, beginning with the Germans early in the republic's history, Irish in the mid-nineteenth century, and Eastern and Southern Europeans and Hispanics by the twentieth century.[18] Scholars like David Roediger, Noel Ignatiev, and Matthew Frye Jacobson, writing in the 1990s, were the first to argue that ethnic groups like the Irish had to work to prove their whiteness, and to gain that preferred status, they rejected alliances with free African Americans despite their similar social class.[19] Eighteenth- and nineteenth-century Americans, Jacobsen argues, employed terms like *Anglo-Saxon, Celtic, Hebrew, Slav, Alpine, Mediterranean,* or *Nordic* to describe the various races of white people and not ethnic differences. They created "a system of 'difference' by which one might be both white *and* racially distinct from other whites."[20] While certainly not as rigid a distinction as that between black and white, the perception of these "white races" influenced the status and treatment of these peoples in the United States. Anglo-Americans embraced Germanic and Scandinavian peoples because they worked hard, tended to have fair complexions, and often belonged to various Protestant religious denominations. The Irish Celtic race, however, supposedly lacked the self-control and intelligence to be white—at least until the late nineteenth century. Southern Europeans and Jews (the Hebrews, Slavs, and Mediterranean peoples) tended to have darker complexions and large families, and they belonged to the Catholic Church or, in the case of Jews, practiced Judaism. Their cultures, religions, skin tones, and physiognomies made them suspect.

In the trans-Mississippi West, settled at the end of the nineteenth century, many of these issues of acceptance also played out. Elliott Robert Barkan, in his 2007 synthesis of immigration in the American West, writes, "For a number of peoples in the American West the quest for whiteness was largely irrelevant—that is, it was scarcely a hurdle to be surmounted (notably for Canadians and Scandinavians)." For other groups, especially ethnic groups like the Greeks and Armenians, whiteness proved elusive for a long time. Barkan traces how many of these ethnic groups "gradually met sufficient criteria to be regarded as whites, however fluid and inconsistent those standards were. In the West many ethnic groups went from non-whiteness to 'probationary whiteness' to full incorporation."[21] Similarly, uncertainty attached to the status of Hispanics in the West, despite their being officially considered citizens and therefore white.[22] Westerners, though, typically considered Hispanics a non-white group—despite their legal status as white citizens. Linda Gordon recounts an obscure incident in Arizona that illustrates the conditional and contested meanings of race in the West. Gordon follows the story of the adoption of several Irish orphans by Hispanic Catholic families in Arizona. Eager to find the orphans homes, church leaders in New York happily sent them to fellow Catholics in the far-off Arizona Territory. Arizona white women, appalled that Irish children (considered white in Arizona) could be placed in non-white homes, demanded that the children be relocated to Anglo homes. At the behest of these white women, a male vigilante group forcibly removed the Irish children and found them new homes with Anglo families. Being white could, in effect, depend on where one lived.[23]

Attaining whiteness proved critical to success in America because it conferred both citizenship and the right to own property. The nation's first naturalization act, passed by Congress in 1790, limited citizenship to "white persons"—a requirement that continued until 1952 (with the exception of African Americans after ratification of the Fourteenth Amendment in 1868 and some Indian peoples under the 1889 Dawes Act).[24] Such a limitation made sense to American leaders, who held reservations about granting rights to groups they considered incapable of making the difficult decisions needed to maintain the new republic. Whiteness also brought privileges beyond freedom and citizenship, as in ownership of property. Being free meant being an independent property owner. Slaves, conversely, could never rise above being property, and American Indian peoples typically did not own and use property in the same way as white Americans and subsequently lost their lands to whites.[25] Neither group, therefore, could be expected to become citizens.

Americans, to be sure, arrived at these views with a great deal of influence from racial scientists in Europe and the United States. Early racial theorists, like Carolus Linnaeus and his disciple, Johann Friedrich Blumenbach, harbored relatively egalitarian views of the differences between the races of humans and argued that racial differences were really only skin deep and resulted from environmental differences, but by the early nineteenth century their views were increasingly challenged.[26] Linnaeus, who created the system to order and name various species of plants and animals that remains influential today, struggled with the classification of humanity, but by the 1758 edition of *System of Nature* he had identified four major types of humanity (and two fictitious ones: *homo ferus*, a species of wild humans incapable of speech, and *homo monstruosus*, which included "freaks" such as giants, dwarfs, and eunuchs). He named the four races of humanity *Americanus, Europeus, Asiaticus*, and *Afer*, corresponding to the Americas, Europe, Asia, and Africa, respectively. In doing so, he merely classified humanity by geography.[27] Blumenbach modified his hero's classification and inadvertently created the science of white supremacy.[28] The German scientist offered five categories of mankind instead of four: Caucasian, American Indian, Oriental, Malay, and African. He rejected racial differences as merely adaptations to climate, reasoning that all humans had roughly the same intellectual capabilities.

Jettisoning race as a marker of difference, however, forced him to develop another way of classifying humanity. He chose the rather subjective criterion of beauty. Not surprisingly, he decided that Europeans stood at the pinnacle of beauty, and the most perfect specimens, he felt, came from the Caucasus Mountains in Russia. These most beautiful of all people he named Caucasian, a name that became a synonym for white.[29] Together, his five races of man formed a pyramid. As the most beautiful—though equal in all other mental and physical aspects—Caucasians occupied the apex. American Indians and the Malays occupied the level below Caucasians, and Orientals and Africans formed the base of the pyramid. Blumenbach deduced that the most attractive people would be found at the place of mankind's emergence, and other groups, over time, moved away and eventually changed physically to adapt to new climates. Thus, Blumenbach provided a strong argument for *monogenesis*, the scientific theory that mankind had a single place of origin. He intended this pyramid to show the distance from the origin of humanity, with the most beautiful Caucasians signifying the ideal of human beauty and the Malay and American Indians next in his hierarchy of beauty. Orientals and Africans, he concluded, represented the least attractive peoples. Blumenbach was thinking only of "beauty," but it did not take much imagination to see the European view of man's racial hierarchy laid out in his orderly pyramid.[30] Likely unaware of the ramifications of his system, Blumenbach had provided an intellectual justification for European conquest and imperialism.

Blumenbach's monogenesis found a home in the United States, as did his argument that environmental change accounted for racial differences. The Reverend Dr. Samuel Stanhope Smith became the leading proponent of the theory in the United States, reaching his views largely independent from Blumenbach.[31] Smith wore his religious and scholarly titles comfortably, but as the divergence between science and religion widened in the early nineteenth century, the Presbyterian minister, professor of moral philosophy, and president of the forerunner of Princeton University found himself increasingly at odds with both religious scholars (who disliked the questions science asked) and scientists who mocked literal interpretations of the Bible. Smith believed both camps were mistaken and asserted that rational, scientific inquiry could elucidate the unity of man, a unity that was explicit in the Bible. His *Essay on the Causes of Variety of Complexion and Figure in the Human Species*, published in 1787 and reprinted in an expanded form in 1810, became an early and respected American ethnological treatise. He argued that mankind had been created by God in one place, most likely the Middle East where the earliest civilizations could be found. Over time, groups of people expanded and colonized other environments. This colonization of markedly different environments in turn led to the creation of distinct races. A change in climate, therefore, could rapidly alter an individual, and these acquired traits would be inherited by the individual's children. As proof Smith offered the then widely known case of Henry Moss, a black man who had slowly turned white (quite likely from the skin disease vitiligo). The beneficent climate of North America—so different from the sun-baked world of Africa—appeared to be curing Moss of his blackness. Benjamin Rush, America's preeminent medical mind of the day and a signer of the Declaration of Independence, also saw Moss's case as a possible cure for the problem of blacks in America and therefore a solution to one of the nation's most troublesome issues.[32]

Smith endorsed monogenesis in part because it fit with the origin story in Genesis. Yet it also spoke to especially nettlesome questions for the young republic, offering hope that lesser peoples could be improved and one day be integrated into the nation.[33] Given enough time, perhaps African American slaves and American Indians could be improved through changes in environment and assimilation into American culture. Missionaries, especially those to the Indians of the West, predicated their efforts on the idea that Christianization and education could transform the savage into a civilized person.[34]

However, if inferior races could be improved through changes in environment and exposure to civilization, then the opposite could also be true. Monogenesis held out the unpleasant possibility that whites could degenerate when placed in inappropriate environments or in close contact with inferior peoples—both of which would invariably happen in the trans-Mississippi West. Western expansion could therefore lead the individual into a state of savagery and the race into degeneracy. Smith noted, for example, that poor whites in the South already approached the dark hue of the native Cherokee Indians: "Compare these [poor white] men with their British ancestors, and the change which has already passed upon them, will afford the strongest ground to conclude that, if they were thrown, like our native indians [*sic*], into a state of absolute savagism, they would, in no great length of time, be perfectly marked with the same complexion."[35] Environment, he argued, explained this. The sun and bilious gases from stagnant water changed people's complexions and even body types. Over time, whites could atrophy and decline. There existed hope, however. In a footnote Smith addressed the issue of white degeneration and concluded, "The arts of civilization may be expected, in a considerable degree, to correct the effects of the climate."[36] Indians, with no knowledge of civilization, faced the fury of the elements and had inevitably become savages, but whites, with their technology and intelligence, would fare better. Or so he hoped.

The negative possibilities of monogenesis forced Americans to remain vigilant if they hoped to keep racial degeneration from destroying the nation. As the first explorers made their way back from the Louisiana Territory in the years after 1803, their reports spoke of a brutal and harsh environment, a place of savage mountains and vast deserts, a place, in short, that would surely change settlers, and probably not for the better.

Fortunately, for a young nation with imperial designs on the territory west of the Mississippi River, a new racial theory emerged in the 1840s (just as Americans began the manifesting of their destiny), a theory that promised to soothe concerns about degeneration. The monogenetic views of Blumenbach and Samuel Stanhope Smith faded before the rising view of *polygenesis*, which promised to cement the wall between the races and provide a modicum of comfort for people worried about the effects of westward expansion on whites. Polygeneticists believed God had created the races of man separately and had endowed them with innate and immutable characteristics that could not be changed by climate.[37]

This new theory found favor with an array of American intellectuals, including scientists like the world-famous naturalist Louis Agassiz, Samuel George Morton (America's preeminent ethnologist), the renowned Egyptologist George Gliddon, archaeologist Ephraim G. Squier, and Josiah Nott, a southern physician and racial theorist. Together they formed the "American school" of anthropology and dedicated themselves to the idea that the races of humanity had evolved separately. This idea found an eager lay audience among slaveholders and those eager to see the young republic expand to the Pacific. Polygenesis, by asserting that inferior races had developed separately and could not therefore improve, justified slavery as the best possible situation for blacks and the removal or eradication of Indians. It also promised that whites could settle in any climate or environment without fear of racial degeneration.

Agassiz, a Swiss émigré whose arrival in the United States instantly gave American science credibility, quickly became the nation's most prominent proponent of polygenesis, a belief he adopted after coming into contact with American slaves.[38] In an 1850 article in the *Christian Examiner*, he outlined his support for the polygenic theory. He argued that the creation story in the book of Genesis referred only to whites; other peoples had been created separately. Further, he rejected the idea that climate accounted for racial differences, noting, "These races [of man,] with all their diversity, may be traced through parts of the world which, in a physical point of view, are most similar, and similar branches occur over tracts of land the physical constitution of which differs to the utmost."[39] American Indians provided an example of both climatic diversity and racial consistency: "Over the whole continent of America . . . all the numerous tribes of Indians have the same physical character."[40] From Canada to South America, through a variety of different climates, American Indians appeared to be the same. Thus, Agassiz concluded, climate could not account for racial differences.

Since God created the races of mankind separately and endowed them with inherent and immutable characteristics, it would be cruel, the Harvard professor warned, to encourage the lesser races to think of themselves as capable of improving to the level of the superior white race. Far better to "foster those dispositions that are eminently marked in them, rather than . . . treating them on terms of equality," he concluded.[41] Slaves should, in short, remain slaves as nature intended. Agassiz admitted that science needed more study to prove the relative worth of each of the races, but he reminded readers that another renowned scientist, Samuel George Morton, had done much to prove the superiority of whites.

An avid collector of human skulls, Morton believed the size of the braincase, or cranium, directly reflected the intelligence of the individual and the individual's race. Through exhaustive (if heavily biased) research on cranial volume, he came to the conclusion in his *Crania Americana*, published in 1839, and in *Crania Aegyptiaca*, in 1844, that Native Americans and Africans did not match the cranial capacity and therefore the intelligence of whites.[42] Josiah Nott, an Alabama physician, helped popularize Morton's ideas while also making a name for himself as a leading racial theorist and an articulate and intelligent proponent of slavery.[43] Much more than an apologist for the South and its "peculiar institution," his ideas placed him very much in the main-stream of American and European thought on race. He wrote, "Nations and races, like individuals, have each an especial destiny: some are born to rule, and others to be ruled. And such has ever been the history of mankind. No two distinctly-marked races can dwell together on equal terms."[44] Slavery benefited blacks, for as lesser creatures they needed the regimentation and control it imposed, and, he argued, freeing them would place the superior race—outnumbered in many parts of the South—in the hands of an inferior race. More than folly, such a plan amounted to race suicide.

Nott also justified westward expansion by arguing that Anglo-Saxon whites had a duty to take these lands and write the next chapter in the westward march of Caucasians. Nott observed:

> Some races, moreover, appear destined to live and prosper for a time, until the destroying race comes, which is to exterminate and supplant them. Observe how the aborigines of America are fading away before the exotic races of Europe. Those groups of races heretofore comprehended under the generic term Caucasian, have in all ages been the rulers; and it requires no prophet's eye to see that they are destined eventually to conquer and hold every foot of the globe where climate does not interpose an impenetrable barrier. No philanthropy, no legislation, no missionary labors, can change this law: it is written in man's nature by the hand of his Creator.[45]

Here, he asserted, lay immutable natural laws governing white supremacy, and little could change this destiny of conquest, though even Nott hedged a bit, noting that Native Americans might still thrive in climates inappropriate to the white race.[46]

These beliefs and ideas, the cultural baggage carried by any society, informed Americans' views and justified their conquest, and they willingly toted them along with the rest of their baggage into the West. Some of this baggage, aptly captured in John O'Sullivan's phrase *Manifest Destiny*, foretold God's plan for Americans to "overspread and possess the whole of the continent."[47] God sanctioned this conquest and blessed the success of America's divine mission, but God had an ally in science. Race science claimed the inherent superiority of Anglo-Americans and the inevitability of their conquest over lesser peoples, an argument that buttressed the divine mandate in Manifest Destiny. Filtering the new environments of the West— its vast plains, high mountains, and desiccated deserts—and the people who lived in them through their own biases and perceptions, they struggled to comprehend these seemingly strange landscapes and peoples, but racial science seemed to offer solace in the face of uncertainty. As Americans ventured into the West, they wore their beliefs in Manifest Destiny and their own racial superiority like armor, but like all armor it covered up their own uncertainty and vulnerability.

Would the academic arguments of polygenesis stand up to the West? Anglo-Americans, after all, would inevitably come into contact with supposedly inferior Indian and Hispanic peoples and unfamiliar climates that differed markedly from the East Coast or the ancestral homeland of Europe. Would white racial vigor triumph, or would racial degeneration and savagery overwhelm these newcomers, leaving them as weak and impotent as the Spaniards in the Spanish empire had allegedly become? If there existed a chance of degeneration, then could the West, on the other hand, be used as a kind of racial dumping ground, a place where freed African Americans and eastern American Indian peoples could be relegated to racially cleanse the nation? All of these seemed like possibilities as Americans stood on the shore of the Mississippi and looked west into the Louisiana Territory.[48] It was here that Americans first glimpsed the racial potential of the West. Would it be a dumping ground, an American Siberia, where the least desirable and compatible groups could be forever consigned to the margins of the nation, or would the region offer white Americans a never-ending frontier? It was here that the story of the white man's West began.

Notes

1. Charles Fletcher Lummis, "Los Angeles: Metropolis of the Southwest," *Land of Sunshine* 3, no. 1 (June 1895): 43–48; quote on 46.

2. "Parade Characteristic of Wild and Wooly West," *San Angelo Standard Times*, October 4, 1910.

3. Ibid.

4. For more on this minor battle but major event, see Paul H. Carlson and Tom Crum, *Myth, Memory, and Massacre: The Pease River Capture of Cynthia Ann Parker* (Lubbock: Texas Tech University Press, 2010).

5. "He Fought for a White Man's Country," *San Angelo Standard Times*, October 5, 1910. I am indebted to Matthew Johnston, an MA student in the Angelo State University history department, for finding this extraordinary quote.

6. See Gary Clayton Anderson, *The Conquest of Texas: Ethnic Cleansing in the Promised Land, 1820–1875* (Norman: University of Oklahoma Press, 2005).

7. Elliott West, "Reconstructing Race," in *The Essential West: Collected Essays* (Norman: University of Oklahoma Press, 2012), 100–126, quote on p. 117.

8. On Russell and Remington's work, see Richard W. Etulain, *Re-Imagining the Modern American West: A Century of Fiction, History, and Art* (Tucson: University of Arizona Press, 1996), 52–68.

9. This interesting comparison is discussed in Peter Coates, *American Perceptions of Immigrant and Invasive Species: Strangers on the Land* (Berkeley: University of California Press, 2006).

10. An interesting group of essays wrestles with this issue. See Stephanie Cole and Alison Parker, eds., *Beyond Black and White: Race, Ethnicity, and Gender in the U.S. South and Southwest* (College Station: Texas A&M University Press, 2004).

11. West's most recent discussion of these themes appears in West, "Reconstructing Race," 100–126.

12. David M. Wrobel, *Promised Lands: Promotion, Memory, and the Creation of the American West* (Lawrence: University Press of Kansas, 2002), 176.

13. On the scary aspects of wilderness, see Roderick Nash, *Wilderness and the American Mind* (New Haven, CT: Yale University Press, 1967). For the West as a land of promise and desire, see Henry Nash Smith, *Virgin Land: The American West as Symbol and Myth* (Cambridge, MA: Harvard University Press, 1950).

14. Frederick Jackson Turner, "The Significance of the Frontier in American History," in John Mack Faragher, ed., *Rereading Frederick Jackson Turner* (New York: Henry Holt, 1994), 31–60.

15. Benjamin Franklin, "Observations Concerning the Increase of Mankind," in Leonard Labaree, ed., *The Papers of Benjamin Franklin* (New Haven, CT: Yale University Press, 1961), 4:234.

16. Ibid.; italics in original.

17. The most recent effort to trace the development of whiteness theory, and a very helpful synthesis, is Nell Irvin Painter, *The History of White People* (New York: W. W. Norton, 2010).

18. Ibid., especially chapters 9, 14, and 26.

19. Some of the more important works on whiteness theory are David R. Roediger, *The Wages of Whiteness: Race and the Making of the American Working Class* (New York: Verso, 1991); Noel Ignatiev, *How the Irish Became White* (New York: Routledge, 1995); Matthew Frye Jacobson, *Whiteness of a Different Color: European Immigrants and the Alchemy of Race* (Cambridge, MA: Harvard University Press, 1998); George Lipsitz, *The Possessive Investment in Whiteness: How White People Profit from Identity Politics* (Philadelphia: Temple University Press, 2006).

20. Jacobson, *Whiteness of a Different Color*, 6; italics in original.

21. Elliott Robert Barkan, *From All Points: America's Immigrant West, 1870s–1952* (Bloomington: Indiana University Press, 2007), 6–13. For the story of Anglo and Hispanic interactions, see David J. Weber, ed., *Foreigners in Their Native Land: Historical Roots of the Mexican-Americans* (Albuquerque: University of New Mexico Press, 1973; reprint, 2003); David J. Weber, ed., *New Spain's Far Northern Frontier: Essays on Spain in the American West* (Albuquerque: University of New Mexico Press, 1979); Arnoldo De León, *Racial Frontiers: Africans, Chinese, and Mexicans in Western America, 1848–1890* (Albuquerque: University of New Mexico Press, 2002); Arnoldo De León, *They Called Them Greasers: Anglo Attitudes toward Mexicans in Texas, 1821–1900* (Austin: University of Texas Press, 1983); Mark M. Carroll, *Homesteads Ungovernable: Families, Sex, Race, and the Law in Frontier Texas, 1823–1860* (Austin: University of Texas Press, 2001). David M. Emmons traces the history of the Irish in *Beyond the American Pale: The Irish in the West, 1845–1910* (Norman: University of Oklahoma Press, 2010).

22. Numerous works have addressed the status of Hispanics in the United States. For more on their generally poor treatment, see De León, *They Called Them Greasers*. For the political debates over ethnicity and citizenship, see David Gutierrez, *Walls and Mirrors: Mexican Americans, Mexican Immigrants and the Politics of Ethnicity* (Berkley: University of California Press, 1995).

23. Linda Gordon, *The Great Arizona Orphan Abduction* (Cambridge, MA: Harvard University Press, 1999).

24. Ian Haney López, *White by Law: The Legal Construction of Race* (New York: New York University Press, 1996), 1.

25. Cheryl Harris, "Whiteness as Property," *Harvard Law Review* 106, no. 8 (June 1993): 1709–91.

26. On the origins of racial science, see William Stanton, *The Leopard's Spots: Scientific Attitudes toward Race in America, 1815–59* (Chicago: University of Chicago Press, 1960); Thomas F. Gossett, *Race: The History of an Idea in America* (Dallas: Southern Methodist University Press, 1963), 54–83; Robert E. Bieder, *Science Encounters the Indian, 1820–1880: The Early Years of American Ethnology* (Norman: University of Oklahoma Press, 1986); Reginald Horsman, *Race and Manifest Destiny: The Origins*

of American Racial Anglo-Saxonism (Cambridge, MA: Harvard University Press, 1981), 116–57; Gustav Jahoda, *Images of Savages: Ancients [sic] Roots of Modern Prejudice in Western Culture* (New York: Routledge, 1999), 63–96; Joseph L. Graves Jr., *The Emperor's New Clothes: Biological Theories of Race at the Millennium* (New Brunswick, NJ: Rutgers University Press, 2001); Stephen J. Gould, *The Mismeasure of Man* (New York: W. W. Norton, 1981); Audrey Smedley, *Race in North America: Origin and Evolution of a Worldview* (Boulder: Westview, 1993); Bentley Glass, Owsei Temkin, and William L. Straus Jr., eds., *Forerunners of Darwin: 1745–1859* (Baltimore: Johns Hopkins University Press, 1959).

27. Gould, *The Mismeasure of Man*, 66, 401–12; Gossett, *Race*, 35; Jahoda, *Images of Savages*, 40–41; Graves, *The Emperor's New Clothes*, 38–39. Not everyone believes that Linnaeus was as color-blind as Gould asserts. See, for example, Patrick Brantlinger, *Dark Vanishings: Discourse on the Extinction of Primitive Races, 1800–1930* (Ithaca, NY: Cornell University Press, 2003), 2, 17.

28. Gould, *The Mismeasure of Man*, 401–12; Graves, *The Emperor's New Clothes*, 40.

29. Gould, *The Mismeasure of Man*, 401–12; Horsman, *Race and Manifest Destiny*, 47–48; Painter, *History of White People*, 72–90.

30. Gould, *The Mismeasure of Man*, 401–12; Horsman, *Race and Manifest Destiny*, 47–48.

31. A concise biographical account of Smith's life and work, including his knowledge of Blumenbach, is found in the introduction by Winthrop D. Jordan in Samuel Stanhope Smith, *Essay on the Variety of Complexion and Figure in the Human Species* (Cambridge, MA: Belknap Press of Harvard University Press, 1965), vii–liii. Also see Gossett, *Race*, 39–41; Stanton, *The Leopard's Spots*, 3–23.

32. On Rush and the problem of including African Americans in American society, see Ronald T. Takaki, *Iron Cages: Race and Culture in Nineteenth-Century America* (New York: Alfred A. Knopf, 1979), 28–35.

33. Bruce Dain, *A Hideous Monster of the Mind: American Race Theory in the Early Republic* (Cambridge, MA: Harvard University Press, 2002), viii.

34. For the early period of US Indian policy and early missionary efforts, see Francis Paul Prucha, *American Indian Policy in the Formative Years: The Indian Trade and Intercourse Acts, 1790–1834* (Lincoln: University of Nebraska Press, 1970); Francis Paul Prucha, *The Great Father: The United States Government and the American Indians*, 2 vol. (Lincoln: University of Nebraska Press, 1984); James P. Ronda, *Lewis and Clark among the Indians* (Lincoln: University of Nebraska Press, 1984); Julie Roy Jeffrey, *Converting the West: A Biography of Narcissa Whitman* (Norman: University of Oklahoma Press, 1991). For general discussions of reformers' efforts to "civilize" Indian peoples after 1865, see Francis Paul Prucha, *American Indian Policy in Crisis: Christian Reformers and the Indian, 1865–1900* (Norman: University of Oklahoma Press, 1977);

Robert M. Utley, *The Indian Frontier of the American West, 1846–1900* (Albuquerque: University of New Mexico Press, 1984), 203–26.

35. Smith, *Essay on the Variety of Complexion and Figure in the Human Species*, 44. It is interesting that poor whites have often been considered racially inferior; see, for example, Painter, *History of White People*, 256–77; Matt Wray, *Not Quite White: White Trash and the Boundaries of Whiteness* (Durham, NC: Duke University Press, 2006).

36. Smith, *Essay on the Variety of Complexion and Figure in the Human Species*, 45.

37. Discussions of *polygenic* versus *monogenic* origins are found in Conevery Bolton Valenčius, *The Health of the Country: How American Settlers Understood Themselves and Their Land* (New York: Perseus Books Group, 2002), 235–36; Horsman, *Race and Manifest Destiny*, 44–45; Gould, *The Mismeasure of Man*, 71–74; Stanton, *The Leopard's Spots*, 1–15; Curtis M. Hinsley Jr., *Savages and Scientists: The Smithsonian Institution and the Development of American Anthropology, 1846–1910* (Washington, DC: Smithsonian Institution Press, 1981), 22–28; Gossett, *Race*, 44–51, 58–67; Graves, *The Emperor's New Clothes*, 37–52; Smedley, *Race in North America*, 234–43.

38. Gould, *The Mismeasure of Man*, 74–82; Stanton, *The Leopard's Spots*, 100–109.

39. Louis Agassiz, "The Diversity of Origin of the Human Races," *Christian Examiner* 49 (1850): 123.

40. Ibid., 126.

41. Ibid., 144.

42. Reginald Horsman discusses Morton's influence in *Race and Manifest Destiny*, 125–27, and Stephen J. Gould exposes the flaws in Morton's work in *The Mismeasure of Man*, 82–104.

43. Josiah Nott's life is analyzed in depth in Reginald Horsman, *Josiah Nott of Mobile: Southerner, Physician, and Racial Theorist* (Baton Rouge: Louisiana State University Press, 1987). Nott's importance is also covered in Gould, *The Mismeasure of Man*, 101–2; Valenčius, *Health of the Country*, 234–35; Horsman, *Race and Manifest Destiny*, 129–57.

44. J[osiah] C[lark] Nott and Geo[rge] R. Gliddon, *Types of Mankind: or, Ethnological Researches, Based upon the Ancient Monuments, Paintings, Sculptures, and Crania of Races, and upon Their Natural, Geographical, Philological and Biblical History* (Philadelphia: Lippincott, Grambo, 1855), 79.

45. Ibid.

46. On the supposed extinction of inferior peoples, see Brantlinger, *Dark Vanishings*; Brian Dippie, *The Vanishing American: White Attitudes and US Indian Policy* (Lawrence: University Press of Kansas, 1982).

47. Quoted in Richard White, *"It's Your Misfortune and None of My Own": A New History of the American West* (Norman: University of Oklahoma Press, 1991), 73.

48. Winthrop Jordan, *White over Black: American Attitudes toward the Negro, 1550–1812* (Chapel Hill: University of North Carolina Press, 1968), discusses the aborted attempts at establishing colonies for freedmen in the West. See especially pp. 546–69. On the creation of Indian Territory, see James P. Ronda, "'We Have a Country:' Race, Geography, and the Invention of Indian Territory," in Michael A. Morrison and James Brewer Stewart, eds., *Race and the Early Republic* (New York: Rowman and Littlefield, 2002), 159–76.

PART I

FROM DUMPING GROUND TO REFUGE

IMAGINING THE WHITE MAN'S WEST, 1803–1924

"FOR ITS INCORPORATION IN OUR UNION"

The Louisiana Territory and the Conundrum of Western Expansion

With the stroke of a pen, the United States acquired the Louisiana Territory from France and doubled the size of the nation in 1803. While many Americans, filled with an insatiable hunger for land, obviously wanted to settle the new territory as rapidly as possible, a few worried about the influence of such massive territorial growth on the nation, fearing that democracy could not flourish in such a large expanse. They worried as well about the influence of expansion on America's dominant white race. Going west into territory held by Indians and the weak but still large Spanish empire meant coming into contact with groups Americans considered inferior. Expansion could therefore undermine democracy and even white racial superiority, for beneath the surface of the young nation, racial tensions strained its unity.

Would going west inevitably weaken settlers, and, if so, could the land be put to better use? Perhaps this new territory could instead be used to racially cleanse the nation and solve some of the pressing racial issues that threatened its survival. It could be used to segregate and relegate free African Americans and eastern Indians to the periphery of the American empire, and

DOI: 10.5876/9781607323969.c001

these groups could in turn act as a buffer zone against "savage" Indians and the crumbling, racially impure Spanish empire. Before seeing the West as a white man's refuge, therefore, there existed an opposite vision of the West as a dumping ground for incompatible and incongruent members of society.

President Thomas Jefferson, aware of his critics' reservations about Louisiana, used his third annual message to Congress, in October 1803, to answer them and outline an ambitious vision of expansion for the nation. While his message meandered through a variety of foreign and domestic issues, Jefferson focused on explaining the importance of the recently acquired Louisiana Territory and the related issue of negotiating with Indians for their land between the Appalachian Mountains and the Mississippi River, an area still sparsely populated by white settlers. Settlers would come, and the Indians would have to give way.

Of course, Jefferson purchased Louisiana to secure access to the Mississippi River for Ohio Valley farmers, but he saw much more of value in the acquisition of the vast territory. He remarked on "the fertility of the country, its climate and extent." Its cultivation would "promise in due season important aids to our treasury," and its vast size would provide "an ample provision for our posterity, and a wide-spread field for the blessings of freedom and equal laws."[1] The future, Jefferson believed, lay in the West. While his administration had done its part to negotiate the treaty, only the US Senate could ratify it. Deferring to congressional authority, he hoped lawmakers would soon act to provide the necessary measures for the quick and efficient "incorporation in our Union" of the Louisiana Territory.[2] Some Americans had balked at the price and at the possible threat such dramatic expansion portended for democracy in the new republic. Nevertheless, the Senate quickly ratified the treaty by a vote of twenty-four to seven.[3]

During his second inaugural address in March 1805, the president again outlined a vision for the Louisiana Territory. He acknowledged that "the acquisition of Louisiana has been disapproved by some" on the grounds that a larger republic would be unwieldy, but, he asked, "is it not better that the opposite bank of the Mississippi should be settled by our own brethren and children, than by strangers of another family?"[4]

Jefferson's federalist opponents questioned the benefits of acquiring this new territory and its current inhabitants. The text of the treaty, however, stipulated that the residents of French Louisiana would "be incorporated in the Union of the United States and admitted as soon as possible according to the principles of the federal Constitution to the enjoyment of all these rights, advantages and immunities of citizens of the United States." Further, the United States would guarantee "the free enjoyment of their liberty, property and the Religion which they profess."[5] The treaty, therefore, required that these people be accorded the same rights as citizens in America's original thirteen states.

The pro-federalist *Gazette of the United States* warned, "Two Spaniards from New-Orleans [would have] the same influence in the Senate with two Senators from Virginia, Pennsylvania or Massachusetts." The *Gazette* doubted if such people "with their ignorance of our constitution, language, manners and habits [were] qualified" for citizenship.[6] The federalist Gouverneur Morris complained, "I always thought that, when we should acquire Canada and Louisiana it would be proper to govern them as provinces, and allow them no voice in our councils."[7] In a January 1804 letter, Morris again argued that the denizens of Louisiana lacked the qualifications for citizenship: "The stipulation [in the treaty] to admit the inhabitants into our nation will prove injurious to this country" and to democracy, since they would be easily swayed by those seeking to create a dictatorship or a monarchy. In the end, Morris declared, "No man without the support of at least one thousand American bayonets can duly restrain the inhabitants of that region."[8] Implicit in these statements was a belief in the inferiority of Louisiana's residents. These peoples, indeed many of whom were of mixed race and ethnicity, could be too easily swayed and led by power-hungry tyrants, detractors asserted. Further, such degraded peoples could not comprehend the complexities and nuances of the American system and thus made fit pawns for would-be tyrants and demagogues. Fears of such "mobocracy" had long simmered in the nation, but acquiring Louisiana added a racial and ethnic dimension to these concerns. Surely, as the United States expanded, participation could only be extended to Anglo-American Protestants, with lesser peoples controlled as imperial subjects. Bestowing citizenship and whiteness—since the two were inextricably linked—on these peoples seemed too high a price for the land, in Morris's view.

Morris's criticism, as he conceded, mattered little, and in time new states would be carved from the region and admitted on equal footing with the rest of the nation. Before new states could be added to either Louisiana or the lands immediately east of the Mississippi, though, something had to be done about the presence of Indians. Thomas Jefferson, in his second inaugural address, argued, "Humanity enjoins us to teach them [the Indians] agriculture and the domestic arts; to encourage them to that industry which alone can enable them to maintain their place in existence, and to prepare them in time for that state of society, which to bodily comforts adds the improvement of mind and morals."[9] Civilization for Jefferson meant giving up the ways of the hunter and becoming farmers. Converting Indians to farming and then getting access to their supposedly excess lands had been an ongoing strategy of Jefferson's administration. In a confidential message to Congress on the western lands, written in January 1803, Jefferson argued that the government should encourage Indians to become farmers rather than hunters "and thereby prove to themselves that less land and labor will maintain them . . . the extensive forests necessary in the hunting life will then become useless, and they will see advantage in exchanging them for the means of improving their farms and of increasing their domestic comforts."[10] Here, then, was Jefferson's iron hand of imperialism wrapped in kid gloves. Better to convince the Indians to willingly give up their land instead of taking it, but, regardless, the result would be the same. The president's western policy encouraged settlement by whites while simultaneously, as he saw it, helping the Indians adapt to the realities of the modern world. The acquisition of the Louisiana Territory later in 1803 opened up another possibility: moving Indians from the Ohio River Valley and the Southeast to some location west of the Mississippi. Despite his interest in and appreciation of Indians and their cultures, when Jefferson looked West he did not see the frontier filled with Indians but instead envisioned an opportunity to realize his dream of an agrarian, utopian society of independent Anglo-American farmers.

The moral and hardworking farmer metaphorically stood in sharp contrast to the Indian or even the rough-and-tumble frontiersman.[11] Settled rather than transient, the pioneer farmer represented civilization itself. The farmer, in reality and also mythology, would help remake the West, planting crops where previously only wilderness existed. This, in the historian Henry Nash Smith's estimation, evoked a myth that had deeper meaning and resonance with Americans than the frontier as a violent land of Indians and frontiersmen. The settling of the garden epitomized a "collective representation, a poetic idea . . . that defined the promise of American life" and encapsulated a variety of meanings, including "fecundity, growth, increase, and blissful labor in the earth."[12] Jefferson, in his 1785 book *Notes on the State of Virginia*, argued that the yeoman farmer personified the most moral and desirable figure for the settlement of the West and the perpetuation of democracy. Crowded Europe needed manufacturing to feed its population, but wage labor in factories led to the loss of freedom and the destruction of democracy because "dependence begets subservience and venality, suffocates the germ of virtue, and prepares fit tools for the designs of ambition." Worse, it would only be a matter of time before the same conditions applied to the United States.[13]

Agriculture, however, promoted morality and virtue, traits that were essential to democracy. He wrote, "Those who labour in the earth are the chosen people of God, if ever he had a chosen people, whose breasts he has made his peculiar deposit for substantial and genuine virtue . . . Corruption of morals in the mass of cultivators is a phaenomenon [*sic*] of which no age nor nation has furnished an example." Americans should not worry about becoming manufacturers, for they could import all they needed from Europe: "While we have land to labour then, let us never wish to see our citizens occupied at a work-bench, or twirling a distaff."[14]

As a lawmaker, Jefferson sought to bring his vision of a West of white yeoman farmers to reality long before he acquired Louisiana. Only by somehow extending the frontier could Jefferson keep the dreaded distaffs at bay. During the Articles of Confederation government in the 1780s, he authored a plan for western expansion that he hoped would prevent both the spread of slavery and the presence of powerful, titled aristocrats, creating the yeoman republic of which he dreamed. Jefferson, in his 1784 "Plan for the Temporary Government of the Western Territory," wrote that the "respective governments [of new states] shall be in republican forms, and shall admit no person to be a citizen who holds any hereditary title," and "after the year 1800 of the Christian era there shall be neither slavery nor involuntary servitude in any of the said States."[15] Thus, he envisioned a free, white yeoman society in the West. In white male landowners, Jefferson and others felt, lay the keys to the perpetuation of democracy. The Northwest Ordinance, based in part on Jefferson's plan for the western territory, became law in 1787, remaining even after the US Constitution replaced the Articles of Confederation. Jefferson's ban on slavery north of the Ohio River also remained a part of it and would in time become a significant border between freedom and slavery.[16]

These motivations compelled Jefferson to acquire the Louisiana Territory because as long as future generations of Americans had enough land, America could remain a nation of free, landholding democrats. In his first inaugural address he wrote that Americans possessed "a chosen country, with room enough for our descendants to the hundredth and thousandth generation."[17] In an 1801 letter to James Monroe, however, he imagined a time in the near future when America's rapid population growth would inevitably result in the United States expanding "to cover the whole northern, if not southern continent, with a people speaking the same language, governed in similar forms, and by similar laws; nor can we contemplate with satisfaction either blot or mixture on that surface."[18] His euphemistic "blot and mixture" were references to miscegenation and the presence of non-white peoples, respectively. Despite being a prominent slave owner, he imagined a time when a continental nation would also be a homogeneous nation, a white nation. Here, then, from Jefferson's formidable pen appeared what is likely the earliest articulation of the white man's West. The historian Winthrop Jordan observes that, for Jefferson, "America's destiny was white."[19] How that destiny could be achieved given the large populations of African Americans and Indians already in the nation appeared problematic—it was one thing to think of a distant time a thousand generations in the future but quite another to plan for settlement in the trans-Appalachian and, later, trans-Mississippi West. Jefferson, like his nation, felt conflicted about the role of Indians in American society, but expansion had continued apace without question—or at least until it met the Mississippi River.

Jefferson's dream of a West occupied by yeoman farmers seemed to evaporate in light of early assessments on the region. Zebulon Montgomery Pike's report of his 1805–7 expedition across the Great Plains, Rocky Mountains, and Mexico painted a bleak portrait of the land beyond the Mississippi River. While the lower Missouri River would "admit of a numerous, extensive, and compact population," farther West it would "be only possible to introduce a limited population." Aridity was the problem. Of the Great Plains he wrote, "But here a barren soil, parched and dried up for eight months in the year, presents neither moisture nor nutrition sufficient to nourish the timber. These vast plains of the western hemisphere may become in time as cele-brated as the sandy deserts of Africa." He crossed a desert "of many leagues," populated by undulating waves of ever-changing sand dunes "on which not a speck of vegetable matter existed." Hoping to salvage some semblance of optimism, Pike opined, "From these immense prairies may arise one great advantage to the United States, viz.: The restriction of our population to some certain limits, and thereby a continuation of the Union." It would prove an impossible task, Pike implied, to govern a continental nation. Here, then, was a natural limit to western expansion, the spread of agriculture, and the spread of American society: "Our citizens . . . will, through necessity, be constrained to limit their extent on the west to the borders of the Missouri and Mississippi [Rivers], while they leave the prairies incapable of cultivation to the wandering and uncivilized aborigines of the country."[20]

Like Pike, Stephen Harriman Long asserted that a desert environment dominated this new territory. To describe it, he coined the term "Great American Desert," tempering Americans' enthusiasm to settle the lands beyond the Mississippi.[21] Long wrote of a vast sandy desert along the Front Range of the Rocky Mountains. He noted that the region seemed prone to violent thunderstorms and large hailstones. Inhospitable fluctuations in temperature promised to stymie human habitation. Long observed that the temperature increased by fifty degrees between sunrise and the hottest part of the day. "These rapid alternations of heat and cold," he concluded, "must be supposed to mark a climate little favourable to health."[22]

Pike's and Long's warnings about the Great Plains seemed to preclude any hope that the area could support traditional Anglo-American agrarian settlement. This seemed, as Pike suggested, to hem in the United States. As the historian William Goetzmann observes, Pike and Long did not offer entirely wrong information. Given the technology of the early nineteenth century, "The Southwestern plains were unfit for widespread settlement." Lacking communication and transportation infrastructure, irrigation, and dryland farming techniques, the Great Plains were ill-suited to agriculture and therefore to civilization as Americans saw it.[23]

Pike and Long, however, concerned themselves with the suitability of the Great Plains not only to agriculture but more generally to Anglo-American settlement, for agriculture was the handmaiden of American civilization. If agriculture could not thrive on the plains, then neither could Americans. Both explorers and other early visitors to the West returned with dire warnings about the dangers of potential settlement there. Should Anglo-Americans be foolish enough to venture into North America's heart of darkness, they could expect to degenerate into half-civilized, semi-nomadic bandits.

The image of the Great American Desert lodged in the American consciousness. Visitors from the East, touring the West, invariably described the Great Plains as a trackless wasteland for hundreds of miles, populated by savage Indians and desperadoes forced from the more civilized lands of the American frontier and the Spanish empire.[24] Washington Irving, among the first writers with a distinctively American voice and arguably its most famous man of letters, saw little to recommend in the plains, concluding that no good could come from owning such a place. Only recently returned from a long sojourn in Europe, he set out on a tour of America in 1832. The writer soon met Henry Leavitt Ellsworth on a Lake Erie steamer. Ellsworth, a government official bound for the newly created Indian Territory, convinced Irving and his two European companions to join the expedition as gentleman explorers. They agreed and soon lit out for the frontier.[25]

The Ellsworth party arrived at Fort Gibson in Indian Territory in early October 1832. On October 10 they made their way to the trading post and Osage Indian agency a few miles from the fort.[26] There, Irving encountered the frontier in microcosm. He was not impressed: "Besides these [Creek and Osage Indians] there was a sprinkling of trappers, hunters, half breeds, creoles, negroes of every hue; and all that other rabble rout of nondescript beings that keep about the frontiers, between civilized and savage life, as those equivocal birds the bats, hover about the confines of light and darkness."[27] His metaphor spoke of boundaries between light and darkness, civilization and savagery, good and evil. The bat's strange position as a creature of neither daylight nor darkness symbolized the mixed races he saw. His "nondescript beings," neither black, white, nor Indian, seemed the manifestation of one of America's darkest fears.

The mixture of races and cultures portended potential dangers for whites, of course, but also for Indians. Thus it was with pleasure that Irving described the Osage as still wild and romantic, "like so many noble bronze figures" dressed in "their simple Indian garb" and practicing "the habits of the hunter and warrior."[28]

Irving viewed his mixed-race cook and jack-of-all-trades, Antoine or "Tonish," however, as far less noble or romantic. Over the course of the journey Antoine would prove his worth time and again (once by swimming across

FIGURE 1.1. The writer Washington Irving, touring Indian Territory in the 1830s, warned that western expansion could lead to white racial decay. He worried that the vast spaces of the West could never truly be settled by Anglo-Americans and would instead be populated only by bloodthirsty Indians and outlaws. Within a decade, however, his uninhabitable plains would become the center of a continental nation. Photo by Matthew Brady, ca. 1855. *Courtesy,* Library of Congress, Washington, DC.

the Arkansas River, a rope clenched in his teeth, while towing the rather effete writer in a makeshift raft), but Irving refused to see him as anything other than a "braggart and a liar of the first water."[29] Applying his experience with Tonish to all French Creole trappers in the West, he concluded that they came dangerously close to degenerating into savages. In his work *Astoria,* he described such trappers as having "separated almost entirely from civilized life . . . [becoming] so accustomed to the freedom of the forest and the prairie that they look back with repugnance upon the restraints of civilization."[30]

Francis Parkman, who toured the Great Plains in 1847, agreed with much of Irving's assessment. He described a group of trappers he encountered on the Platte River as "uncouth" and "half-savage," and their faces "looked out from beneath the hoods of their white capotes with a bad and brutish expression, as if their owners might be willing agents of any villainy. And such in fact is the character of many of these men."[31] Contact with the wilderness could have a corrosive effect on civilization, making savages out of civilized people.[32]

To writers like Irving and Parkman, separation from civilization and giving in to the base desire to mix with inferior peoples led to racial degeneration. Savagery and miscegenation flourished in conducive natural environments, and the western frontier was just such a place. Americans regarded trees as indicators of a soil's fertility and suitability for agriculture. The plains lacked trees and therefore the civilizing influence of agriculture. Thus, savagery thrived on the Great Plains.[33] Irving wrote that the barren wasteland of the far West "apparently defies cultivation, and the habitation of civilized life . . . it is to be feared that a great part of it will form a lawless interval between the abodes of civilized man, like the wastes of the oceans or the deserts of Arabia; and like them be subject to the depredations of the marauder."[34] The western frontier was even more dangerous than Arabia because men from civilized societies lived alongside savages, and in time a "mongrel" society like the one near Fort Gibson would emerge that alloyed the ferocity of the Indian with the superior intellect of the civilized Anglo-American—a volatile combination. Irving wrote: "Here may spring up new and mongrel races, like new formations in geology, the amalgamation of the 'debris' and 'abrasions' of former races, civilized and savage; the remains of broken and almost extinguished tribes; the descendants of wandering hunters and trappers; of fugitives from the Spanish and American frontiers; of adventurers and desperadoes of every class and country, yearly ejected from the bosom of society into the wilderness."[35]

Americans could, he felt, easily sink to the level of the inferior peoples around them, victims of miscegenation and uncultivable environments. Most other

visitors to the plains endorsed the prevailing notion of aridity and its atten-
dant savagery. Even as late as 1857, US Army lieutenant Governeur K. Warren
could report that Anglo-American settlement in Nebraska had reached the
97th parallel, the limit of agriculture and civilized settlement. These settlers
"are, as it were, upon the shore of a sea, up to which population and agriculture may advance, and no further," he claimed.[36]

Irving's and Parkman's belief in the rapid degeneration of whites in the
West reflected the dominant cultural belief in the contingency of race.
According to the best scientists of the day, it was alarmingly easy for whites
to become less white. Given Samuel Stanhope Smith's analysis of race
and environment, the Great American Desert seemed to indeed present
a formidable impediment to the spread of civilization. The belief in the
West as hostile to white settlement played into the larger debate on race
and ethnicity in the early republic. Certainly, the Indians and half-civilized
people of the plains threatened democracy and perhaps even the stabil-
ity of the nation itself. Writers like Irving and Parkman readily warned of
the dangers of an American version of the warlike Tartars and Bedouins
attacking isolated outposts.[37] But such external threats comprised just one
of the myriad racial challenges facing the nation. Anomalous and undesirable racial groups already lived inside the boundaries of the United States.
These complex racial questions vexed the young nation, but the West
offered a possible solution.

If sending Anglo-American settlers into the West would undermine democracy and compromise the racial purity of the nation, what, then, to do with
the lands acquired in the Louisiana Purchase? Some advocated using the
region as a kind of racial dumping ground and thereby racially cleanse the
United States east of the Mississippi. The two most anomalous groups in the
nation, and therefore the most likely candidates for removal, were American
Indians and free African Americans. The Cherokee and other semi-civilized
Indians could be moved west of the Mississippi where, their alleged defenders
argued, they would have time enough to adapt to the ways of the white man's
world and give up title to their lands in the East. The Jefferson administration
first minted this idea, and it remained in circulation throughout the ensuing
decades. Similarly, free blacks, occupying a strange borderland between slaves
and free whites, could be evacuated to the West. Together, these groups could
provide a buffer against the savage and warlike Indians farther west.

Removing "civilized" Indians and free blacks seemed acceptable since Americans considered neither group capable of participating in American democracy. Indeed, the law excluded both groups from citizenship on the grounds that their instincts and base passions enslaved them. Democracy required rational thought and self-control, characteristics that neither Indians nor free blacks could supposedly possess. Without these traits, neither group could attain an understanding of republicanism or civic virtue.[38] Similarly, the legal system extended true citizenship only to white men (and not even all white men at first), while African American slaves occupied the lowest rung of the social order.[39] American leaders felt it vital to exclude African Americans (both the free and the enslaved) and American Indians for the good of the nation's survival. Blacks and Indians had been denied real participation in society, but even their continued presence in the nation remained a lingering problem. Removal might offer a practical solution, and the open lands of the Louisiana Territory beckoned with possibility.

The desire to colonize freed slaves somewhere outside the country appeared earlier than Jefferson's *Notes on the State of Virginia*, but his work attracted the most attention to the scheme in the late eighteenth century. Jefferson argued that young blacks should be "colonized to such a place as the circumstances of the time should render most proper, sending them out with arms, implements of household and of the handicraft arts, seeds, pairs of the useful domestic animals, etc. to declare them a free and independent people, and extend to them our alliance and protection, till they shall have acquired strength." To make up for the loss of their labor, America could "send vessels at the same time to other parts of the world for an equal number of white inhabitants."[40] Jefferson, as an advocate of white settlement of the West, preferred to send these freed slaves out of the country, but others thought a destination closer to the United States would be more practical.

Following the publication of Jefferson's *Notes*, several others offered proposals for colonization as a solution to the vexing question of how best to end slavery and prevent miscegenation. In 1788 "Othello," supposedly a free black from Baltimore, asserted that slaves should be freed and sent to a territory in the West.[41] In 1795 an anonymous New Hampshire writer argued in *Tyrannical Libertymen* that "a portion of our new territory be assigned for the purpose [of colonization]; and let the great body of negroes be sent to colonize it." The author imagined "a large province of black freemen, industrious and well regulated," who could develop some section of the West, provide revenue and strength to the nation, and act as a place where Christianized blacks could be recruited to spread "light, liberty, and benevolence" to the darkest corners of Africa.[42] By regulated, he no doubt meant controlled by laws but also through means that would smother the base passions and dark desires blacks supposedly harbored.

Thomas Branagan, a prolific anti-slavery writer, similarly felt that ending slavery and removing free blacks represented the best solution to the race question. Branagan asserted in *Serious Remonstrances* that slaves would eventually rise up and claim their natural rights as human beings. This would happen, he felt, at the most inopportune moment, most likely during a war with a foreign nation. Ending slavery peacefully was far better, he felt, than fighting both a foreign invader and a slave insurrection. While some had advocated the forced removal of free blacks, Branagan instead proposed a plan "for the accommodation of the blacks" that offered land as an incentive. Branagan claimed, "I would . . . joyfully embrace [such an incentive] myself and consider it as the most advantageous circumstance of my life to have the offer made me."[43] This advantageous offer would "allow them [blacks] a certain number of acres of land for a new settlement . . . Thus many an honest family would be provided for comfortably."[44] Branagan admitted that the South would not agree to his scheme (at least not for some time), but morally it fell to the North to do so as the right thing: "We have like true Christians and patriots, relinquished our ill-gotten slaves [in the North]; we have made them free virtually, but not politically; let us then from motives of generosity, as well as self-preservation, make them free and happy in every sense of the word, in a republic of their own."[45] All the plan required, he asserted, was a few hundred thousand acres of land in the Louisiana Territory that "will not be worth a cent to [our] government this five hundred years."[46] In a footnote he added, "The new state might be established upwards of 2000 miles from our population. It is asserted that the most distant part of Louisiana is farther from us than some parts of Europe."[47] In essence, northerners (and perhaps someday southerners) could exculpate themselves for the sin of slavery, strengthen the frontier by sending settlers to the West, and spatially segregate free blacks thousands of miles away.

Even Jefferson entertained the idea of sending freed slaves to the Louisiana Territory (although he preferred locations in Africa or the Caribbean, since

he dreamed about settling the Louisiana Purchase lands with white settlers).
In a late 1803 letter to Virginia governor John Page, the president wrote, "The
acquisition of Louisiana may also procure the opportunity" to colonize
blacks outside of the eastern United States.[48] He warned, however, that such
decisions ultimately rested with Congress.

The hope for a mass manumission and relocation of freed slaves proved
chimeric. By 1806, several factors had doomed the idea of a black territory in
Louisiana. The growing crisis with European powers, for example, focused
the nation's attention on international matters. The official end of the
African slave trade, as specified in the US Constitution, and a temporarily
flagging interest in abolition stopped the momentum for some sort of black
expatriation—although in time colonization would return and see the creation
of Liberia in 1822 under the auspices of the American Colonization Society.[49]

Yet as hope for colonizing blacks in the trans-Mississippi West faded, the
colonization of eastern American Indians became more likely. The creation
of Indian Territory, as historian James P. Ronda has argued, rested on "a set
of assumptions about race and geography, national sovereignty and cultural
identity." Once again, Jefferson figured prominently in the early debate over
the Louisiana Territory and its settlement. Certainly, he felt that much of
the land should be dedicated to his white yeoman farmers, but within such
a massive amount of land some territory could be set aside for Indians as
"a means of tempting all our Indians on the East side of the Mississippi to
move West," he explained in a letter to General Horatio Gates. This territory
would give Indians time to fully assimilate into American society and allow
their former lands to be opened to white settlement.[50] Jefferson never acted
on the idea, but it remained in circulation throughout the early 1800s.

President James Monroe made Indian removal a priority of his administration. In 1817 the Committee on Public Lands endorsed the creation of an
Indian Territory west of the Mississippi River. The current state of frontier
development, with its uneven pattern of white and Indian settlement, benefited neither group, the authors of the committee's report argued, because it
exposed whites to savagery and Indians to the worst attributes of American
culture, including alcohol consumption. Better, then, to move the Indians
into a clearly delineated space. In the words of Ronda, the committee proposed "a geography of race, a geography that promised a sovereign solution
to the Republic's 'Indian Problem.'"[51]

John Quincy Adams's administration also sought a way to relocate Indians, but it was under Andrew Jackson that Indian removal began in earnest. Elected in 1828, the new president had a long and checkered association with Indian peoples, having fought alongside them and often simultaneously against them, most notably at the Battle of Horseshoe Bend in 1814. That battle and the subsequent Battle of New Orleans in 1815 catapulted the Tennessean to national prominence, and following a protracted and circuitous journey he ascended to the presidency in 1828. Jackson announced his interest in Indian removal in his first State of the Union Address in December 1829, calling on Congress to enact legislation to remove eastern Indians. Hugh Lawson White in the US Senate and John Bell in the US House (both Tenneesseans) chaired their respective Committees on Indian Affairs and shepherded the bills through both chambers. Despite substantial opposition and close votes in both houses of Congress, the removal bill passed. Jackson immediately signed it on May 28, 1830.[52]

Jackson claimed that "no one can indulge a more friendly feeling than myself" toward Indian peoples, but a "benevolent policy" of Indian removal provided the best of all possible solutions to the Indian question, enabling "them to pursue happiness in their own way, and under their own rude institutions." With Indians situated beyond the Mississippi River, a "civilized population [can instead be given] large tracts of country now occupied by a few savage hunters."[53] In other words, drawing on Jefferson's humanitarian argument, removal would allow Indians the freedom to adapt at their own pace, and their former lands could be opened to settlement by productive white farmers. By 1833 Jackson had abandoned the pretense of removal as chiefly a humanitarian policy, emphasizing instead the Indians' innate inferiority to whites as justification to spatially segregate them forever. In his 1833 message to Congress the president singled out recalcitrant members of the last remaining southern tribes (most likely the Cherokee and Creeks) and hoped they "will realize the necessity of emigration and speedily resort to it." He declared that these Indians possessed "neither the intelligence, the industry, the moral habits, nor the desire for improvement which are essential to any favorable change in their condition. Established in the midst of another and a superior race . . . they must necessarily yield to the force of circumstances and ere long disappear."[54] The 1836 Report on the Committee of Indian Affairs similarly insisted on the Indians' irredeemable inferiority to whites. Celebrating the "successful" implementation of Indian removal, the report exclaimed that Indians "are on the outside of us, and in a place which will ever remain an outside."[55]

Jackson and his supporters could congratulate themselves on having finally solved the vexing "Indian problem," but not everyone believed the problem had really been solved. Washington Irving observed that the policy of removal, which he had seen firsthand in his tour of Oklahoma, only added more people to "this singular and heterogeneous cloud of wild population." Even worse, the removed tribes "consider themselves expatriated beings, wrongfully exiled from their hereditary homes, and the sepulchers of their fathers, and [they] cherish a deep and abiding animosity against the race that has dispossessed them."[56] Irving warned that the removed Indians felt betrayed by the United States and their jaundiced view of America would likely color encounters with other Indian peoples. Irving's negative assessment of Indian relocation, however, did not seem to matter. The point, after all, was that the eastern Indians no longer inhabited the eastern woodlands, and it mattered little if they sank to an even lower state of savagery on the isolated plains—or so the proponents of removal argued.

Imagining Indian Territory as remote from the rest of the nation, as being outside and Indians therefore as un-white outsiders, politicians in the 1830s felt they had solved one of the nation's most pressing issues. Once only socially and politically marginalized, Indian peoples were now spatially marginalized as well, literally on the outside looking in. Jackson, in his 1830 message to Congress, had stated that Indian removal would "relieve the whole State of Mississippi, and the western part of Alabama, of Indian occupancy," but it could accurately be said that this relief extended to the nation as well.[57]

Yet politicians had not solved the other pressing racial issue—the presence of African Americans and the issue of slavery. As government agents removed Indians from Georgia, Alabama, and Mississippi, planters increasingly replaced them with slaves as King Cotton became rooted in the southern economy. Indian removal, therefore, created a vacuum soon filled by slaves, further entrenching slavery in the American South and propelling the nation toward civil war. Indians, whose lands were the only things Americans coveted, were easy to separate, but the spread of labor-intensive cotton agriculture made controlling blacks more important and emancipation less likely. Indeed, the development of the American capitalist economy required their labor. In the North this labor could be provided by immigrants, but in the South the "bio-power" required to make cotton profitable came from the muscles of slaves. Capitalism "would not have been possible without the controlled insertion of bodies into the machinery of production," as Michel Foucault observed, and in few places was that insertion more obvious and more important than in the American South. Southern society existed only if institutions of power and control "ensured the maintenance of production relations."[58] Put simply, American development required both the Indians' land and the bodies of slaves, making the former expendable and the latter essential.

For more than three decades American policymakers saw the West as a racial dumping ground, an American Siberia where unwanted Indian peoples could be relocated and forgotten, but renewed expansion smothered this conceit. Little more than a decade after the removal of many eastern Indians to Indian Territory, the annexation of Texas, the acquisition of the Southwest following the Mexican-American War, and the discovery of gold in California put Indian Territory at the heart of a now continental nation. The periphery, stubbornly, would not remain peripheral.

By the late 1840s, Indian Territory and the surrounding Great Plains occupied the center of the country. However, the region still had an image, created in part by Pike and Long, as a desert, and subsequent travelers agreed with these early judgments. Thomas Fitzpatrick, a mountain man turned Indian agent, wrote in 1853 that the heart of the country loomed as "a great and disconnecting wilderness" separating the East from the Pacific Coast. Between the Mississippi River and California, therefore, lay an arid, vast hole dividing the fecund coasts.[59] "That hole," according to Elliott West, "began suddenly to fill on July 6, 1858, the day a party of thirteen prospectors found gold dust in a small creek flowing from the Front Range of the Rocky Mountains."[60] Their small discovery set off a frenzied race to the Rockies.

As tens of thousands of prospectors hurtled across the plains, the image of the center, of plains and mountains, began to change. Miners washed gold from nascent towns like Central City and Idaho Springs in the Colorado Rockies, proving the land to be literally valuable and giving credence to those who believed in America's place as God's new chosen nation. To feed these miners, farmers began to cultivate along the rivers that poured from the mountains, apparently drowning the memory of the Great American

Desert. To the east, farmers spilled out beyond Missouri into neighboring Kansas and Nebraska. Town boosters and railroads began to extol the virtues of the plains as uncommonly suited to agriculture. Transformed from desert into garden and finally into heartland, the hollow center had been filled.

Yet some fears remained. What of the racial degeneration Irving had warned of in the 1830s, and what would happen to Anglo-Americans and others of Northern European ancestry when they settled in the unquestionably warmer and drier West? Certainly, a new generation of scientists like Aggasiz doubted the environmental determinism of monogenesis, offering polygenesis as an inoculation against fears of degeneration. It was one thing to talk of the immutable nature of race from the safety of eastern universities but quite another to head to the West and apply theory to practice. With more than a little trepidation, settlers set off into the unknown.

NOTES

1. Thomas Jefferson, "Third Annual Message," October 17, 1803, in Saul K. Padover, ed., *The Complete Jefferson, Containing His Major Writings, Published and Unpublished, Except His Letters* (New York: Tudor, 1943), 401.

2. Ibid.

3. Jon Kukla, *A Wilderness So Immense: The Louisiana Purchase and the Destiny of America* (New York: Alfred A. Knopf, 2003), 306.

4. "Treaty between the United States of America and the French Republic." The full text of the treaty is available at Yale University's Avalon Project, http://avalon.law.yale.edu/19th_century/louis1.asp (accessed July 12, 2012).

5. Ibid.

6. Quoted in Kukla, *Wilderness So Immense*, 308.

7. Jared Sparks, *The Life of Gouverneur Morris* (Boston: Gray and Bowen, 1832), 3:198.

8. Gouverneur Morris to John Dayton, January 7, 1804, in ibid., 202.

9. Thomas Jefferson, "Second Inaugural Address," March 4, 1805, in *The Complete Jefferson*, 412.

10. Thomas Jefferson, "Confidential Message Recommending a Western Exploring Expedition," January 18, 1803, in *The Complete Jefferson*, 398.

11. Henry Nash Smith recounts the agrarian myth in *Virgin Land: The American West as Symbol and Myth* (Cambridge, MA: Harvard University Press, 1970), 123–262.

12. Ibid., 123.

13. Thomas Jefferson, *Notes on the State of Virginia*, in *The Complete Jefferson*, 678–79.

14. Ibid.

15. Thomas Jefferson, "Plan for the Temporary Government of the Western Territory," in *The Complete Jefferson*, 237.

16. See Donald W. Meinig, *Continental America, 1800–1867*, vol. 2: *The Shaping of America: A Geographical Perspective on 500 Years of History* (New Haven, CT: Yale University Press, 1993), 432–35, 450.

17. Thomas Jefferson, "First Inaugural Address," March 1801, in *The Complete Jefferson*, 384.

18. Quoted in Winthrop Jordan, *White over Black: American Attitudes toward the Negro, 1550–1812* (Chapel Hill: University of North Carolina Press, 1968), 547.

19. Ibid.

20. Zebulon Montgomery Pike, *The Expeditions of Zebulon Montgomery Pike, to Headwaters of the Mississippi River, through Louisiana Territory, and in New Spain, during the Years 1805–6–7*, Elliott Coues, ed. (New York: F. P. Harper, 1895), 2:524–25.

21. Walter Prescott Webb, *Great Plains* (Lincoln: University of Nebraska Press, 1981), 147.

22. Stephen Harriman Long, *Account of an Expedition from Pittsburg to the Rocky Mountains* (London: Longman, Hurst, Rees, Orme and Brown, 1823), 2:314.

23. William H. Goetzmann, *Exploration and Empire: The Explorer and the Scientist in the Winning of the American West* (New York: Alfred A. Knopf, 1966), 62.

24. Smith, *Virgin Land*, 174–79.

25. John Francis McDermott provides an excellent description of the meeting and preparation for the trip in his introduction to Washington Irving, *The Western Journals of Washington Irving*, John Francis McDermott, ed. (Norman: University of Oklahoma Press, 1944), 3–66.

26. Ibid., 111–12; and in the published account Washington Irving, *A Tour on the Prairies*, in *Three Western Narratives* (New York: Library of America, 2004), 20–22.

27. Irving, *Tour on the Prairies*, in *Three Western Narratives*, 20–22.

28. Ibid.

29. Ibid., 15.

30. Irving, *Astoria*, in *Three Western Narratives*, 275.

31. Francis Parkman, *The Oregon Trail: Sketches of Prairie and Rocky-Mountain Life*, 4th ed. (Boston: Little, Brown, 1905), 64.

32. Roderick Nash, *Wilderness and the American Mind* (New Haven, CT: Yale University Press, 1967), 27–30; Richard Slotkin, *The Fatal Environment: The Myth of the Frontier in the Age of Industrialization, 1800–1890* (Norman: University of Oklahoma Press, 1985), 120–22; Richard Slotkin, *Regeneration through Violence: The Mythology*

of the American Frontier, 1600–1860 (Norman: University of Oklahoma Press, 1973); Smith, *Virgin Land*, especially chapter 5.

33. Smith, *Virgin Land*, 175.

34. Irving, *Astoria*, 359.

35. Ibid.

36. Quoted in Smith, *Virgin Land*, 178.

37. Ibid., 176–77.

38. Ronald T. Takaki, *Iron Cages: Race and Culture in Nineteenth-Century America* (New York: Alfred A. Knopf, 1979), 12.

39. The classic discussion of the relationship between white freedom and black slavery is Edmund S. Morgan, *American Slavery, American Freedom: The Ordeal of Colonial Virginia* (New York: W. W. Norton, 1975).

40. Quoted in Jordan, *White over Black*, 546.

41. Ibid.

42. Anonymous, *Tyrannical Libertymen: A Discourse upon Negro Slavery in the United States* (Hanover, NH: Eagle Office, 1795), 10.

43. Thomas Branagan, *Serious Remonstrances: Addressed to the Citizens of the Northern States, and Their Representatives* (Philadelphia: Thomas T. Stiles, 1805), 17–18.

44. Ibid., 18.

45. Ibid., 23–34.

46. Ibid., 22.

47. Ibid.

48. Thomas Jefferson to Governor John Page, Washington, DC, December 23, 1803, in *The Writings of Thomas Jefferson*, Andrew A. Lipscomb and Albert Bergh, eds. (Washington, DC: Thomas Jefferson Memorial Association, 1905), 19:138.

49. Jordan, *White over Black*, 565.

50. James P. Ronda, "'We Have a Country': Race, Geography and the Invention of Indian Territory," in Michael A. Morrison and James Brewer Stewart, eds., *Race and the Early Republic: Racial Consciousness and Nation-Buildings in the Early Republic* (New York: Rowman and Littlefield, 2002), 159–75.

51. Ibid., 161.

52. Theda Perdue and Michael D. Green, *The Cherokee Removal: A Brief History with Documents* (New York: Bedford, St. Martins, 2005), 121–23.

53. Andrew Jackson, "Second Annual Message," December 6, 1830, in James D. Richardson, *A Compilation of the Messages and Papers of the Presidents.* US Congress (New York, 1896–99), 10:1082–86.

54. Andrew Jackson, "Fifth Annual Message," December 3, 1833, in *Compilation of the Messages and Papers*, 10:1252.

55. Quoted in Ronda, "We Have a Country," 164.

56. Irving, *Astoria,* 359.

57. Jackson, "Second Annual Message."

58. Michel Foucault, *The History of Sexuality,* vol. 1: *An Introduction* (New York: Vintage Books, 1990), 1:140–41.

59. Elliott West, "Golden Dreams," in *The Essential West: Collected Essays* (Norman: University of Oklahoma Press, 2012), 47.

60. Ibid., 44.

2

A CLIMATE OF FAILURE OR ONE "UNRIVALED, PERHAPS, IN THE WORLD"

Fear and Health in the West

While early observations of the Great Plains by Zebulon Montgomery Pike, Stephen Harriman Long, and Washington Irving painted the vast grasslands as an awesome barrier to white civilization, in time other travelers would begin to assess the far West more positively. These reports, in turn, began to transform American conceptions of the West as a wasteland and dumping ground for the nation's unwanted peoples. The descriptions of a harsh, trackless wilderness soon gave way to glowing accounts of sunny, warm regions. American sailors, for example, involved in the hide trade with far distant California, remarked on the beauty and potential of the region. They marveled at the temperate climate with its mild winters and cool summers. There existed, however, a danger implicit in the sun and fair climate of California and the Southwest, for too much good weather could harm individuals as much as inhospitable climates and savagery.

Americans saw themselves as descendants of the hardy races of Northern Europe. Their work ethnic—considered a hallmark of alleged Anglo-Saxon superiority—emerged from an age-old, relentless battle with a harsh and

DOI: 10.5876/9781607323969.c002

unforgiving Mother Nature. In struggle lay the key for tempering Northern Europeans into the fittest, strongest people on the planet, but this domination could only be renewed by constant competition with nature, and the Southwest was simply too warm. A salubrious climate could be detrimental to racial vigor, and indeed, early Anglo-American visitors saw proof of the dangers of a pleasant climate in the allegedly lazy Indians and Hispanics of California and the Southwest. This belief justified American conquest, but would not the same fate befall the vigorous, expansionistic Americans?

Richard Henry Dana's *Two Years before the Mast*, which recounted his experiences as a sailor engaged in the hide trade between the East and California from 1834 to 1836, ranks among the earliest works to argue that good climates could hurt white American racial vigor. He noted that California possessed tremendous natural resources, fertile soil, a temperate climate, vast plains for grazing, little disease, and numerous great ports. "In the hands of an enterprising people," he declared, "what a country this might be . . . Yet how long would a people remain so, in such a country? The Americans . . . and Englishmen [who live in California] . . . are indeed more industrious and effective than the Spaniards; yet their children are brought up Spaniards, in every respect, and if the 'California fever' (laziness) spares the first generation, it always attacks the second."[1]

Dana consciously equated laziness with an endemic disease. What worried him and others was the prospect that inferiority might be contagious.

Despite the fact that he was merely a sailor, Dana's Harvard education and manners enabled him to mix with the highest stratum of Mexican California. Among the many important Southern Californians he met was Don Juan Bandini, whom he described as a prime example of the kind of "decayed gentleman" he had often seen in California. Dana described Bandini as slim, delicate, and highly articulate, a nobleman characteristically "ambitious at heart, and impotent in act."[2] Masculinity, for Dana and the legions of Americans who followed him, meant action, strength, and competitiveness, not decay and impotence—the latter the opposite of virility, a chief attribute of the vigorous man. The Southwest's pleasant climate, Dana believed, created such infirmities. Only by struggling against a harsh, unrelenting nature could men avoid growing weak and effeminate. The mild climate of the Southwest seemed to make the ancient struggle between man and nature obsolete, and comfort invariably came at the expense of racial vigor.

Hispanic women, although widely praised for their beauty, also suffered from evident racial degeneration. If Anglo-Americans considered ideal women to be chaste, modest, and virtuous, then Mexican women represented the opposite. Dana summed up the views of many when he wrote, "The women have but little education, and a good deal of beauty, and their morality, of course, is none the best." Marital indiscretions nonetheless occurred rarely since husbands and other male family members stood ready with "a few inches of cold steel [to] punish . . . an unwary man."[3] The beauty of California women still struck Dana when he returned to the Golden State in 1859. Upon getting reacquainted with Don Juan Bandini and his wife, Doña Refugio, Dana still found the lady quite stunning, perhaps because of "the preserving quality of the California climate."[4]

Dana and other early adventurers in the West certainly had reason for concern given their understanding of race at the time, but the emerging racial science of polygenesis seemed to offer a panacea to racial fears. Polygenesis argued that the races of humanity had been created in different locations and been endowed with innate and immutable characteristics. Anglo-Americans, as white-skinned Europeans, unquestionably occupied the pinnacle of human development, and their whiteness could not be fundamentally altered (except perhaps through miscegenation or residence in the most extreme climates). Africans, created as supposedly docile and stupid creatures, seemed destined to serve as slaves, and American Indian peoples, with their alleged savagery and inability to adapt to change, appeared doomed to vanish before the superior race, as in the oft-used simile "like snow melting before the sun." In addition to justifying slavery and expansion, polygenesis promised that whites could colonize any environment without fear of degenerating.

During his 1859 visit to California, Richard Henry Dana marveled at the essential differences in the races—a marked change for a man who had once warned about the dangers of California's climate. After leaving San Francisco, he headed for China. While crossing the Pacific he met a Chinese family with a newborn. Dana wrote, "Travelling as I do gives one a strong notion as to the differences of races. The differences seem almost of the essence and ineradicable—not to speak of the original unity, but of the present state of things. Mixtures of races seem doomed to extinction. There is a Chinese infant on board, born in Cal., but its little eyes are as Chinese, from the moment they were opened as any 'oldest inhabitant.'"[5] Climate, as in the case of the Chinese infant, did not change the baby into something else, he noted with almost palpable relief.

Yet Dana did not endorse all aspects of polygenesis and remained a believer in the original unity of the human family. He did concur with polygeneticists that mixed races faced inevitable extinction. "I do not," he continued, "believe the Kanakas [Hawaiians] can . . . increase and maintain themselves long as an equal race with the whites, or that a mixed race will multiply at all. These facts, and even that most striking one respecting the intermarriage of mulattoes, do not disprove the orig. unity, nor relieve the difficulties in the theory of orig[inal] diversity."[6]

Polygenesis had provided a salve to those worried about whites sinking to the levels of the savage races, but it did not entirely relieve the fear that whites could degenerate to a degree at least from climates like that of the American West. Had this not, in fact, happened in Latin America? Even polygeneticists agreed that certain races should avoid climates foreign to them. The racial theorist and leading polygeneticist Josiah Nott wrote that whites were "destined eventually to conquer and hold every foot of the globe where climate does not interpose an impenetrable barrier."[7] But climate did pose barriers that could undermine white racial vigor. Scientists uniformly considered hot and humid climates dangerous to whites while convinced that peoples of African descent possessed unique adaptations to such climates. As the historian Conevery Bolton Valenčius notes, "Black immunity to [tropical diseases like malaria], real and perceived, was a powerful argument for white Americans about the rightness of black servitude."[8] Slaves belonged in the South, working in the heat of muggy cotton fields or rice paddies. This was not cruel, slaveholders argued. It was natural.

While polygenesis opened the door for possible Anglo-American settlement of the West, most experts agreed that already weak members of society could benefit from the West's salubrious climates. The chronically ill, especially those suffering from pulmonary ailments like tuberculosis, could find hope in the region.[9]

The perception of the West as a healthy region developed slowly over the first half of the nineteenth century. Early explorers to the West made infrequent references to the region's healthfulness, although they did not report many diseases either. Stephen Long, for example, noted that among the Omaha Indians, the "catalogue of diseases, and morbid affections, is infinitely less extensive than that of civilized men." Common ailments like rheumatism, gout, jaundice, and phthisis (tuberculosis) did not occur among them, he claimed.[10] Long did not feel optimistic about the prospects of western settlement, and he asserted that the temperature fluctuations in Colorado's Rocky Mountains would not promote good health, though he believed the dry air would be better than that in the humid Mississippi Valley.[11] John C. Frémont conversely observed in 1842, "The climate [on the plains] has been found very favorable to the restoration of health, particularly in cases of consumption," a fact he attributed not to the climate (as most observers did) but rather to the presence of sagebrush and other "aromatic plants."[12]

Spurred by more favorable reports, like those of Frémont, the belief that the West offered a genial, healthy landscape had begun to take hold in the American consciousness by the 1840s. Josiah Gregg, an American trader, for example, marveled at the "salubrity of climate [in] . . . New Mexico. Nowhere—not even under the much boasted Sicilian skies[—]can a purer or a more wholesome atmosphere be found. Bilious diseases—the great scourge of the valley of the Mississippi—are here almost unknown." Except for epidemics of typhoid and smallpox, "New Mexico has experienced very little disease of a febrile character; so that as great a degree of longevity is attained there, perhaps, as in any other portion of the habitable world."[13]

Susan Shelby Magoffin, a young bride whose husband, like Gregg, participated in the trade between Missouri and Santa Fe, found the Great Plains not "very beneficial to my health so far," an impression exacerbated by a miscarriage she suffered at Bent's Fort.[14] New Mexico, however, proved markedly better, and in her diary for September 10, 1846 she wrote, "The air is fine and healthy; indeed the only redeeming quality of this part of New Mexico is its perfectly pure atmosphere, not the damp unhealthy dews of the States."[15]

California similarly developed a reputation for healthfulness. Mrs. Louise Amelia Knapp Smith Clappe (better known by her nom de plume "Dame Shirley") accompanied her physician husband to the California goldfields in 1851. Shirley's husband selected the mining camp Rich Bar "as the terminus of his health-seeking journey, not only on account of the extreme purity of the atmosphere, but because there were more than a thousand people there already, and but one physician, and as his strength increased, he might find in that vicinity a favorable opening for the practice of his profession, which, as the health of his purse was almost as feeble as that of his body, was not a bad idea."[16] Upon leaving the mining camps fourteen months later, Shirley boasted to her sister of the physical and mental changes resulting from the experience. "I took kindly to this existence, which to you seems so sordid and mean," she wrote. In California she "gained an unwonted strength in what seemed to you such unfavorable surroundings. You would hardly recognize the feeble and half-dying invalid . . . in the person of your *now* perfectly healthy sister."[17]

Walter Colton, writing in the 1850s about his experiences a decade earlier, also boasted of California's healthfulness. He claimed, "The fecundity of Californians is remarkable and must be attributed in no small degree to the effects of climate. It is no uncommon sight to find from fourteen to eighteen children at the same table, with their mother at the head." One Monterey woman, he asserted, had twenty-two surviving children. Indeed, California's climate seemed so salubrious that once transportation improved, Colton predicted, "The day is not distant when a trip to California will be regarded rather as a diversion than a serious undertaking. It will be quite worth the while to come out here merely to enjoy the climate for a few months. It is unrivaled, perhaps, in the world."[18]

Following the Civil War and the completion of the transcontinental railroad, people did flock to California for the climate. The state's international reputation as a gigantic sanitarium encouraged often extravagant claims. Norman Bridge, a physician specializing in pulmonary ailments, noted that even California could not cure everyone. He wrote in Charles Fletcher Lummis's promotional magazine *Land of Sunshine*, "There has been no exaggeration about the climate of Southern California. One who recovers from pulmonary tuberculosis is excusable for some enthusiasm about the climate; while he who fails to recover will hardly be loud in his praises."[19] California, Bridge continued, could make the weak strong, and cured invalids could live fulfilling and productive lives, but for advanced cases, he cautioned, it extended little hope.

The naturalist John Muir, writing in the late 1870s, held a largely pessimistic opinion of California's reputation for healthfulness. Invalids "come here only to die, and surely it is better to die comfortably at home . . . It is indeed pitiful to see so many invalids, already on the verge of the grave, making a painful way to quack climates, hoping to change age to youth, and the darkening twilight of their day to morning. No such health-fountain has been found, and this climate, fine as it is, seems, like most others, to be adapted for well people only."[20] Muir, however, found some places in the West healthy not only for the body but also for the soul. "The summer climate of the fir and pine woods of the Sierra Nevada would," he wrote, "be found infinitely more reviving [than sanitariums]; but because these woods have not been advertised like patent medicines, few seem to think of the spicy, vivifying influences that pervade their fountain freshness and beauty."[21] Reflecting on the healing power of wild country, in a letter on Mount Shasta Muir wrote, "The mountains are fountains not only of rivers and fertile soil, but of men. Therefore we are all, in some sense, mountaineers, and going to the mountains is going home. Yet how many are doomed to toil in town shadows while the white mountains beckon all along the horizon!"[22] In the mountains the sick, the weak, the world-weary could all be healed, but California's climate could only do so much.

California's main competition in the growing business of health tourism came from the mountainous territory of Colorado. The English traveler Isabella Bird observed in 1873, "The climate of Colorado is considered the finest in North America, and consumptives, asthmatics, dyspeptics, and sufferers from nervous diseases, are here in hundreds and thousands, either trying the 'camp cure' for three or four months, or settling permanently." So numerous were health seekers, she claimed, that "nine out of every ten [Colorado] settlers were cured invalids."[23] Dr. Samuel Edwin Solly, a supposedly noted English physician and health seeker, gave a lower but still considerable estimate of the number of health seekers as roughly one-third of Colorado's total population. The "one-lung army" totaled perhaps 30,000 in Denver by 1890—a fifth of the city's population.[24] Rose Georgina Kingsley, an English friend of Denver and Rio Grande Western Railway (D&RGW) president William Jackson Palmer, provided a typical endorsement of Colorado's "bracing and healthy" climate. In one case, she explained, a young man she knew "came out in the summer of 1871 apparently dying of consumption, obliged to be moved in an invalid carriage. In the spring of 1872 we wished him good sport as he started on foot for a week's shooting and camping in the mountains!"[25] A few years later one observer declared, "The Centennial State, while it is no more a cure-all than the patent nostrums of the period, can indeed afford blessed relief, and life itself, to many a forlorn and despairing sufferer."[26]

The D&RGW extolled the virtues of the state in its advertising material. Colorado, it claimed, possessed superior health resorts to those of Switzerland and France, and the infirm could easily access them by way of rail lines from the East.[27] Manitou Springs, located near Colorado Springs and owned and heavily promoted by the D&RGW, became Colorado's premier health resort. The railroad company charged Dr. Solly with explaining the superiority of Manitou Springs's hot springs pools to those of other famous resorts around the world. Not surprisingly, he found those in Manitou the equal of even the most renowned resorts in Europe. The various springs, with their differing temperatures and chemical content, could treat virtually any ailment known to humanity, including congestion, inflammation, dyspepsia, and nervous and sexual disorders, to name a few.

The superiority of Colorado's environment set it apart from Europe's resorts. Its dry, inland location meant that humidity, which Doctor Solly warned endangered consumptives, would not be a problem, and Manitou's sheltered location assured sunny and mild winter weather. Health seekers, the doctor advised, should plan on winter as the best time to stay at Manitou Springs, since the winter sun and desiccated air could have the greatest "effect . . . upon the human body." He concluded, "There is probably no climate in the world where out-door life is so thoroughly enjoyable through every season of the year as that of Manitou."[28] Consumptives might not be completely cured, but many would be able to live longer and healthier lives in Colorado. Solly, who had recovered his health in Colorado Springs, used his growing professional reputation to advertise the city to an eager invalid audience.[29]

The healthy western lifestyle therefore compared quite favorably with the urban East. Tuberculosis, which Dr. Joseph W. Howe called the "scourge of humanity" in 1875, particularly thrived in crowded, unsanitary factories and urban environments.[30] Tenements filled with dozens of workers, weakened by long and tiring shifts in close quarters with infected people, made contracting TB likely. Samuel Hopkins Adams, in a 1905 McClure's Magazine article, argued that tuberculosis could be effectively controlled with the creation of large sanitariums, better sanitation methods, and improvements in urban tenement houses. A lack of proper sanitariums meant that "we must either dump the vast majority of our consumptive poor into the contagious wards of our hospitals, send them to the pest-houses, or—this is the common and approved method—let them die in their dark tenements or their wretched dwellings."³¹ Simply changing one's environment could cure this scourge. "Fresh air, sunlight, and good food will save any case of tuberculosis that has not progressed too far—and nothing else will," Adams explained. These conditions readily existed in cities, exclusive of the slums, and therefore, "the sufferer doesn't need to go to Arizona or California. Climate, while it may be an aid in some cases, has much less influence on tuberculosis, except in the later stages, than is generally supposed."³² Adams lamented the plight of the urban poor, forced to live in cramped, infected dwellings, and his article, like those of other Progressives, functioned to goad Americans into action.³³

The polluted city was the offspring of industrialization, and poor urban workers kept its factories humming. The laboring poor, though, did not always live isolated from their social betters and could therefore spread tuberculosis. The railroad provided a technological solution to the problems of urbanization that came with the Industrial Age.³⁴ Great distances, even for the ill, no longer served as obstacles, and people with money and leisure time could easily access places like Santa Fe or Los Angeles, towns that had once sounded distant and exotic. Western promoters never tired of extolling the virtues of their beneficent climate and the lucrative industry it spawned.

The healthy West continued to beckon, promising escape for those who could afford the price, but this was merely part of a growing dissatisfaction wealthier Americans felt toward the city. The September 17, 1891, issue of the *Nation* juxtaposed the alien city against the healing countryside. An article on the new immigration noted that an increasing number of unskilled or unemployed immigrants headed for the nation's ports. Unfortunately, the magazine observed, "[as] the influence of the Teutonic races declines, that of the Latin and Slavic increases" from year to year. Even worse, these immigrants were predominately male, of the "lowest class," and "not related to us [Anglo-Americans] in race or language." Such immigrants might be appropriate, the author noted, for "an undeveloped frontier; but the statistics of the reported destination of immigrants show that the bulk of them intend to settle in New York, Pennsylvania, and Massachusetts."³⁵ The next article in the magazine noted the increasing numbers of middle- and upper-class people who escaped the cities for quiet country cottages where they could spend the summers. This phenomenon reflected "a growing national love of Nature and her quietudes."³⁶ The juxtaposition of the two articles, while likely coincidental, reflected the tensions of the Gilded Age; and escaping the city, with its immigrants and diseases, became a common pursuit of those with leisure time and money. The West, therefore, seemed an ideal place: free of the smoke, pollution, and lowest class of immigrants and brimming with nature in all her myriad grandeur and quietudes.

Railroads and resort owners (often one and the same) promised rejuvenation to a select few. Railroad fares and the cost of living for months in a resort or sanitarium precluded all but the wealthy from coming. Those with money could get access to peaceful, healthy environments far from the pollution and problems of industrial urban cities. Across the Southwest, railroads erected impressive and exclusive sanitariums and hotels. The Southern Pacific Railroad created the Del Monte Hotel in Monterey, California, in 1880, the first of the West's elaborate resorts. In 1882 the Atchinson, Topeka and Santa Fe answered with the massive Montezuma Hotel in Las Vegas, New Mexico, and the D&RGW built the Antlers Hotel in Colorado Springs in 1883 and developed exclusive resorts in Manitou Springs and Glenwood Springs.[37] Only wealthy whites could stay in resorts like Manitou Springs that were both racially and class exclusive.[38] Disease knew no distinctions of class or race, but treatment regimes certainly did.

Colorado, California, and New Mexico might all be blessed with an agreeable climate, but only a few places had the conditions suitable for constructing sanitariums, and Colorado Springs vied to be the best of them all. "An invalid needs not only good climate," Lewis Morris Iddings opined in Scribner's, "but the best of food and many comforts. Roughing it for sick people has been much over-estimated."[39] Accompanying Idding's article were drawings of fashionable Colorado Springs "invalids," seemingly in the bloom of health, enjoying outdoor activities and attending evening balls. Iddings noted the civilized nature of the city and its residents: "The residents are Eastern people of considerable wealth . . . and their scheme of life is intended to take in such means of enjoyment as they have been accustomed to at home. It is Eastern life in a Western environment." Filled with beautiful architecture (the handiwork of an eastern architect forced to relocate for his health), a fledgling university staffed with professors from fine eastern and European schools teaching cultivated but sickly youth ("and thus care is taken not to press them with too much study"), and the Cheyenne Mountain Country Club, Colorado Springs seemed anything but a frontier outpost.[40]

FIGURE 2.1. Railroads eagerly courted invalids, promising them health and rejuvenation in fine resorts throughout the West. While people debated whether the
West's climate would be beneficial to Anglo-Americans generally, there was little
debate about the vivifying effects of the West's climate on tuberculosis patients and
others with debilitating ailments. View of the "Colorado" Hotel and hot springs
bathhouse built by the Denver and Rio Grande Western Railway in Glenwood
Springs. *Courtesy,* Denver Public Library, Western History Collection, Denver, CO.

While the rich could convalesce in style, many young men and women of
lesser means also went west to build up their strength and find a place for
themselves in the world. Julian Ralph of Denver declared that the Mile-High
City's "good taste, good society, and progressiveness" were a result not of its
mineral wealth but rather of its invalid population: "It was not [mining and]
oil that gave us college-bred men to form a Varsity Club of 120 members, or
that insisted upon the decoration of the town with such hotels as ours. The
influence of invalids is seen in all this. They are New Yorkers, Bostonians,
Philadelphians, New Orleans men, Englishmen—the architects, doctors,

lawyers, and every sort of professional men being among them."[41] Denver welcomed invalids, and it seemed all the better for it.

These glowing reports of "bracing air" and ocean breezes, of former invalids risen like Lazarus and strolling under the purple skies of a Pikes Peak sunset, did much to contradict early negative reports of the West that warned of the region's isolation, savage population, and inappropriateness for white settlement. Many early visitors, like Richard Henry Dana, worried that the mild climate represented a greater threat to white racial vigor than did savagery. Polygenesis alleviated some of these fears, but even Josiah Nott hedged when it came to the question of white superiority and climate. Fears remained, however, that racial vigor could not thrive in warm climates. Many easterners, in fact, criticized California and the Southwest as too healthy. Climates that might suit invalids could nevertheless be harmful to the overall racial vigor of the white race. It fell to promoters and western mythmakers in the last third of the nineteenth century to once again defend their region from detractors and convince Anglo-Americans that the region offered all Americans—not just the sick—an opportunity to achieve a level of development unprecedented in human history.

Notes

1. Richard Henry Dana Jr., *Two Years before the Mast and Other Voyages*, Thomas Philbrick, ed. (New York: Library of America, 2005), 166.

2. Ibid., 227.

3. Ibid., 165.

4. Ibid., 377.

5. Richard Henry Dana Jr., *Journal of a Voyage Round the World, 1859–1860*, in ibid., 638.

6. Ibid.

7. J[osiah] Nott and Geo[rge] R. Gliddon, *Types of Mankind; or, Ethnological Researches, Based upon the Ancient Monuments, Paintings, Sculptures, and Crania of Races, and upon Their Natural, Geographical, Philological and Biblical History* (Philadelphia: Lippincott, Grambo, 1855), 79.

8. Conevery Bolton Valenčius, *The Health of the Country: How American Settlers Understood Themselves and Their Land* (New York: Perseus Books Group, 2002), 237.

9. For a history of tuberculosis, see Thomas Daniel, *The Captain of Death: The Story of Tuberculosis* (Rochester: University of Rochester Press, 1999). The definitive

study of the influence of health on western settlement remains Billy Mack Jones, *Health-Seekers in the Southwest, 1817–1900* (Norman: University of Oklahoma Press, 1967).

10. Stephen Harriman Long, *Account of an Expedition from Pittsburg to the Rocky Mountains* (London: Longman, Hurst, Rees, Orme, and Brown, 1823), 1:238.

11. Ibid., 314.

12. John C. Frémont and Samuel M. Smucker, *The Life of Colonel John Charles Fremont* (New York: Miller, Orton, and Mulligan, 1856), 136.

13. Josiah Gregg, *Commerce of the Prairies*, Max L. Moorhead, ed. (Norman: University of Oklahoma Press, 1954), 105.

14. Susan Shelby Magoffin, *Down the Santa Fé Trail and into Mexico: The Diary of Susan Shelby Magoffin*, Stella M. Drumm, ed. (New Haven, CT: Yale University Press, 1926), 65–68.

15. Ibid., 115.

16. "Dame Shirley to Molly," September 13, 1851, in Thomas C. Russell, ed., *The Shirley Letters from California Mines in 1851–52* (San Francisco: Thomas C. Russell, 1922), 4–5.

17. "Dame Shirley to Molly," November 21, 1852, in *Shirley Letters*, 350; italics in original.

18. Walter Colton, *Three Years in California* (New York: S. A. Rollo, 1859), 27, 181.

19. Norman Bridge, "Common Sense and Climate," *Land of Sunshine* (May 1895): 104. Bridge continued his discussion of California's place in healing consumptives in the June 1895 issue.

20. John Muir, *Steep Trails*, William Frederic Badé, ed. (New York: Houghton Mifflin, 1918), 143–44.

21. Ibid.

22. Ibid., 47.

23. Isabella L. Bird, *A Lady's Life in the Rocky Mountains* (Norman: University of Oklahoma Press, 1960), 41–42.

24. Cited in Jones, *Health-Seekers in the Southwest*, 96–97.

25. Rose Georgina Kingsley, *South by West, or, Winter in the Rocky Mountains and Spring in Mexico* (London: W. Isbister, 1874), 143.

26. "Vacation Aspects of Colorado," *Harper's New Monthly Magazine* 60 (March 1880): 544.

27. Passenger Department of the Denver and Rio Grande RR, "The Opinions of the Judge and the Colonel as to the Vast Resources of Colorado . . ." (Denver: Denver and Rio Grande Railroad, 1894), 11.

28. Samuel Edwin Solly, *Manitou, Colorado, USA: Its Mineral Waters and Climate* (St. Louis: J. McKittrick, 1875), 35.

29. For more on Solly's life and career, see Jones, *Health-Seekers in the Southwest*, 155–59.

30. Quoted in ibid., 124.

31. Samuel Hopkins Adams, "Tuberculosis: The Real Race Suicide," *McClure's Magazine* 24 (January 1905): 236.

32. Ibid., 248.

33. On cities and the Progressive Era, see Martin Van Melosi, *Pollution and Reform in American Cities, 1870–1930* (Austin: University of Texas Press, 1980).

34. Jones, *Health-Seekers in the Southwest*, 124.

35. "The New Immigration," the *Nation* 53 (September 17, 1891): 209–10.

36. "Changes in Summer Migration," the *Nation* 53 (September 17, 1891): 210–11.

37. Jones, *Health-Seekers in the Southwest*, 151–52.

38. Earl Pomeroy, *In Search of the Golden West: The Tourist in Western America* (Lincoln: University of Nebraska Press, 1990), 3–30. See also Thomas A. Chambers, *Drinking the Waters: Creating an American Leisure Class at Nineteenth-Century Mineral Springs* (Washington, DC: Smithsonian Institution Press, 2002); Jones, *Health-Seekers in the Southwest*. In an exception that proves the rule, Janet Valenza mentions a small resort in Marlin, Texas, that had separate bath quarters for African Americans. See Janet Mace Valenza, *Taking the Waters in Texas: Springs, Spas, and Fountains of Youth* (Austin: University of Texas Press, 2000), 131.

39. Lewis Morris Iddings, "Life in the Altitudes: Colorado's Health Plateau," *Scribner's Magazine* 19 (February 1896): 139.

40. Ibid., 142.

41. Quoted in Jones, *Health-Seekers in the Southwest*, 97.

3

"THE ABLEST AND MOST VALUABLE
FLY RAPIDLY WESTWARD"

*Climate, Racial Vigor, and the
Advancement of the West, 1860–1900*

As railroads grafted the West to the nation with iron stitches and sanitariums and luxury hotels for invalids boasted of the region's healthfulness, some critics argued that too much sun and invigorating air, though good for invalids, might prove detrimental to the continued domination of the Anglo-Saxon race. This fear had long simmered in the debate between those who favored monogenesis versus proponents of polygenesis, but now the new racial science of Social Darwinism and eugenics reignited the debate. The region could never become the white man's West until these questions of racial degeneration had been laid to rest.

In the 1830s, Richard Henry Dana warned against the "disease" of laziness that appeared endemic in California society. His prediction of possible racial decay echoed throughout the rest of the nineteenth century. Bayard Taylor, a popular travel writer in the mid-nineteenth century, for example, summed up the paradox of racial development and climate, writing: "In regard to climate, we are met by this difficulty, that that which is most enjoyable is not best adapted to the development of the human race." This phenomena

DOI: 10.5876/9781607323969.c003

existed because "the zone of action and achievement lies between lat[itudes] 35th and 55th North. On either side of this belt we have a superabundance of the benumbing [cold] or relaxing [hot] element."[1] In extremely cold climates people struggled to survive, and the harsh weather precluded the development of real civilization; thus groups like the Inuit and the Laplanders never advanced beyond the primitive stages of human development, or so Taylor claimed. In warmer climes nature was too easy on humanity. With nature providing food and a warm and pleasant environment, work did not motivate humankind, and peoples in these warm climates likewise did not advance beyond primitive stages of development. Taylor predicted that an end to the ancient struggle with a harsh and unrelenting nature would lead whites into the inferiority characteristic of the native Hispanics and Indians of the West.

White racial vigor, the hallmark of progress, emanated from climates that were neither too hot nor too cold. Northern Europeans, born struggling against an inhospitable climate, had evolved as superior beings to the darker peoples of the world because they had learned to survive through struggle. As the fittest, strongest peoples on the planet, they told themselves, it seemed self-evident that they had emerged as the dominant power on the globe. Colonialism closely tied notions of race to imperial conquest, but in the American West, as Taylor suggested, contact with the region's beneficent climate might lead to racial degeneration. Underneath the bravado of Manifest Destiny lingered the fear that Anglo-Americans would soon sink to the level of their non-Anglo neighbors.[2]

It would fall to westerners themselves to argue against the belief in climate-induced racial degeneration, and they, too, would draw on an environmental explanation to justify the superiority of their culture and society. Charles Fletcher Lummis, Joseph Pomeroy Widney, and others argued that under sunny western skies, Anglo-Americans would advance to an unprecedented state in world history. These western boosters, challenging the assumption that they inhabited a frontier society, argued that the West had grown into the most civilized, moral, progressive, advanced, and whitest region of the nation. Freed from the hardships of a repressive eastern or European winter, Anglo-Saxons in the temperate West would achieve a level of comfort and development unprecedented in the history of the world. Far from a place of racial decline, they argued, the West would become a new, ideal homeland for the fittest people on the planet, and along the shores of the Pacific would emerge a new empire greater than any that had come before in human history.

Bayard Taylor, in 1861, addressed the issue of climate and racial degeneration. He found native Californians "vastly superior to the Mexicans," with "larger frames, stronger muscle, and a fresh, ruddy complexion."[3] Significantly, these people now enjoyed citizenship in the United States. Native Mexicans presented a very different story. Mexico, he explained, while exceedingly fertile and pleasant, did not foster racial vigor. In Mexico, he wrote, "under the influence of a perpetual summer, the native race becomes indolent and careless of the future. Nature does everything for them." Beans emerged from the ground in limitless profusion, and fruits literally fell from the trees into their hands. While appearing "lithe and agile" and utterly free (or at least Taylor thought so), theirs was a pointless existence, which allowed them to "never step out of the blind though contented round which their fathers walked before them."[4] As a result, their intellect and racial vigor atrophied.

Helen Hunt Jackson, touring California more than forty years after Richard Henry Dana and a decade after Taylor, echoed their opinions. Jackson observed, "Climate is to a country what temperament is to a man—Fate." In the tropics, she explained, "human activities languish; intellect is supine; only the passions, human nature's rank weed-growths, thrive." Colder climates lacked the fecundity of the tropics and held no prospects of appeal for Americans. There existed a few places, however, "Florida, Italy, the South of France and of Spain, a few islands, and South California," warm enough to inspire animal and plant productivity without leading to the languishing of intellect.[5] Jackson became infatuated with Southern California, and her California novel, *Ramona*, became a national bestseller and the inspiration for a revival of the region's Hispanic and Indian cultures, albeit in a heavily romantic way.[6] Yet even she had doubts about California's suitability for Anglo-Americans. She wrote, "One never escapes from an undercurrent of wonder that there should be any industries or industry [in Southern California]. No winter to be prepared for; no fixed time at which anything must be done or not done at all; the air sunny, balmy, dreamy, seductive, making the mere being alive in it a pleasure; all sorts of fruits and grains growing a-riot, and taking care of themselves." In such an environment "it is easy to understand the character, or, to speak more accurately, the lack of character, of the old Mexican and Spanish Californians."[7] Their life of ease and contentment had been replaced by a more productive and ambitious race. She imagined California's Spanish founders "shuddering, even in heaven, as they look down to-day on his [the Yankee's] colonies, his railroads, his crops— their whole land humming and buzzing with his industries."[8]

Yet had the conquerors themselves been conquered? Americans may have taken California, but in the end California might triumph. The laziness of Californios, Hispanic Californians, Jackson warned, could return:

> One questions also whether, as the generations move on, the atmosphere of life in the sunny empire they lost will not revert more and more to their type, and be less and less of the type they so disliked. Unto the third and fourth generations, perhaps, pulses may keep up the tireless Yankee beat; but sooner or later there is certain to come a slacking, a toning down, and a readjusting of standards and habits by a scale in which money and work will not be the highest values. This is "as sure as that the sun shines," for it is the sun that will bring it about.[9]

Jackson could see racial degeneration resulting from California's pleas-ant climate, but a sense of ambivalence whispered in her work, a belief that something could be said for a life not measured by money and hectic activity. This reevaluation of priorities would be a theme in the work of later defend-ers of California and the West such as Charles Fletcher Lummis.

Evidence of this climatic degeneration, as Jackson intimated, supposedly existed among the native peoples of the Southwest. Americans criticized Hispanics and Indians for being lazy because nature did too much for them. Josiah Gregg's influential travelogue, *Commerce of the Prairies* (first published in 1844), like Dana's work, helped foment attitudes toward Hispanics. New Mexicans, he asserted, were indolent, immoral, fanatical in their religious beliefs, lacking in intelligence "except in artifice [and exhibiting] no profun-dity except for intrigue."[10] John Hanson Beadle, writing in the 1870s, agreed with Gregg. "Take [New Mexicans] all in all," Beadle claimed, "they are a strangely polite, lazy, hospitable, lascivious, kind, careless and no account race."[11] A *Rocky Mountain News* contributor in Santa Fe concurred: "The Mexican people . . . are a mixture of the Spanish and the old native, or Indian, races and seem to have inherited the vices and bad qualities of each," including ignorance, superstition, laziness, and lack of ambition. Americans, conversely, "with their thrift, intelligence, and progress [are] making a new era for New Mexico."[12] Anglo-Americans offered remoteness, the domination of the lower classes by the Catholic Church and the wealthy, a lack of democracy and education, and miscegenation as additional explanations for Hispanic inferiority, but climate also played a key role.[13]

Climatic degeneration made men cowardly, weak, and effeminate, while women became lascivious, as Dana had asserted when discussing the Bandinis of California, an influential couple he had met during his visit in the 1830s. Many later observers agreed with both assessments. Frederick Law Olmsted admired the Hispanic women he met in Texas and Mexico. He attributed their beauty, at least in part, to the climate. "Their dresses," he wrote with barely restrained glee, "seemed lazily reluctant to cover their plump persons, and their attitudes were always expressive of the influences of a Southern sun upon national manners."[14] Being plump signified healthfulness, which Texas provided, and the sun made these women eager to expose more of themselves than American women would have dared. Sexual forwardness resulted from this solar seduction.

Hispanic women did not enchant every American man, or at least they did not admit to it in print. Beadle demurred from the perspective of Dana and Olmsted. He wrote, "Barbarous people are never really beautiful; and where women are freest, there most beauty is found." Free from the control of superstitions and a false religion, American women remained the most beautiful. With patriotic zeal he even appropriated Patrick Henry's famous quote, declaring, "Give me an American woman or give me death!"[15] A superior culture, Beadle asserted, could only develop from a superior civilization; a debased civilization would inevitably succumb to the environment, and no red-blooded American man should surrender to the temptations of a seductive climate or the flirtatious women who inhabited it.

At the end of the nineteenth century, Charles Fletcher Lummis, a Hispanophile in every sense of the word, came to a much different conclusion. He had long been captivated by the women of the Spanish Southwest (a fact that drew considerable comment from his detractors and apparently with good reason, as his wife accused him of infidelity with several women, including at least one Hispanic woman, during divorce proceedings in 1909). He set out to defend their beauty and morality in the January 1895 issue of *Land of Sunshine*, the magazine he edited in the late 1890s and early 1900s. Lummis described all the women of Spanish America as fair, but the fairest could be found on the northern and southern extremes, far from the heat and "African" influences.[16] California's Hispanic women, not surprisingly, ranked as his favorites. He wrote, "As a rule, the facial types of the cooler Spanish-American countries are . . . finer, more spiritual, than those nearer the equator."[17] The accompanying illustrations showed that when he wrote "finer" and "more spiritual," he meant whiter. His rhetoric assumed implicitly that being far away from the heat of the tropics, where Africans thrived, made the women lighter skinned and therefore more Spanish and attractive.

Clearly, therefore, the idea that genial climates could lead to racial degeneration remained in circulation in the second half of the nineteenth century. Lummis and other western defenders, however, had a new scientific tool at their disposal, a tool that would enable them to address their critics and lay to rest fears of climatic degeneration: evolutionary theory and its bastardized progeny, Social Darwinism and eugenics. These new ideas indelibly shaped the argument over the appropriateness of Anglo settlement in the American West.

Charles Darwin's *Origin of the Species*, published in 1859, marked a dramatic breakthrough in the natural sciences, accounting for the tremendous variation in the world's flora and fauna by postulating that plants and animals gradually adapted to changes in the environment over many millennia. This slow rate of change, over the course of centuries, made the fears of rapid racial degeneration suddenly seem laughable.

Evolutionary theory quickly spread beyond a small group of scientists to historians, ethnologists, the newly emerging sociologists, and scores of other thinkers, all applying evolutionary principles to their disciplines and society at large. America in the late nineteenth century latched on to the theory with tremendous enthusiasm for, in the hands of Social Darwinists like Herbert Spencer, it made sense of a rapidly changing and industrializing nation and justified the continued domination of Anglo-Americans over supposedly inferior and less well-adapted immigrants. According to historian Richard Hofstadter, Americans took to Darwin's theory and its supposed social implications so rapidly that post-bellum America could be called "*the* Darwinian country. England gave Darwin to the world, but the United States gave to Darwinism an unusually quick and sympathetic reception."[18] The theory, moreover, argued against radical social changes and reforms like socialism, communism, and even more modest reforms, because would not social

A

B

FIGURE 3.1. Charles Fletcher Lummis loved the Del Valle family, spending a great deal of time with them. No doubt when he celebrated the beauty of Hispanic women, he had the Del Valle girls in mind. *Courtesy*, Braun Research Library Collection, Southwest Museum, Autry National Center, Los Angeles, CA.

change, like biological change, be slow, spanning generations? Furthermore, in a system based on competition, the wisest men would naturally be the most powerful and affluent, and the inferior laboring classes would be below them. Both of these observations spoke to a conservative impulse among America's Anglo elite.

Herbert Spencer became the most influential thinker to articulate and popularize the social implications of Darwin's theory. Adapting Darwin's ideas, Spencer wrote several volumes of his *Synthetic Philosophy* in the 1860s and 1870s. These essentially summarized the latest scientific findings, not just those relating to Darwinism but also to geology, embryology, physics, and even philosophical meditations like those of Thomas Malthus. Spencer's genius lay in making these varied ideas accessible and applicable to modern society, but Darwin's theory was clearly the focal point of Spencer's system of human society. Coining the term *the survival of the fittest* (seven years before Darwin published *Origin*), he argued that each generation represented the triumph of the best humans over the less-adapted ones. The poor were the least fit to survive, and for the betterment of humanity as a whole the state should not aid the poor in any way. It might seem cruel, he argued, but if the poor "are not sufficiently complete to live," he wrote, "they die, and it is best they should die."[19]

Social Darwinism should not be blamed for causing American imperialism, but it certainly helped justify it. Americans, after all, had long harbored a sense of mission that had a racial dimension. Just as the supposedly scientifically factual racial Anglo-Saxonism of polygenesis justified the Mexican-American War, Darwin's theory gave late-nineteenth-century racism and imperial expansion a basis in cutting-edge science. Social Darwinism explained war as beneficial. In the hands of imperialistic thinkers, war became not something to be avoided but instead a competition pitting man against man, with the strongest emerging victorious. It fell upon Americans as heirs to the legacy of the Anglo-Saxons to continue the westward expansion of the race.[20] In the 1880s John Fiske, an acolyte of the pacifistic Spencer, gave a series of lectures celebrating the Anglo-Saxon legacy of Americans and their English cousins. He argued that the democratic legacy of ancient Rome had been carried forward by the hardy Anglo-Saxon and Germanic tribes after the fall of the Roman empire. Anglo-Saxons had a duty to continue the expansion of freedom and democracy. The next step in world history, he argued, was the global domination by Anglo-Saxons, which would, perhaps somewhat iron-ically given their supposed martial prowess, usher in an era of worldwide peace. Americans and Englishmen would soon outbreed other, lesser races, transforming the Americas and perhaps even Africa into new Anglo-Saxon strongholds. Fiske's lectures so captivated Americans that more than twenty newspapers published his 1885 lecture on Manifest Destiny. He had lectured in England and before a crowd that included President Rutherford B. Hayes, General William Tecumseh Sherman, and numerous other dignitaries.[21]

Aline Gorren, in *Anglo-Saxons and Others*, also explicitly linked imperialism and industrial acumen to evolutionary theory, arguing that Anglo-Saxons, alone among the white races of the world, seemed suited to industrial devel-opment and imperial expansion. Modern society, with its great factories and mechanized armies, differed markedly from any that had preceded it. This was the new environment of the modern age, and, as with any environmen-tal change, only the strongest and fittest would thrive. Gorren claimed, "The Anglo-Saxons are the only peoples who [are in] perfect accord with the char-acteristic conditions of modern life. They are in absolute harmony with their environment as it is constituted by those conditions. Other peoples . . . are striving to adapt themselves, but they fail in part because their organs are not prepared for the new functions demanded of them."[22]

A pragmatic philosophy and a desire to work hard enough to procure material comfort separated the Anglo-Saxons from all other races, even the other white peoples of Europe. "Evolution," Gorren noted, "had sanctified the wisdom of their practical view of life. It might be said that one must never again speak slightingly of material instincts, of a like for good food, and good clothes, and a good home . . . provided one have the love of action which makes the hard work necessary for the obtaining of these things not too desperately irksome." From this self-interest would come a desire to show the rest of the world how best to live or, in short, how best to be like the Anglo-Saxons. The Anglo-Saxon lifestyle of pragmatism and material comfort would appear "like a revelation directly from on high and which lift[s] up the Anglo-Saxon as a beacon light to humanity."[23] Some would see that beacon and change; others would not. The twentieth century, Gorren warned, would "be one fierce fight for self-preservation, in which it is cer-tainly the weakest that will go to the wall, those, that is, whose equip-ment is the least complete for the special business at hand." Evolution had dictated that only those best suited to the industrial world would survive. With a flair for understatement he wrote, "It is safe to assume that the Anglo-Saxons will not be of that number, for it has been observed that they are the most perfect."[24]

Evolutionary theory not only justified white supremacy and imperial expansion but also alleviated guilt over conquest. Gorren and others could speak in euphemisms such as "going to the wall," but in practice that meant extinction of the "lesser" races. For support of the view that inferior races would disappear, one need not look far. Darwin's theory stressed confrontation and the triumph of the strongest over the weakest. As Hofstadter noted, "Imperialists, calling upon Darwinism in defense of the subjugation of weaker races, could point to *The Origin of [the] Species*, which had referred in its subtitle to *The Preservation of Favored Races in the Struggle for Life*."[25] Darwin, indeed, indulged in the stock racism of his age, writing in *The Descent of Man*, "The civilized races of man will almost certainly exterminate and replace throughout the world the savage races. At the same time the anthropomorphous apes . . . will no doubt be exterminated." The result would be a greater gap between man and animal as struggle wiped out Africans and Australian Aborigines on the human side and gorillas and other primates on the animal side.[26]

Extinction discourse, as contemporary scholars have called the belief that "savage" peoples were fated to disappear, issued from racism and imperialism. Often, the phrasing of arguments implied extinction as something natural and therefore unavoidable, not the product of European invasion. Primitive peoples would naturally vanish before the onslaught of European immigration. Warfare and disease—the latter mysterious and often attributed to forces beyond human understanding—contributed to the passing of races. Another cause existed as well: savagery would be self-extinguishing. "Savage" practices like infanticide and human sacrifice would lead these races to commit "race suicide." The historian Patrick Brantlinger has observed that this notion amounted to "an extreme form of blaming the victim." The widespread belief in extinction also created a consensus among Europeans, even those working to save the primitive races, that extinction was inevitable, creating a self-fulfilling prophecy that nevertheless ameliorated white guilt. Whites themselves had not caused the precipitous decline in native populations; it had simply resulted from natural Darwinian competition or perhaps the will of a dispassionate God.[27]

Westerners certainly agreed with much of Social Darwinism and the later eugenics movement. Some like Stanford University president David Starr Jordan, even shaped the debate, and there existed distinctive regional variations on these issues in the West. Extinction discourse, for example, assuaged westerners' guilt over the supposed disappearance of American Indians. With the conquest of the West complete by the last third of the nineteenth century, attention could be shifted to the issue of climate and racial degeneration. Whites had clearly taken up residence in the region, and one day the region would become important and powerful, but the predictions of writers from Richard Henry Dana to Bayard Taylor haunted westerners who worried that their region would produce only an inferior population. To put these ghosts to rest, westerners needed to arrive at a belief that whiteness could thrive in a climate that seemed so alien to anything in the race's past.

Charles Fletcher Lummis, for one, brandished Darwinism like a club, striking fiercely at the notion that western expansion would lead to racial decay.[28] As editor of the influential magazine *Land of Sunshine* (later renamed *Out West*), Lummis argued that California's climate would improve the race and make the state the most powerful in the nation.[29] Addressing the issue in his first *Land of Sunshine* editorial in January 1895, he asserted that the Golden State's development represented not just another chapter in the story of American settlement but rather the beginning of a new era in the history of humanity: "Here for the very first time the Saxon has made himself fully at home in a perfect type of the semi-tropics." Historically, "Our blood has befalled [*sic*] climes where to keep alive was in itself a reasonably active occupation. What will be the human outcome of this radical change[?]" Lummis answered his own rhetorical question, arguing that a new society would emerge superior to both the old, indolent Hispanic one and the vigorous but stodgy society of Lummis's native New England: "Southern California is not only the new Eden of the Saxon home-seeker, but part, and type, of Spanish-America; the scene where American energy has wrought miracles . . . but under the skies of New Spain."[30]

A year later, in one of many editorials Lummis wrote comparing California to the East, he again defended his adopted state's weather. Referring to himself in the third person he wrote, "He is not a Southwesterner because he has to be, but because he chooses. He counts it the most important venture his Saxon tribe ever made—this trying on of its first comfortable environment.

And by so much as he believes in evolution, he believes that in this moth-
erly climate the race now foremost in the world will fairly outstrip itself in
achievement; and most of all in what is best of all—the joy of life."[31]

A large portion of the February 1896 issue addressed the question of racial
degeneration and California's climate. Lummis charged Charles Dudley
Warner, an alleged expert on the relationship between race and climate
(though in reality an eastern writer and editor most famous for coauthoring
The Gilded Age with Mark Twain), with defending Southern California's climate.[32] Warner explained that Anglos did poorly in exceptionally hot climates,
such as the Caribbean. Blacks in these climates indeed appeared healthier
than whites, he conceded, but the heat and humidity sapped their vigor, leaving them lazy and unmotivated. Civilization needed a cooler environment in
which to thrive. He wrote, "It is the lesson of experience that the white races
thrive best, produce the best results of civilization, in temperate and even
in rough climates. Greece, Italy, Spain, furnish no exceptions to this, for in
each [a] very appreciable winter prevails." A winter's chill, it seemed, could
create civilization, and Anglos excelled in such frigid conditions.[33] Warner
was essentially arguing that California was nice but, like Italy and Greece, the
wellsprings of Western civilization, not too nice.

He next addressed the question of environment and racial vigor, asking,
"Will the settlers hold their northern vigor and enterprise, or will they follow the example of their occupiers, the Spanish Americans?"[34] The answer
was neither. A healthier climate, Warner argued, would not hurt Anglos,
who were strong enough to endure the nicest weather, and they might even
benefit from it. Southern California perhaps could become a place "reasonably prosperous, not without energy, industrially and intellectually, and yet
not have the restlessness of some others I know, and not be in a continuous exasperating war with nature and with man."[35] Lummis, in his editorial
for the same issue, succinctly answered those who argued that California
threatened the survival of the race. He quipped, "If that gentleman's [i.e.,
Anglo-Saxon's] . . . stamina is of such poor sort that it will spoil if not kept
on ice—then it isn't quite so essential to the world's development as he is
inclined to deem it."[36]

Lummis would spend most of the next thirty years recapitulating his belief
in California's destiny. Every issue of the Land of Sunshine/Out West showcased at least one of Southern California's rapidly growing towns. On the

surface these articles were simply intended to lure home-seekers and investors, detailing such prosaic things as the number of schools and churches, the size and productivity of farms, and so on; but the subtext behind the black-and-white photos and the narrative of promotion maintained that Southern California merged Anglo-Saxon vigor with the climate of the Mediterranean, creating an area of unprecedented wealth and growth. California's destiny as a great and powerful area seemed assured.

Like Lummis, Joseph Pomeroy Widney, a former army surgeon during the wars against the Apache in Arizona and later a promoter of Southern California, believed in the racial destiny of California and the West. Widney felt the West offered the American Anglo-Saxon (or in his terminology the Engle-American) a chance at world domination. While Lummis and Warner argued that whites had never experienced a climate as nice as those of California and the Southwest, Widney argued that the conquest of the West represented a return to the distant past, a time when Aryan horsemen had claimed not the American West but the plains of Asia. In the second volume of his two-volume epic *The Race Life of the Aryan Peoples* he wrote, "The cowboy of the Western plains of America is only the cowboy of the uplands of Mid-Asia of three thousand years ago come to life again. His prototype is more than hinted at in the cow songs of the Hymns to the Maruts and in the earlier *Avestas*, even to the 'round-ups,' lacking only the grim crack of the revolver, but not lacking the grim spirit of battling."[37] Unlike Washington Irving, who feared the wild plains, Widney believed losing some of the "settled habits" of European life would not lead to savagery but instead would represent a return to Aryan racial destiny: "As America east of the Mississippi is Europe, only a modified Europe; so America west of the Mississippi is Asia, only a modified Asia."[38] Settling the West was not an attempt at settling in a new climate but rather a homecoming. Best of all, Anglo-Americans could have Mexico as well because its high, dry central plateau was not unlike the Asian high plains or California.[39]

Widney did, however, agree with most observers about the debilitative effects of tropical climates on the Aryan races, ranking climate as the second-most-important influence on racial degeneration behind only miscegenation. Races would remain true to their ancestry as long as they continued to live in climates conducive to them. Canada's cold climate had proven unfavorable to the French, and the Spanish, likewise, had succumbed to racial degeneration in the New World. He claimed, "The Spaniard landed south of his normal climatic home . . . to the hot, humid shores of the West Indies . . . the Gulf of Mexico, and . . . the east slope of the Andes." Spain's tropical settlements were therefore capable of breeding malaria and yellow fever but not "the iron-sinewed [conquistadors] of the high dry mesas of Castile and Leon . . . who, clad in armor, could toil through the everglades of Florida battling their way on to the banks of the Mississippi, [braving] the marshy plains of *tierra caliente* with their dread *vomito*." Instead, miscegenation and climatic degeneration destroyed the race and banished the conquistador to memory. Widney continued, "The half-breed children of these men of storm and stress swung in the hammock under tropical shades, smoking the cigarette, and dreaming away the noonday hours, while men of a sterner breed despoiled them of their patrimony. The life of storm and stress for them did not exist; and the empire their fathers had won in toil and battling slipped unheeded from nerveless hands."[40] The Spanish-American War closed, he argued, the final chapter in the story of Spanish racial degeneration, and their defeat at the hands of the racially vigorous Aryan Americans provided a cautionary tale about the limits of imperialism. Environment determined race, and empires that overreached, expanding into climates unfamiliar to their racial past, were destined to fall; but, excepting the tropics, it was America's duty to spread its control over the temperate sections of the globe. He concluded, echoing Social Darwinists like Herbert Spencer, "The end of it all is the survival of the fittest; and this is Imperialism. And it has been the race law of the world from the beginning."[41]

Lummis's and Widney's use of Social Darwinism to defend the western climate from its detractors marked only the beginning of their argument. Western intellectuals, keen on using Social Darwinism and eugenics to their advantage, argued that westerners, in fact, collectively constituted the most advanced people on the planet. Anglo-Americans in the late nineteenth century faced the danger of too much civilization. A beneficent climate would not cause racial degeneration, but life in comfortable cities could. Without a frontier to conquer and battles to win, Anglo-Americans would become weak and effeminate. Indeed, perhaps many had already succumbed to inferiority.

Americans might be stronger and more vigorous than Europeans, but they, too, were threatened by comfort and weakness. Colonists to the New World had left behind the insulating civility of Europe to battle with a harsh nature and American Indians. They had been strengthened by the rigors of western expansion and settlement, the weak dying and the strong enduring. Out of this struggle with savages and the wilderness, they had become American. This argument meshed well with Social Darwinism and eugenic theory.

By the early years of the twentieth century, Anglo-Americans seemed increasingly enamored of eugenics, the science of encouraging desirable (middle-class Anglo-American) citizens to breed while discouraging lesser peoples like immigrants and African Americans from doing so. Leading eugenicists like Charles Benedict Davenport and Stanford's David Starr Jordan found an eager audience in westerners. As the historian Alexandra Minna Stern has argued, eugenics was a national and not just an eastern phenomenon that took hold in the West. She noted that "California performed twenty thousand sterilizations, one-third of the total performed in the country, that Oregon created a state eugenics board in 1917, and that the impact of restrictive immigration laws designed to shield America from polluting 'germ plasm' reverberated with great intensity along the Mexican border." The West, she asserted, also provided a racial mythology that eugenicists appropriated, a mythology based on an updated version of the "noble westward march of Anglo-Saxons and Nordics."[42]

Conversely, western proponents declared their region, not the East, the most advanced section of the country. The West, they argued, had become a refuge from the problems of the Gilded Age, a place free of urban slums, machine politics, and "undigestible immigrants." The non-white groups of the West, the Indians, Hispanics, and Chinese, were harmless and romantic— unlike the millions of immigrants flooding the nation's eastern ports who threatened to destroy democracy itself through their willingness to vote for political machines.

Drawing on Social Darwinism and eugenics, westerners justified the inevitable settlement of non-Anglo immigrants as well. Those who made it to the West, whether native-born or foreign, represented the best of the best, the bravest, fittest, most energetic examples of humanity. Immigrants to the region would not pose a threat as did those in the East because they were of a better class and much smaller in number. Limits to this belief existed, however. Many westerners were reluctant to admit that the Chinese were equal members of society, and they considered the clannish and odd Mormons inferior to mainstream Americans, despite the fact that their membership was heavily composed of desirable Northern European immigrant groups.

To convince Americans of the superiority of western society, westerners nevertheless had to confront the dominant view of the region as a frontier. The image of the West as a backward, violent frontier with little civilization and culture had become a well-established stereotype by the middle of the nineteenth century, but its origins preceded the founding of the United States.[43] No less a critic than the Frenchman Alexis de Tocqueville saw the frontier as a threat to American democracy. Every year, Americans "quit the coasts of the Atlantic Ocean to plunge into the Western wilderness," he observed. These were rootless people, often outcasts in their home states, people filled with greedy desires. They entered a world without laws and authority, without family connections and tradition or morality. Still, these inferior peoples could join as equal members of the Union, giving them the right to govern the nation "before they have learned to govern themselves."[44] Tocqueville did not simply observe that westerners could not create effective governments on the frontier but also that they could not "govern" or restrain the passions that life on the frontier undoubtedly exposed. The perpetuation of democracy, however, required restraining such base passions. Tocqueville's criticism of frontiersmen foreshadowed criticism of recent immigrants, who also supposedly lacked the mental acumen necessary for democracy. Nevertheless, other visitors to the frontier echoed Tocqueville's observations.

Isabella Bird, an English traveler, wrote to her sister in 1873 describing life on the Colorado frontier as "moral, hard, unloving, unlovely, unrelieved, unbeautified, [and] grinding." Such "discomfort and lack of ease and refinement . . . seems only possible to people of British stock."[45] Worse, Coloradans cared little for organized religion, and taking advantage of "your neighbor in every fashion which is not illegal, is the quality held in the greatest repute."[46] She assured her sister of her complete safety, despite traveling alone, among such godless heathens, but violence lingered nearby even in her narrative.

Bird herself never encountered the worst aspects of western frontier life, perhaps because of the deference even frontiersmen showed to women, especially genteel women like herself. Yet she met at least one man whose reputation for violence preceded him. He was Mountain Jim, her guide up Longs Peak and a notorious trapper with "'Desperado' . . . written in large letters all over him." Mountain Jim was a shocking sight, missing an eye from an encounter with a grizzly bear and dressed in tatters with a large knife and a revolver tucked into his belt. Yet, "as he spoke I forgot both his reputation and appearance, for his manner was that of a chivalrous gentle-man, his accent refined, and his language easy and elegant."[47] In a footnote Bird explained that nine months after their tour of Estes Park, someone murdered Mountain Jim: "His life, without doubt, was deeply stained with crimes and vices, and his reputation for ruffianism was a deserved one."[48] Still, she had found fears of the harshness of frontier life to be overblown.

The writers of a celebratory sketch of Los Angeles (written in 1876 to com-memorate both the American centennial and the approximately first cen-tury of Los Angeles history) admitted that the Anglo influx into Southern California "was not always made up of the more peaceable elements of society. Men of questionable character, men of no character, drifted in." Yet these "sun-tanned," strong, and vigorous men instantly cast off "the long, slumb'rous years of the old Missions and ranchos," bringing progress and commerce to the region, a fair trade for a period of violence.[49] Thus even boomers like the trio behind the sketch of Los Angeles could not entirely break with the impression of the West as a rough country, filled with rough people. American popular culture, from James Fenimore Cooper onward, had found in the frontier adventure and violence, and dissuading outsiders of the myth of the romantic and adventurous West would prove nearly impossible.[50]

Not everyone, however, found the frontier and its people uncouth and dangerous. Helen Hunt Jackson, a cultured New England writer, found Colorado to her liking—at least once she got over the shock of the move and the radically different landscape. Forced, like many other invalids, to migrate in search of a curative climate, Helen Hunt (not yet a Jackson) moved to Colorado Springs in 1873. A convert to the West, Jackson spent the last decade of her life celebrating the West and its peoples, including the American Indians, whom she believed the federal government and American civiliza-tion had severely mistreated.[51]

She adored her new hometown of Colorado Springs, writing numerous essays extolling the beauty of the scenery and the kindness of her neighbors. Western towns might be rough in character and buildings, but there also prevailed a "helpfulness and sympathy . . . born of the hard-pressing needs and the closely-linked common life." This differed from older eastern com-munities, where "people have crystallized into a strong indifference to each other's affairs, which, if [it] were analyzed, would be found to be nine parts selfishness."[52] Like other western defenders, she believed the West would be different from the East. Surrounded by a benevolent and beautiful natural environment, westerners could lead a purer and more genuine life. In her 1874 essay "Colorado Springs" she declared, "There is to be born of these plains and mountains, all along the great central plateaus of [the] continent, the very best life, both physical and mental, of the coming centuries." Like an echo of antiquity, Colorado would be home to "patriarchal families living with their herds, as patriarchs lived of old on the eastern plains [in the Middle East]." "Of such life, such blood," Jackson continued, "comes culture of a few generations later—a culture all the better because it comes spontaneously and not of effort, is a growth and not a graft." Reinforcing this return to the patriarchs of yesterday and their resurrection in the West, she concluded, "It was in the east that the wise men saw the star; but it was westward to a high mountain, in a lonely place, that the disciples were led for the transfiguration!"[53] Comparing Coloradans to the shepherds of the Bible seemed a bit presumptuous, and clearly there was a racial and ethnic element to her observations. The blood, a signifier of racial and ethnic composition, set Coloradans literally apart, and Colorado's altitude put them a mile closer to heaven. In both cases, this made them better (and racially purer) than people in the East.

The pioneer farmer as an iconic American figure had already established himself by the nineteenth century, and westerners keenly used the myth of the hardworking and moral farmer to their advantage. William Gilpin, a former Colorado territorial governor and Denver promoter, stressed that western emigrants resembled an orderly, peaceful, and disciplined army planting an "empire in the wilderness by a system of colonization at once perfect and inscrutable." Pushed by the tens of thousands of immigrants from the Old World (themselves the chosen, hardest-working members of their nations, Gilpin claimed), "our own people . . . perpetually move up to recruit and reinforce the pioneers."[54] These new pioneers invariably derived from the fittest members of society, and their vigor, Gilpin believed, would create a powerful city at the base of the Rocky Mountains.

Joseph Pomeroy Widney claimed to have studied the racial superiority and biological fitness of immigrants to the West, and, like Hunt and Gilpin, he believed westerners were a breed apart. The pioneers, he claimed, were "a people tall, erect, spare, not an ounce of superfluous flesh, full-chested, clean-limbed, head narrow rather than broad, of the dolichocephalous type, features inclined to the aquiline cast, hair straight, eye[s] keen, alert, restless." They had descended from the rugged trans-Appalachian frontiersmen, the men "who for generations had served as a bumper between the steadily advancing civilization of the Atlantic coast and the wild Indian who was forced back before it."[55] These pioneering sons of pioneers displayed not only great bravery but also admirable intelligence, growing up to be men like George Rogers Clark, Henry Clay, and Abraham Lincoln—esteemed company indeed.[56] Conflict and the rigors of the frontier had made these men the proto-typical Americans, while in the East "people [were] influenced and tinged by the constant influx of alien blood." European ideas, values, and even languages constantly molded easterners. The westerner differed because "his blood yearly is becoming more purely America; for he is breeding out the inherited types."[57] The westerner had no memory of Europe and therefore no compunction to follow its effete values and culture.

Charles Benedict Davenport, a leading eugenicist, outlined how migration could strengthen a group or a race, and he used the West as an example. Migrations "have a profound eugenic significance. The most active, ambitious, and courageous blood migrates. It migrated to America and has made her what she has become; in America another selection took place in the western migrations, and what this best blood—this *crème de la crème*—did in the West all the world knows."[58] Similarly, a Denver and Rio Grande promotional pamphlet, extolling Colorado's considerable virtues, claimed, "Colorado's people are picked from the best communities in the world, and they come this long distance because here they find the best opportunities for health and wealth, and many are attracted by our superb climate. Colorado is just far enough from the denser settlements of the country not to attract the indolent and the shiftless . . . the intelligence and morality of our people is far above the average."[59]

Charles Nordhoff, in *California for Health, Pleasure, and Residence*, first published in the 1870s, predicted greatness for California because its superior population outshone that of eastern cities. New York, according to Nordhoff, deserved credit as the true frontier because there civilized Anglo-Americans came into contact with European immigrants of the basest sort, and the immigrants were clearly winning. "New York receives," Nordhoff wrote, "a constant supply of the rudest, least civilized European populations; that of the immigrants landed at Castle Garden, the neediest, the least thrifty and energetic, and the most vicious remain in New York, while the ablest and most valuable fly rapidly westward . . . [where they became members of California's] settled permanent population."[60]

Even the Chinese, Nordhoff declared, proved more desirable than the teeming masses of immigrants flooding eastern cities because at least they could read their native language and knew their place in society. Nordhoff described meeting an original forty-niner who explained that a kind of natural selection accounted for California's superiority to the East. The pioneer, now a wealthy banker, explained, "When gold was discovered . . . wherever an Eastern family had three or four boys, the ablest, the most energetic one, came hither. Of that great multitude of picked men, again, the weakly broke down under the strain; they died of disease or bad whiskey, or they returned home. The remainder you see here, and you ought not to wonder that they are above your Eastern average in intelligence, energy, and thrift."[61]

Americans considered intelligence, energy, and thrift the most desirable characteristics, the traits that made America great. These marked the very traits Richard Henry Dana had found lacking in Hispanic Californians, a deficiency he attributed to California's climate. Nordhoff's banker saw things differently. He stressed that California's population did not roam because few wanted to return to the East, and they could go no farther west than California. California and the West, therefore, had the best and fittest members of the Anglo population. Even the region's non-Anglo immigrants surpassed their countrymen in the East because of their vigor and ambition. All in all, the banker concluded, "We have much less of a frontier population than . . . [exists] in New York."[62]

The positive influence of migration was also described in John Hanson Beadle's *The Undeveloped West*. California, he declared, would be great because of the influence of the diversity of its population and the influence of migration on improving settlers: "The future Californians will probably be the most inventive race in the world; for only the most resolute settled the country at first, only the most skillful succeeded, and their situation was such as to make invention and contrivance a necessity. Still more will this result from a mixture of races; that state of facts which has made the American what he is, exists tenfold more in California."[63]

A generation later, David Starr Jordan similarly declared that westward movement had created a superior human being in California. In a 1908 article in *Sunset* magazine, Jordan declared, "In my judgment the essential source of

Californianism lies in heredity. The Californian of to-day is of the type of his father of fifty years ago. The Argonauts of '49 were buoyant, self-reliant, adequate, reckless, thoroughly individualistic, capable of all adjustments, careless of conventions, eager to enjoy life and action. And we, their sons, with all admixture of other blood of other temperament are still made in their image. It is blood which tells."[64]

The winnowing process of migration would seem to have been undermined by new technologies. The West, following the completion of the transcontinental railroad, could be easily accessed by even the least vigorous. Yet a promoter as gifted as Charles Fletcher Lummis could find a way to perpetuate the argument put forth by Nordhoff and others. Lummis turned to the free market to explain the West's continued domination by desirable peoples. The West's "transcontinental spaces, the size of fares, the far greater cost of land [were all influential] in determining (by elimination) the extraordinary average of the new California in morals, intelligence, and property. Not only has something attracted a desirable class; something has rather warded the undesirables."[65] Western migration demanded a robust physique and a robust bank account, neither of which recent immigrants possessed.

Though western boosters desired native-born Americans, they accepted immigrants who settled in the region as somehow superior to their countrymen in the East and more willing to assimilate into American culture. The West, so the argument went, compelled immigrants to rapidly abandon their old national and ethnic identities and become American. No less a voice than Frederick Jackson Turner articulated this belief in his famous 1893 essay "The Significance of the Frontier in American History." Turner argued that the rapid assimilation of immigrants into American culture merely illustrated the benevolent power of the frontier. The frontier was the defining feature in American history, a place that provided an outlet for excess population, a home for grassroots democracy, and a fertile land to feed a hungry nation. Turner declared, "The frontier is the line of most rapid and effective Americanization." There, at the "meeting point between savagery and civilization," the immigrant, as many worried, did temporarily become a little savage as he traded the "railroad car" for the "birch canoe." Huddled in clearings hewn from the woods by vanishing Indians, following faint Indian trails, and planting Indian corn, the European immigrant slowly became like an Indian, finding the frontier environment "at first too strong for the man." This changed, however, as slowly, steadily, the settler pushed back the wilderness and brought forth civilization. By this time, after years of struggle, he had left behind his European background and emerged transfigured as an American.[66] Turner, in stark contrast to Washington Irving's early-nineteenth-century analysis, looked back on the era of frontier expansion as the formative experience in American history. Like Widney, Turner believed each successive period of frontier settlement diluted the European influence. The Atlantic Coast settlements acted as "the frontier of Europe," but with each generation "the frontier became more and more American."[67] Turner's view, while perhaps partly nostalgia, reflected the fin de siècle transformation in people's attitudes about the West as a place. No longer did the frontier represent something fearful; it now defined the meaning of American.

Americans recognized the difficult labor inherent in frontier life, especially farming, and they saw hard work as a desirable trait in immigrants to the West. Americans admired those immigrants because their hard work literally made the desert bloom. In their work ethic, many western writers declared, immigrants far outmatched native-born Americans. Frederick Law Olmsted, writing in the 1850s, found immigrants in Texas the hardest-working and most able people in the state. The German immigrants in towns like Neu Branfels, he explained, were poor but industrious, and their fortunes improved each year because of their hard work. They lived in small but well-made houses, with neat fields surrounding them that stood in stark contrast to "the patches of corn-stubble, overgrown with crab-grass, which are usually the only gardens to be seen adjoining the cabins of the poor whites and slaves."[68] This progress, Olmsted asserted, resulted from free labor and a work ethic that made these Germans the equals of the best native-born citizens.

In the late 1870s James Rusling similarly witnessed immigrant labor as transformative in Missouri. They elevated the state from the degenerate condition in which it had existed during slavery: "All along the route, it was plain to be seen, Missouri had suffered sadly from slavery. But the wave of immigration, now that slavery was dead, had already reached her, and we found its healthful currents everywhere overflowing her bottoms and prairies." Vigorous and industrious Germans and Yankees inhabited land that had once known only white laziness and black slave labor. The desirability of freedom-loving, hardworking German immigrants was self-evident, Rusling argued: "The sturdy Rhine-men, as true to freedom as in the days of Tacitus, were already everywhere planting vineyards, and in the near future were sure of handsome returns from petty farms, that our old time 'Pikes' and 'Border Ruffians' would have starved on."[69] He found many of the same characteristics in the German population of Anaheim, California: "Here were some five hundred or more Germans, all industriously engaged, and exhibiting of course their usual sagacity and thrift. They had constructed *acequias*, and carried the hitherto useless Santa Anna River everywhere—around through their lots, and past every door; they had hedged their little farms with willows, and planted them with vines, orange, lemon, and olive trees; and the once barren plains in summer were now alive with perpetual foliage and verdure." Their settlement resembled "a bit of Germany, dropped down on the Pacific Coast. It has little in common with Los Angelos [*sic*] the dirty, but the glorious climate and soil, and was an agreeable surprise [in] every way."[70] From Texas to Missouri to California, these industrious immigrants transformed the landscape, putting down roots and rapidly remade these places into the white man's West.

The transformative power of the West and its need for good, hardworking immigrants was the subject of a 1910 article by Herbert Kaufman in the magazine *Everybody's*, titled "Southwestward Ho!" The essay extolled the virtues of immigrant settlement in Texas and Oklahoma. Ideally, Kaufman declared, young Americans would finally turn their backs on the corrupt and evil cities and return to the countryside. Despite being raised in urban enclaves, these young people would unconsciously remember their agrarian ancestral past: "They are Americans, the native-born, the sons and the daughters of pioneer strain, hearkening to the impulse which in another day drove forth their forbear[s]."[71] Yet they did not return in great enough numbers to alleviate the Southwest's "help problem." Kaufman continued: "The native whites will not enter service. Colored help is insolent and inefficient. But this simply means the coming of the immigrant girl, who in turn will lead her man after her; and both will benefit the region."[72] The best solution to the immigrant problem, Kaufman declared, was to divert Eastern European immigration to Galveston: "Italy could empty herself into Texas alone, and Texas would still have room for Germany and France to boot."[73] Italians and other "Latins," considered a scourge in other parts of the country, could easily adapt to Texas's warm climate (since they were from the warm Mediterranean), and they would quickly assimilate into American society, benefiting Texas and the nation.

Immigrants' thrift, industry, and desire for hard work made them acceptable to westerners, many of whom believed that only these kinds of immigrants should settle in the region. Yet hard work would not necessarily
allow westerners to appreciate groups that seemed too radically different.
Westerners singled out the Chinese and the Mormons of Utah as undesirable,
despite their work ethics. The former were racially too different and the latter acolytes of religious heresy in the minds of most Americans. Regardless
of their willingness to labor, westerners roundly discriminated against the
Chinese. James G. Eastman, the orator of Los Angeles's centennial celebration in 1876, for example, declared that the nation had room for "the inge-
nious Swiss, the practical Englishman, the polished Frenchman, the philo-
sophic German, the gallant Spaniard, the busy, country-loving Irishman, and
the sturdy Swede." These Europeans worked hard and appreciated freedom
and democracy. America would remain a haven, he declared, "to all who
come with brain or muscle or skill to enjoy the blessings of our government
because they believe in its principles and love its doctrines, and desire to con-
tribute to its success, the invitation is irrevocable, and the doors are open
forever. They are brothers in blood, in thought, in aspiration and inheritance."
The Chinese, by contrast, were inclined to idolatry, consented to monarchy,
and despised American values and institutions, Eastman claimed. He concluded, "This grand continent, with its civilization and wondrous development, its cultivating valleys and happy homes, is not the lap into which China
may spew its criminals and paupers, its invalids and idiots, its surplus moral
and physical leprosy."[74]

Even worse, as many observers asserted, the Chinese could survive on
very little. Edwin R. Meade, in the explorer F. V. Hayden's popular book on
the West, declared that the Chinese would hurt white laborers: "It is impossible that the white laborer can persist in the presence of these conditions
[low Chinese wage rates]. Not only substantial food, comfortable clothing,
and decent household accommodations are necessary to him, but his family must be supported in a respectable manner and schooling and religious
training be provided for his children. These latter have become essential, and
are the glory of our race and nation."[75] The Chinese, conversely, lived in a
largely male society sans families and children, an arrangement intolerable
for whites. To resolve the matter, Meade argued, laws should forever ban
Chinese immigration to the United States.

Not everyone adamantly opposed the Chinese. James Rusling, for example, argued that the Chinese would assimilate in time and until then would provide a much-needed labor source to develop the West Coast: "The first generation passed away, the next[,] de-Chinaized, Americanized, and educated, would soon become absorbed in the national life . . . As the ocean receives all rains and rivers, and yet shows it not, so America receives the Saxon and the Celt, the Protestant and the Catholic, and can yet receive the Sambo and John, and absorb them all." Setting aside the obviously demeaning racial epithets, Rusling nevertheless advocated for a multiracial society. This society could be achieved, he asserted, by American institutions: "The school-house and the church, the newspaper and the telegraph, can be trusted to work out their logical results; and time, our sure ally, would shape and fashion even these [Chinese] into keen American citizens."[76] Rusling's relatively egalitarian and progressive view, however, gained little public support, and legislation soon prevented Chinese entry into the nation with the passage of several acts, most notably the 1882 Chinese Exclusion Act, that forbade their entry into the United States. Their laudable thrift and hard work could not, in the end, overcome Americans' widespread opposition.[77]

At the fin de siècle, westerners sought to create a civilization in which Anglo-Americans could find refuge from a changing world. Westerners argued for the superiority of their region because it lacked the racial and ethnic problems of the rest of the country. Undesirable immigrants wielded power in the East, overwhelming native-born Americans, but the difficulty and expense of western migration prevented a massive influx of these undesirable citizens. Anglo-Americans could, however, embrace desirable immigrants if they worked hard and could be easily assimilated into American culture. The Chinese in particular differed too much to be welcomed into the West by most Anglo-American westerners.

The West, especially California and the Southwest, nevertheless remained the home of the nation's largest populations of American Indian peoples, Hispanics, and Asians (both the Chinese and, beginning around the turn of the twentieth century, an increasing number of Japanese). This diversity might appear to give lie to the imagining of the West as a white man's homeland. Western image makers, however, romanticized and appropriated these cultures, adding an exotic veneer over the political and social domination of Anglo-Americans. In comparison, they argued, the East seemed doomed to sink under the weight of inferior white but non-Anglo immigrants. Explaining this process, showing that the ills of industrialization and non-Anglo immigration did not affect the West, proved to be the last stage in the intellectual and imagined creation of the white man's West.

NOTES

1. Bayard Taylor, *At Home and Abroad, a Sketch-book of Life, Scenery and Men* (New York: G. P. Putnam, 1860), 497–98.

2. The best analysis of the alleged effects of the environment on race is in Conevery Bolton Valenčius, *The Health of the Country: How American Settlers Understood Themselves and Their Land* (New York: Perseus Books Group, 2002), 229–58. Another work of interest on the relationship between the body and the environment is Linda Nash, *Inescapable Ecologies: A History of Environment, Disease, and Knowledge* (Berkeley: University of California Press, 2006).

3. Bayard Taylor, *Eldorado; or, Adventures in the Path of Empire* . . . (New York: G. P. Putnam's Sons, 1861), 144.

4. Ibid., 340.

5. Helen Hunt Jackson, *Glimpses of Three Coasts* (Boston: Roberts Brothers, 1886), 3–4.

6. William Deverell, *Whitewashed Adobe: The Rise of Los Angeles and the Remaking of Its Mexican Past* (Berkeley: University of California Press, 2004), 215.

7. Jackson, *Glimpses of Three Coasts*, 28–29.

8. Ibid.

9. Ibid., 29.

10. Josiah Gregg, *Commerce of the Prairies*, Max L. Moorhead, ed. (Norman: University of Oklahoma Press, 1954), 154.

11. J[ohn] H[anson] Beadle, *The Undeveloped West: or, Five Years in the Territories* (Philadelphia: National Publishing, 1873; reprint, New York: Arno, 1973), 460.

12. W.R.T., "From Trinidad to Santa Fe—Six Days in the Oldest City in the United States," *Rocky Mountain News* (Denver, CO), March 4, 1869.

13. On the causes of alleged Hispanic inferiority, see Robert W. Johannsen, *To the Halls of the Montezumas: The Mexican War in the American Imagination* (New York: Oxford University Press, 1985), 165–69; David J. Weber, *The Spanish Frontier in North America* (New Haven, CT: Yale University Press, 1992), 335–41; Arnoldo De León, *They Called Them Greasers: Anglo Attitudes toward Mexicans in Texas, 1821–1900* (Austin: University of Texas Press, 1983); David Montejano, *Anglos and Mexicans in the Making of Texas* (Austin: University of Texas Press, 1987).

14. Frederick Law Olmsted, *A Journey through Texas, or, A Saddle-Trip on the Southwestern Frontier* (New York: Dix, Edwards, and Co., 1857), 349. Olmsted is later quite taken with a teenage Spanish woman with a "beautiful little bust" that she exposed as she ground corn for him and his companions.

15. Beadle, *Undeveloped West*, 459.

16. For an example of Lummis's fascination with Mexican women, see the story of Susie del Valle, the daughter of an old California family, in Mark Thompson, *American Character: The Curious Life of Charles Fletcher Lummis and the Rediscovery of the Southwest* (New York: Arcade, 2001), 122–24; for his apparent infidelity, see pp. 278–82.

17. Charles Fletcher Lummis, "The Spanish American Face," *Land of Sunshine* 12, no., 2 (January 1895): 21–23.

18. Richard Hofstadter, *Social Darwinism in American Thought* (New York: George Braziller, 1959), 5; italics in original.

19. Ibid., 41.

20. See especially Hofstadter's chapter "Racism and Imperialism," in ibid., 170–200.

21. Ibid., 176–78.

22. Aline Gorren, *Anglo-Saxons and Others* (New York: Charles Scribner's Sons, 1900), 2.

23. Ibid., 14.

24. Ibid., 22–23.

25. Hofstadter, *Social Darwinism*, 171.

26. Quoted in Stephen J. Gould, *The Mismeasure of Man* (New York: W. W. Norton, 1981), 69.

27. Patrick Brantlinger, *Dark Vanishings: Discourse on the Extinction of Primitive Races, 1800–1930* (Ithaca, NY: Cornell University Press, 2003), 1–4. Brantlinger looks mostly at the American and British experiences. The idea of the vanishing American Indian is also recounted in Brian Dippie, *The Vanishing American: White Attitudes and U.S. Racial Policy* (Lawrence: University Press of Kansas, 1982).

28. In addition to works written by Lummis, many of which are still in print, see also Edwin R. Bingham, *Charles F. Lummis: Editor of the Southwest* (San Marino, CA: Huntington Library Press, 1955); Turbese Lummis Fisk and Keith Lummis, *Charles F. Lummis: The Man and His West* (Norman: University of Oklahoma Press, 1975); Sherry L. Smith, *Reimagining Indians: Native Americans through Anglo Eyes, 1880–1940* (New York: Oxford University Press, 2000), 119–44.

29. For discussion of Lummis's plan for an Anglo-Saxon California, see Kevin Starr, *Inventing the Dream: California through the Progressive Era* (New York: Oxford University Press, 1985), 89–90.

30. Charles F. Lummis, "Editorial," *Land of Sunshine* 2, no. 2 (January 1895): 34–35.

31. Charles F. Lummis, "In the Lion's Den," *Land of Sunshine* 4, no. 3 (February 1896), 183. "In the Lion's Den" was Lummis's monthly editorial in *Land of Sunshine*.

32. Cited in Thompson, *American Character*, 181.

33. Charles Dudley Warner, "Race and Climate," *Land of Sunshine* 4, no. 2 (February 1896): 103–6. The creation of Southern California as a new Mediterranean is recounted in Kevin Starr, *Americans and the California Dream* (New York: Oxford University Press, 1973), 365–414.

34. Warner, "Race and Climate," 104.

35. Ibid., 106.

36. Charles Lummis, "In the Lion's Den," *Land of Sunshine* 4, no. 2 (February 1896): 141.

37. Joseph P[omeroy] Widney, *The Race Life of the Aryan Peoples*, vol. 2: *The New World* (New York: Funk and Wagnalls, 1907), 65.

38. Ibid.

39. Widney's views on the annexation of Mexico are in ibid, 149–51.

40. Ibid., 10–11.

41. Ibid., 211.

42. Alexandra Minna Stern, *Eugenic Nation: Faults and Frontiers of Better Breeding in Modern America* (Berkeley: University of California Press, 2005), 7.

43. The historiography of violence in the West is extensive. See, for example: David T. Courtwright, *Violent Land: Single Men and Social Disorder from the Frontier to the Inner City* (Cambridge, MA: Harvard University Press, 1996), especially 47–130; Richard Maxwell Brown, *No Duty to Retreat: Violence and Values in American History and Society* (Norman: University of Oklahoma Press, 1991); Robert M. Utley, *High Noon in Lincoln: Violence on the Western Frontier* (Albuquerque: University of New Mexico Press, 1987); Richard Slotkin's trilogy, *Regeneration through Violence: The Mythology of the American Frontier, 1600–1860* (Norman: University of Oklahoma Press, 2000); *The Fatal Environment: The Myth of the Frontier in the Age of Industrialization, 1800–1890* (Norman: University of Oklahoma Press, 1998); *Gunfighter Nation: The Myth of the Frontier in Twentieth-Century America* (Norman: University of Oklahoma Press, 1998). An excellent example of the social conditions of frontier life, at least on the mining frontier, is Susan Lee Johnson, *Roaring Camp: The Social World of the California Gold Rush* (New York: W. W. Norton, 2000).

44. Alexis de Tocqueville, *Democracy in America* (New York: Vintage Books, 1990), 1:396; translated by Henry Reeve, corrected by Francis Bowen, and edited by Phillips Bradley.

45. Isabella L. Bird, *A Lady's Life in the Rocky Mountains* (Norman: University of Oklahoma Press, 1960), 50.

46. Ibid., 69.

47. Ibid., 79.

48. Ibid., 89.

49. J. J. Warner, Benjamin Hayes, and J. P. Widney, *An Historical Sketch of Los Angeles County, California: From the Spanish Occupancy, by the Founding of the Mission San Gabriel Archangel, September 8, 1771, to July 4, 1876* (Los Angeles: Louis Lewin, 1876), 67.

50. On the literary creation of the mythic West, see two examples from a large historiography: Henry Nash Smith, *Virgin Land: The American West as Symbol and Myth* (Cambridge, MA: Harvard University Press, 1970), 51–122; Slotkin, *Fatal Environment*, especially 81–106, 191–208, 499–532.

51. Mark I. West, "Introduction," in Mark I. West, ed., *Westward to a High Mountain: The Colorado Writings of Helen Hunt Jackson* (Denver: Colorado Historical Society, 1994), 1–9. See also Ruth Odell, *Helen Hunt Jackson* (New York: D. Appleton-Century, 1939); Evelyn I. Banning, *Helen Hunt Jackson* (New York: Vanguard, 1973).

52. Helen Hunt Jackson, "A Colorado Week," in West, ed., *Westward to a High Mountain*, 21–52.

53. Helen Hunt Jackson, "Colorado Springs," in West, ed., *Westward to a High Mountain*, 11–20.

54. William Gilpin, *Mission of the North American People, Geographical, Social, and Political* (Philadelphia: J. B. Lippincott, 1874), 99.

55. Widney, *Race Life of the Aryan Peoples*, 2:80.

56. Ibid., 81.

57. Ibid., 93.

58. Charles Benedict Davenport, "The Geography of Man in Relation to Eugenics," in William Ernest Castle, John Merle Coulter, Charles Benedict Davenport, Edward Murray East, and William Lawrence, eds., *Heredity and Eugenics* (Chicago: University of Chicago Press, 1912), 299.

59. Denver and Rio Grande Western Railway, *The Opinions of the Judge and the Colonel as to the Vast Resources of Colorado* (Denver: Denver and Rio Grande Western Railway, 1894), 23.

60. Charles Nordhoff, *California for Health, Pleasure, and Residence: A Book for Travellers and Settlers* (New York: Harper Bros., 1882), 18–19.

61. Ibid.

62. Ibid.

63. Beadle, *Undeveloped West*, 178.

64. "Two University Presidents Speak for the City," *Sunset* 20, no. 6 (1908): 546; quoted in Stern, *Eugenic Nation*, 132.

65. Charles Fletcher Lummis, "The Right Hand of the Continent, Part Three," *Out West* (August 1902): 139–71.

66. Frederick Jackson Turner, "The Significance of the Frontier in American History," in John Mack Faragher, ed., *Rereading Frederick Jackson Turner* (New York: Henry Holt, 1994), 33–34.

67. Ibid., 34.

68. Olmsted, *Journey through Texas*, 140.

69. James F. Rusling, *Across America: or the Great West and the Pacific Coast* (New York: Sheldon, 1874), 24.

70. Ibid., 340–41.

71. Herbert Kaufman, "Southwestward Ho! America's New Trek to Still-Open Places," *Everybody's* 22, no. 6 (June 1910): 725.

72. Ibid., 730.

73. Ibid., 731.

74. Eastman quoted in Warner, Hayes, and Widney, "Historical Sketch," 86.

75. Edwin R. Meade, "A Labor Question," in F. V. Hayden, ed., *The Great West: Its Attractions and Resources* (Bloomington, IL: Charles R. Brodix, 1880), 391.

76. Rusling, *Across America*, 317–18.

77. Najia Aarim-Heriot, *Chinese Immigrants, African-Americans, and Racial Anxiety in the United States, 1848–1882* (Urbana: University of Illinois Press, 2003), 228. Other works on the Chinese experience in the West include Liping Zhu, *A Chinaman's Chance: The Chinese on the Rocky Mountain Mining Frontier* (Niwot: University Press of Colorado, 1997); George Anthony Peffer, *If They Don't Bring Their Women Here: Chinese Female Immigration before Exclusion* (Urbana: University of Illinois Press, 1999); Kil Young Zo, *Chinese Emigration into the United States, 1850–1880* (New York: Arno, 1978); Stuart Creighton Miller, *The Unwelcome Immigrant: The American Image of the Chinese, 1785–1882* (Berkeley: University of California Press, 1969); Alexander Saxton, *The Indispensable Enemy: Labor and the Anti-Chinese Movement in California* (Berkeley: University of California Press, 1971).

4

INDIANS NOT IMMIGRANTS

Charles Fletcher Lummis, Frank Bird Linderman, and the Complexities of Race and Ethnicity in America

Charles Fletcher Lummis and Frank Bird Linderman were painfully aware that they had missed the show. It would be the better part of a decade before the US Census Bureau and Frederick Jackson Turner announced the end of the frontier, but by the mid-1880s its passing already seemed obvious. Timing, no doubt, had a profound influence on both men. They came to understand the West not in terms of progress and settlement, as had an earlier generation, but rather as a place threatened by those same forces. Lummis and Linderman underwent a process of transformation, of becoming westerners, or, to use historian Hal Rothman's term, *neo-natives*, people from outside the region who became westerners and, in their cases, self-appointed experts and defenders of the region's culture.[1] The transformation into westerners forever altered their conception of the West and its people. Seeing the West through the lens of romanticism and anti-modernism, they envisioned a region where Native Americans (and in Lummis's case Hispanics) would remain a vital part of the culture and society and where the negative characteristics of modern America, especially Southern and Eastern European immigration, would be

DOI: 10.5876/9781607323969.c004

kept at bay. The West would emerge as a haven for Anglo-Americans where the region's colorful racial groups could be preserved while remaining little more than quaint. The West could be a refuge for whiteness, they hoped, a last chance to create an ideal society. In celebrating a romantic version of diversity while arguing for the continued dominance of Anglo-Americans, Lummis and Linderman put the last touches on the intellectual creation of the white man's West.

Like many people before him, the lithe, twenty-five-year-old Charles Fletcher Lummis set out for opportunity in the West, although in his case opportunity came in the form of a job at the *Los Angeles Times*. It was the fall of 1884. Unlike his contemporaries in an age of transcontinental railroads, Lummis decided to walk. He intended this roughly 2,500-mile journey from Chillicothe, Ohio, to Los Angeles to be equal parts publicity stunt and a sincere attempt to discover the West for himself. Like his Harvard classmate and friend Theodore Roosevelt, Lummis believed in the strenuous life, and he hoped to find himself in the arid land of mesas and canyons. He was far from unique in his desire to find meaning in the West. Roosevelt, the writer Owen Wister, and the artist Frederic Remington also went west to act out an increasingly common ritual of national and self-discovery—all believing that the West remained authentic, preindustrial, and Anglo-dominated. Going west, quite simply, meant returning to a time when (white) men were men. Roosevelt, Wister, and Remington sojourned in the West before returning to the East, where they mingled with the most powerful elements in the nation, but their time in the West had transformed them into supposedly stronger and better men. The West, for these men and others, remained an "agrarian, rural, egalitarian, and ethnically and racially homogenous" region, which compared favorably to the "industrial, urban, elitist, ethnically heterogeneous, and racially mixed" East, according to the historian G. Edward White.[2] Perhaps somewhat ironically, the western experience prepared Roosevelt, Wister, and Remington to lead and shape an eastern-dominated, ethnically diverse, industrial society. All these men emerged from the experience changed in important ways, but Lummis and Linderman, unlike Roosevelt, Remington, and Wister, went west and stayed.

Lummis and Linderman set out to celebrate the West and its cultures, one in Southern California and the other in Montana. They argued that the region still offered an antidote to the problems of industrialization,

FIGURE 4.1. *Studio Portrait of Lummis before His Tramp,* 1884. Part publicity stunt and part a genuine effort to learn about his new home, Charles Fletcher Lummis walked from Chillicothe, Ohio, to Los Angeles, California. As he said, the trip enabled him to transcend from a "little, narrow, prejudiced, intolerant Yankee" into a westerner who appreciated Hispanic and American Indian cultures. These cultures helped make the West unique and superior in many ways to the East, he believed. *Courtesy,* Braun Research Library Collection, Southwest Museum, Autry National Center, Los Angeles, CA

pollution, and non-Anglo immigration. A writer, reporter, editor, and self-taught combination of ethnologist, archaeologist, and historian, Lummis's varied career became the consummate example of the active intellectual, the uniquely American type of thinker and doer. Eventually, his opinions and reputation would carry weight far beyond Southern California. His fiery zeal for the Southwest, rather than any intellectual achievements, made him well-known in his era. He was certainly a popularizer, but in being so he left a lasting legacy.

Frank Bird Linderman, trailing Lummis by less than a year, went west in 1885 at age sixteen. He chose as his destination the Flathead Lake country of the Montana Territory, the most isolated place he could find on a folded and refolded map of the nation. In his memoir, he called the place the "farthest removed from contaminating civilization," no mean consideration for a boy who feared "that the West of my dreams would fade away before I could reach it."[3] A friend and an African American coachman employed by his friend's family accompanied him. The coachman had been a cavalryman in the West, and he filled the boys' minds with stories of the wild and untamed region.[4] Following an eventful train trip to Montana, the trio settled in the Flathead country, but after a few days his companions grew homesick and returned to Ohio. Linderman decided to stick it out and learn to be a trapper.[5]

In the Flathead country Linderman found a landscape as romantic as his fantasies, a place filled with howling wolves and marked only by the tracks cut by deer and Indians. The latter in particular stoked his imagination and, in time, inspired his anthropological works, works deeply tinged by his belief in the vanishing West and a threatening modern, industrial world. According to the historian Sherry L. Smith, Indians "represented, for him, the most powerful symbols of a West that was no more."[6] Linderman in *Montana Adventure* never gave a name to the black man with whom he went West, referring to him only as "the negro," but American Indians left him awestruck. He stared, dumbfounded, when encountering a Flathead Indian smoking "with such an air of peace and contentment that I fairly ached to shake hands with him."[7] He explained that the man's name was Red-horn, a "renowned Flathead warrior" whose martial skills were widely respected by his friends and feared by his enemies. Linderman felt grateful that the powerful warrior treated him like a man, though he knew instinctively "that I was a rank pilgrim."[8] This represented, Linderman thought, a sort of acceptance by the Indians and even by the Montana wilderness. Leaving his childhood behind him in the East, he had become a man and, even better, a frontiersman. He flattered himself for a moment, writing, "I feel nearly as they do, I am quite certain." He quickly corrected himself and admitted that this conceit was probably "only imagined success."[9] Nevertheless, he felt pride in being accepted into a world he had once dreamed about, and this acceptance extended beyond Indians to another romantic group: Montana trappers.

Linderman caught up with the aging trappers at the twilight of the fur trade. Later, when he himself had grown gray, he noted that they were "unlike any type that lives today," and being accepted by them "was like joining a fraternity."[10] Linderman would spend the rest of his life believing sincerely that he had glimpsed the end of an era, and he would do his best to preserve the vestiges of that world through print and political action.

Later in life, Linderman would go even farther, asserting that he was in fact even more Indian than younger Indians. In his biography of the Crow woman Pretty-shield, he quoted the old woman as worrying about the condition of modern Indians. One of Pretty-shield's grandsons entered the room during one of Linderman's interviews with her. He described the teenage boy as "decked out in the latest style of the 'movie' cowboy, ten-gallon hat, leather cuffs and all." His appearance prompted Pretty-shield to "wonder how my grandchildren will turn out . . . They have only me, an old woman, to guide them, and plenty of others to lead them into bad ways."[11] Linderman saw older Indians like Pretty-shield as more genuine and noble than modern Indians. Comparing Goes-together, his translator, to Pretty-shield, he remarked, "She [Goes-together], a comparatively young woman of the same blood as Pretty-shield, frequently complained of her physical condition, had done this less than an hour ago. Pretty-shield, nearly twice the age of Goes-together, had remained an old-fashioned Indian, believing as her grandmother had believed. She had nothing to complain of, no affliction, excepting grandchildren."[12] Modern Indians, like Goes-together and Pretty-shield's army of grandchildren, had lost connection with their past and grown lazy, weak, and infirm. They had, in essence, lost what made them Indian. Linderman, in contrast, felt he shared with Pretty-shield the same authentic experiences.

Linderman felt that he, too, belonged to this noble age of heroes. In *Pretty-shield* he went to great lengths to assert his authenticity as a westerner and his affinity with Indians. The first line of his book made this clear: "Throughout forty-six years in Montana I have had much to do with its several Indian tribes, and yet have never, until now, talked for ten consecutive minutes directly to an old Indian woman."[13] While the overall point of the sentence is to pique the reader's interest in the hidden world of Indian women and to assert the importance of the story he is about to tell, it also provides readers with his credentials as an expert and a Montanan.

For Charles Fletcher Lummis, becoming a westerner meant coming to appreciate both the region and its peoples. His 1884 walking tour marked the transformative moment of his life. He went West armed with standard-issue views of Hispanics and Native Americans. Both groups appeared as curious, inferior novelties and anachronisms to the young reporter. He best articulated his early views about American Indians and Hispanics in a series of letters for his former employer in Ohio, the *Chillicothe Leader*. He first encountered Native Americans at the Indian school in Lawrence, Kansas. After laughing at the funny translations of the students' names, Lummis concluded, "The whole institution is under the charge of James Marvin, L.L.D., an educator of almost national reputation, and he shows by deeds his faith that here lies the true solution to the vexed and vexing 'Indian Question.'"[14]

Such an endorsement for educators' assimilation policy made his skin crawl in later years. Indeed, only a few years later, Lummis would become an ardent critic of Indian schools, even going so far as to initiate lawsuits in federal court against the policies of Indian educators.[15] In August 1899 Lummis launched an assault on Indian education in *Land of Sunshine* (renamed *Out West* in 1902), a California promotional periodical he converted into a respected western magazine. The seven-month series, titled "My Brother's Keeper," excoriated the assimilation policy of schools like those in Carlisle, Pennsylvania, and Hampton, Virginia. Led by the reformer Captain Richard Henry Pratt, these schools sought to transform Indian children by removing them from their families and tribes and forcibly assimilating them into American society.[16] In his first salvo against the policy, Lummis wrote that Pratt's method effectively alienated children from their native cultures while ill-preparing them for life in the larger American world: "The confessed theory is that he [the Indian child] has no right to have a father and mother, and they no right to him; that their affection is not worth as much to him as the chance to be a servant to some Pennsylvania farmer or blacksmith, and generally at half wages."[17] In a letter to President Theodore Roosevelt early in his administration, Lummis congratulated the president and expressed his great optimism that Roosevelt's would be the first administration to have a competent Bureau of Indian Affairs. This was important, Lummis argued, because "I care for Indians not as 'bric-a-brac' but as actual humans."[18]

In *A Tramp across the Continent*, the memoir of his 1884 journey across the West, he marveled at the quiet Pueblo villages he encountered. Like the good New Englander he was, he called the reader's attention to the thrift and hard work of the sedentary Indians of the Rio Grande valley. A highly developed civilization, with irrigated farms and well-built homes, the Pueblos appeared the model of the industrious Indian. Lummis explained to readers that they "had learned none of these things from us, but were living thus before our Saxon forefathers had found so much as the shore of the New England."[19] To be sure, Lummis did not believe all Indians were equal. He liked the Pueblo peoples best, harbored some suspicion of the Navajo, and believed the Hualapais of the Mojave stood out as "a race of filthy and unpleasant Indians, who were in world-wide contrast with the admirable Pueblos of New Mexico . . . They manufacture nothing characteristic, as do nearly all other aborigines, and are of very little interest."[20]

Lummis, like most self-appointed Indian protectors, could also be condescending toward them. The slogan, for example, of his Indian rights group, the Sequoya League, was "To Make Better Indians," something Lummis felt he knew how to do better than men like Pratt. Similarly, he warned Roosevelt that the policy of severalty, by which tribal lands were broken up into individual landholdings, most famously part of the 1887 Dawes Allotment Act, threatened Indian independence. The best solution, he argued, would be to ensure that individual Indian landowners be prohibited from selling their lands for at least fifty years. The reason was that "the Indian is not yet of age and he needs the protection we give to our minors."[21] Needless to say, his paternalism sounded little different than Pratt's, but Lummis at least respected Indian cultures.

Similarly, he entered the West with assumptions about the region's Hispanic population. In southern Colorado he encountered his first Hispanic villages. Of the residents of the village of Cucharas he wrote, "In it, in lousy laziness, exist 200 Greasers of all sexes, ages and sizes, but all equally dirty." He continued, in his November 18, 1884, letter, to describe the Hispanics of southern Colorado in a less than favorable light, concluding with an overtly racist joke. "Not even a coyote," he told his growing number of readers (his letters were widely published by eastern newspapers), "will touch a dead Greaser, the flesh is so seasoned with the red pepper they ram into their food in howling profusion."[22] Only a decade later, in *Land of Sunshine*, he recanted his earlier views and wrote, "'Greaser' . . . is a vulgar phrase which more soils the mouth that speaks it than the person at whom it is aimed. It is precisely on a par with the word 'nigger'; as offensive per se, and as sure [a] brand of the breeding of the user."[23]

As for the Chinese, a group that drew most of the wrath of California and western nativists, Lummis again voiced positive views.[24] Given that he lived in California, it is not surprising that he commented mostly on the Chinese in the state. In the November 1900 issue of *Land of Sunshine*, he praised Sui Sin Fah (the pen name of Edith Maude Eaton, a British Chinese contributor to the magazine).[25] Of her work he wrote, "To others the alien Celestial is at best mere 'literary material'; in these stories he (or she) is a human being."[26] Nevertheless, her exotic pen name considerably augmented her story's literary worth. In the same issue Lummis advocated a harsh response to the Boxer Rebellion but reminded readers, "We have massacred a good many foreigners, ourselves, in this Christian land. Our Boxers have murdered Chinese in Rock Springs and other centers of civilization; Italians in New Orleans; and Negroes everywhere." He warned that the western powers should restrain themselves and not murder innocent people who had no voice in the Chinese government.[27]

Lummis made it clear that becoming a westerner led him to transcend his racist views. In *A Tramp across the Continent*, which did not appear until nearly a decade after his transcontinental hike, he used the story of his ignorance to editorialize on the problems of racism. He sincerely asked his readers: "Why is it that the last and most difficult education seems to be the ridding ourselves of the silly inborn race prejudice? We all start with it, we few of us graduate from it. And yet the clearest thing in the world to him who has eyes and a chance to use them, is that men everywhere—white men, brown men, yellow men, black men—are all just about the same thing. The difference is little deeper than the skin."[28]

Long before finally reaching Los Angeles, he had become a convert to the West and a prophet of a proto-multiculturalism. Reflecting on this late in life, he wrote in his weekly column in the *Los Angeles Times*, "I wasn't born a frontiersman—I Earned it. I was born a little, narrow, prejudiced, intolerant Yankee." Conversely, he argued, "the real Western Spirit is as much broader, freer, braver, richer, more independent and more tolerant than [northeastern] Puritanism or Tenderfootedness."[29] He also believed its native inhabitants, the region's Hispanics and American Indians, offered much to society and should continue to exert some influence in shaping the West. Imbued with the passion of the converted, Lummis would be a defender of the West and its people for the rest of his life.

An exceedingly complex, if often inconsistent, individual, Lummis took a progressive stance on issues of race, but his attitude toward new immigrants proved much less charitable. Lummis often crowed about the superiority of California society in comparison to the East because it lacked the large numbers of "indigestible" immigrants that plagued cities like Boston and New York. In an article in the January 1895 issue of *Land of Sunshine*, Lummis's first month on the job, he explained the superiority of the "golden state" to the East. California was growing rapidly, but, he argued, it was the quality of the immigrants that made it different. People of "wealth and refinement" chose to relocate to Los Angeles, whereas "elsewhere the bulk of immigration has been of at least indifferent stuff." These people of wealth and refinement tended to be Anglo-Americans who left to escape the East and often to find renewed health and a sense of purpose in California. Lummis's native New England, which became a favorite target of the combative editor, witnessed a degradation of its society as a result of "an invasion which has seriously lowered the mean of culture." The difference in the quality of immigrants meant "there is no criminal class [in Southern California]; practically no pauper class." Of course, California had a few undesirable types, "but numerically they are lonely, and politically and socially the good citizen is not ruled by them."[30] Lummis was never subtle and, in case the reader missed the point, he continued by extolling Los Angeles's ethnic virtues: "Our 'foreign element' is a few thousand industrious Chinamen and perhaps 500 native Californians who do not speak English. The ignorant, hopelessly un-American type of foreigners, which infests and largely controls Eastern cities, is almost unknown here. Poverty and illiteracy do not exist as classes."[31] California, therefore, represented a refuge, a still distant land of Anglo domination far removed from the problems of modernity.

Seven years later Lummis recapitulated his belief in California's superiority and the East's increasing inferiority in a seven-part series titled "The Right Hand of the Continent." Los Angeles, he asserted, was more eastern than Boston "in nativity, in politics, in standards. It is less [polluted] with foreign elements, and less ruled by them."[32]

This argument against foreigners formed a key part of Lummis's attempt to justify Los Angeles to the rest of the nation. He used the region's climate and its high proportion of Anglo-American immigrants to subvert notions of frontier backwardness. Yet he was not a "knee-jerk" foe of immigration, and, especially during World War I, when anti-German sentiment reached its peak, he spoke out in defense of immigrants.[33] Similarly, he was impressed with the kindness of Italian immigrants, who shared their meager supplies with him during a chilly Colorado night in 1884. He noted, in a calculated insult to the settlers who had turned him away, "I was glad to find one 'white man' in this God-forsaken place."[34] Here, playing with a common expression of the day, Lummis meant white not only in the racial sense but also as a synonym for honesty and charity.

His fear of immigration melded with a strong opposition to imperialism, an opposition based in his interpretation of American values, economic fears, and racial anxiety. Before and after the Spanish-American War, Lummis attacked his nation's expansionist zeal, warning that American overseas expansion would lead to unintended consequences. Imperialism, he argued, threatened to destroy the Anglo Eden on the Pacific Coast. It represented a rejection of American values of democracy and self-determination and threatened to bring too many non-white peoples into the United States. In his monthly editorial, he pointed out America's dismal record on civil rights. Americans had enslaved Africans, treated American Indians poorly, and they "haven't done much to the Chinese—except exclude, ostraci[z]e, blackmail and occasionally mob and murder them." Lummis concluded with a warning about imperialism: "And in the face of all this [racial injustice] . . . there are optimistic ninnies who believe we are just the right guardians to adopt a few more millions, from inferior races."[35] Rather than racial injustice, the deleterious effect of massive immigration on his adopted state remained his chief concern. Imperialism would mean "the sacrifice of California" because "we cannot keep out nor fine the products of our new 'possessions,' which raise the same things that California does."[36] Importation of cheaper crops would hurt California's economy, but worse was the arrival of cheap, non-white labor: "We cannot shut subjects of the United States out of the United States, as we can—and have been obliged to—the alien Chinese. When we force the unwilling to accept this country as their country, then they must be free in it . . . and the coolies . . . are to come to crowd American farmers. People such as build the homes, which make California the garden of the world, cannot compete with Filipinos." Imperialism, he warned, would only benefit large corporations and syndicates, and the small farmer would be ruined.[37]

Lummis, however, remained a strong supporter of Latin American nations and a staunch advocate of self-determination for the peoples of the Americas. He was deeply suspicious of the expansionist designs of men like Theodore Roosevelt, a personal friend and admirer of the editor of *Land of Sunshine*. In a fiery letter to Roosevelt, Lummis complained of the unjust takeover of Panama. He conceded that the nation of Colombia had problems, but the United States also had its faults—chief of which was racial intolerance:

> The gravest fault and danger, it seems to me, of the American people—and I mean you, with both hands, for you come as near as I reasonably hope to see any one man to realize what I deem the American type—is that composed, infused and made Strong by every blood on earth, we tend to despise the Other Fellow—as if there were any. We keep up the same old medieval, anti-papist, A.P.A. [American Protective Association], lick of burning ev[e]ry man that isn't one of us. And it is a mistake. As even America is mostly populated with human beings, I hope it is not treason to hold that we may have both dangers and faults.[38]

Explaining Lummis's contradictory views seems difficult at first. How could he support the expansion of Anglo settlement while defending the native peoples of the Southwest? How could he fear imperialism and still be friendly with Roosevelt, the nation's preeminent expansionist? How could he defend the rights of immigrants to come to America but crow about how his adopted home was superior because of their absence? Lummis attempted to articulate a vision of place that made sense of these seeming contradictions. California, quite simply, should be a refuge for Anglo whites, a place free of new stock immigrants where non-whites knew their place and added a veneer of exoticism and regional variety.

In terms of the preservation of the special status of Anglos, Californians need not worry about the rise of political machines or slums, which appeared to threaten democracy in eastern cities through manipulation of voting, Lummis believed. Such problems existed in New York, Boston, and other eastern cities where legions of foreigners were easily swayed by the promises of clever politicians. Compared with the flood of immigrants inundating eastern ports, California's Hispanics, Chinese, and few remaining Indians seemed romantic and thus essentially harmless. Hispanics, while extended citizenship, found themselves deprived of real participation in many ways. Asians and Indians, as non-citizens, exerted no influence in California whatsoever.[39] The sociologist Tomás Almaguer argues that the domination of whites in California "represented the extension of 'white supremacy' into the new American Southwest."[40] This system offered Anglo-Americans a privileged position that immigration in the East increasingly challenged.

Lummis had a sincere appreciation for Hispanic and Indian cultures, but he, like other Los Angeles boomers, actively engaged in constructing an image of Southern California as a refuge for Anglo-Saxons that appropriated elements from California's Spanish legacy. Lummis was a major figure in what historian William Deverell aptly calls the "whitewashing" of the Hispanic past. By creating a selective, romanticized version of the Mexican past, Anglo Angelenos fashioned a distinct regional identity that promised material comfort and economic growth while simultaneously stripping actual Hispanic peoples of real political and economic power.[41] California's racial diversity, as Lummis noted, made it far more desirable than the East, in large part because of the small numbers of politically impotent non-whites. These were Lummis's "few thousand" Chinese and "500 native Californians" and a tiny population of Native Americans, including the "Warner's Ranch" Indians, a group of a few hundred "mission Indians" Lummis personally helped move to a reservation in Southern California.[42] The balance and supposed racial harmony would, however, fall apart if thousands of peoples of "inferior races" settled in California. The distance from ports of entry on the Eastern Seaboard, fortunately, seemed to preclude that possibility.

Nevertheless, this celebration of Anglo-Saxonism (and its alleged attributes of American democracy, vigorous capitalism, and economic and technological development) masked a profound sense of anxiety. Lummis proved more egalitarian in his views, at least with respect to Hispanics and Native

FIGURE 4.2. Like Lummis, Frank Bird Linderman came to appreciate American Indians and frontiersmen. He spent his life advocating on behalf of Indian peoples, collecting their stories, and denouncing new immigrants as dangerous and irredeemably foreign. Here, Linderman (*left*) stands with his friend and renowned artist Charles M. Russell (*right*) and Chief Big Rock (*center*) of the Chippewa Indians, a group for whom Linderman helped convince the federal government to create a reservation. *Courtesy,* Linderman Collection, Archives and Special Collections, Mansfield Library, University of Montana, Missoula.

Americans, but he was no less anxious about the American experiment. He sought to preserve the special place Americans like himself (so-called White Anglo-Saxon Protestants [WASPs]) occupied, and the West seemed like the perfect place to do it.

Lummis's vision of an Anglo-American West coexisting with the remnants of American Indian culture also resonated with Frank Bird Linderman. For Linderman as for Lummis, the noble but threatened American Indian became his most important literary subject and the focus of much of his political attention. During his long relationship with the Rocky Boy Band of Cree and Chippewa Indians, he helped them find employment, provided them with clothes, and fought to get a permanent reservation established in Montana. In these battles he revealed his true feelings toward Indians, feelings that demonstrated that he both understood and appreciated Indians in a way most of his fellow Montanans did not.

He fought, for example, to destroy the common belief that Indians were lazy and shiftless, a belief even Linderman's supporters of the reservation idea held. Montana senator Henry L. Myers argued that the Rocky Boy Indians "from all that I can learn . . . will never work or till the land or support themselves."[43] He therefore supported the idea of a small reservation for them on the site of an abandoned military reserve near Harve, Montana, because there "they may be corralled, so as to keep them from wandering around over the country aimlessly and bothering people."[44] Safely removed from the surrounding whites, the band could subsist as best they could on the two townships of land the congressional bill set aside for them. Linderman asserted that the high altitude and infertile character of the land made it unsuitable for agriculture. As for the belief that Indians were lazy, Linderman countered that they had been forced to live in a precarious position, denied their traditional lifeways, and yet kept from participating in the white man's economy in any meaningful way. They were treated as "renegades" by the people of Helena, on whose outskirts they set up threadbare tents and tepees, and "in a sense were just that, since they had no home, no reservation, no place where they might make a living."[45] He replied to Senator Myers, "When people are obliged to beg and prowl in alleys, to feed from garbage cans therein, because no one will give them employment, and because all are turned against them on account of their personal appearance and physical condition, it is easy for the onlooker to cry 'vagabond.' "[46] When given a chance, he asserted, Indians would work as hard as or harder than whites, and, as proof, he cited the story of a Rocky Boy Indian who demanded thirty-five cents an hour for labor performed for Linderman's friend Dr. Oscar Lanstrum. When Lanstrum complained about the rates, Linderman spoke with the Indian, who told him he worked harder than Lanstrum's white employee and therefore deserved more money. In the end, the doctor agreed.[47]

Linderman enlisted other eminent Montanans in his scheme to create a reservation for the Rocky Boy Indians, including the famous cowboy artist Charles M. Russell. Like Linderman, Russell played an important role in conveying the mythic West to Americans and in advocating for the continued presence of Indians in America. At Linderman's request, Russell wrote to Senator Myers in 1913 in support of Linderman's proposed reservation: "These people have been on the verge of starvation for years and I think it no more than square for Uncle Sam, who has opened the west to all foreigners, to give these real Americans enough to live on."[48] Russell, like Linderman and Lummis, believed that Indians, not foreigners, were real Americans and that their noble and romantic culture should be preserved in the face of rapid change. Russell, too, envisioned a white man's West, a refuge for both Anglo-Americans and colorful and subservient American Indians.

Following a protracted battle over what to do with this small band of Indians, Linderman and his allies finally forced a bill through Congress for the creation of the Rocky Boy Reservation in 1916.[49] Securing a reservation for them, however, was only the beginning, and Linderman continued to press politicians and Indian service bureaucrats for better rations, permission for the Indians to practice traditional dances, such as the forbidden Sun Dance, and for an expansion of the reservation. In a 1933 letter to the reform-minded John Collier, head of the Bureau of Indian Affairs, he wrote, "These Indians are real workers, and if encouraged and helped will prove to the doubters that the red man has a future even in the white man's scheme of things."[50] They needed more land to be successful, he believed, to prove themselves.

As a result of Linderman's endless skirmishes with bureaucrats, he earned the Indians' friendship. John Evans, a Harve harness maker friendly to the Indians, wrote Linderman to tell him about the compliment paid him by Day Child, a tribal elder at Rocky Boy. He quoted Day Child as saying, "I want you to know how I like Frank Linderman. My father is dead. I loved him, but if my father came back and stood on one hill and I saw Frank Linderman on another hill I would not go to my father. I would go to Frank Linderman. You know I do not lie, this is the truth."[51] Though filtered through Evans and no doubt intended to flatter Linderman, Day Child's comments reflected the Rocky Boy Band's gratitude for his repeated help and counsel and the important role he played in winning some semblance of security for them.

Linderman's views on both Indians and modern society found expression in his literary works, most notably his biographies of two significant Crow elders, Chief Plenty Coups and Pretty-shield. Plenty Coup's story was published in 1930 under the title *American: The Life Story of a Great Indian,*

FIGURE 4.3. Charles M. Russell dressed as an Indian. Russell embraced and celebrated plains Indian culture in his paintings in a way no other artist had. For Russell, Indians represented a rugged and vanishing America. At Linderman's request Russell wrote to Montana senator Henry L. Myers in support of creating a reservation for the Rocky Boy Band of Cree and Chippewa Indians. *Courtesy,* Frank Bird Linderman Collection, Archives and Special Collections, Mansfield Library, University of Montana, Missoula.

FIGURE 4.4. Frank Bird Linderman and two native men holding an American flag. Indian peoples represented "real Americans," Frank Bird Linderman believed, deserving of rights and respect. Yet America, he professed, seemed on the edge of falling under the control of undesirable immigrants and the political machines they supported. *Courtesy,* Frank Bird Linderman Collection, Archives and Special Collections, Mansfield Library, University of Montana, Missoula.

Plenty Coups, Chief of the Crows, while his biography of Pretty-shield, originally titled *Red Mother*, appeared in 1932. The two works marked the pinnacle of Linderman's literary success. These aging figures were, to Linderman, authentic Indians who recalled the time before the white men came in numbers and dispossessed them of their lands. In comparison, Linderman wrote that younger Indians "know next to nothing about their people's ancient ways." In keeping with his belief in a vanished era he asserted, "The real Indians are gone."[52]

According to historian Sherry L. Smith, Linderman's choice of titles for his biographies reflected his inner fears and beliefs. The titles of the works "underscore Linderman's theme of a vanishing world," not only for Indians "but also one where red-blooded, Anglo-Saxon Americans held supreme against immigrants and one where women knew their place as mothers rather than as congresswomen."[53] The modern world, with its problems (not the least of which was his congressional defeat by Jeanette Rankin), made the world of the Indians all the more desirable and its passing all the more mournful. He summed up his perspective in the title of one of his works: *On a Passing Frontier.* Through his writing career and his political activism, Linderman attempted to preserve some of the West of his memory, but increasingly the transformation going on in Montana challenged his memories of Indians, trappers, and the untrammeled wilderness of the territorial period.

Dirty, industrial, and peopled by hordes of inferior immigrants, Montana's mining towns, like Butte, represented everything he hated about modern existence. Yet despite his best efforts, the modern world pulled him in, and in 1892 the would-be frontiersman had to abandon his anachronistic sojourn as a trapper and find more stable and remunerative employment. He had fallen in love and required a steady paycheck so he could marry and start a family. Linderman worked for a time in Raville and then moved on to the bustling, polluted town of Butte, where he worked for the Butte and Boston Smelter as an assayer and chemist. He described his first night on the job as hellish, filled with "clouds of bluish-green sulphur fumes that inflamed my throat and irritated my nose almost beyond endurance."[54] Linderman's job required him to weigh loads of steaming calcine, a near-molten substance produced in the smelters. His first shift ended with a conflict between himself and a man who refused to weigh his loads, in flagrant violation of the orders of the mine's superintendent. The man was an Italian, which for Linderman was significant. After a brief scuffle with the man, Linderman won, but he was fired for his trouble.[55]

His dislike for immigrant miners extended well beyond this one encounter. He variously described Butte's Italians, Welsh, Austrian, Cornish, and Irish miners as drunks, rabble-rousers, wife beaters, and stooges for a variety of fraternal, political, and reform efforts.[56] He loathed his coworkers at another job in the mining industry, this time as an ash wheeler, an easy job populated by the mining company's professional musicians when their musical skills were not needed. Most of his coworkers were immigrants, and he loathed one in particular. Nicknamed "Joe-joe, the dog-faced one," Linderman described him as ape-like, deformed, and with a blank and vapid expression. His dislike of the "clownish hornblower" grew after the homely musician's negligence caused the death of a highly trained horse when it fell into an ore bin.[57]

Indeed, the foreign element in Butte finally drove Linderman away in search of, literally, greener pastures. Linderman and his family "wished to get away from Butte, where there were no trees, not even a blade of grass." Polluted air and hordes of rough immigrants marked the antithesis of everything he had hoped to find in Montana. He described his neighborhood as unsatisfying, in part because "English was scarcely ever heard there" and Austrian miners swore and sang outside a nearby bar at all hours of the night.[58] Vowing never to force his children to live without being able to play "beneath leafy trees," Linderman decided to leave Butte and its motley population.[59]

The trapper-turned-assayer, however, found it more difficult than he hoped to leave the mining industry behind, but gradually he established a freelance assaying business and a newspaper and eventually became a politician and an insurance agent. He did not forget his dislike of immigrants. In a letter on the quality of beans the US government furnished to the Rocky Boy Indians he quipped, "I have always maintained that it was mighty hard to recognize the 'noble Roman' in a Dago organ grinder, and it is equally hard to recognize an edible bean in the black eyed specimens I forwarded you."[60]

Linderman most feared the threat immigrants posed to the survival of the nation. Anti-immigrationist sentiment grew to a crescendo in the 1920s and Linderman led the chorus, at least in Montana. In a letter to Gertrude Atherton, he praised her article in *Bookman* because it would help draw attention to Madison Grant's *The Passing of the Great Race*, whose thesis argued that the superior Anglo-Saxon race found itself on the losing end of population growth to more fertile, cowardly immigrants, while World War I and the Anglo martial spirit culled the best young men. As he explained to Atherton, "We have not only permitted immigration to injure our country but through apathy have allowed our children's birthright of opportunity to be filched from them." The decline in America's character was obvious: "The great change that has come over our country within the last fifty years is startling indeed to those who think and American ideals are being dimmed or lost in the rabble from other lands."[61] The solution, Linderman told Senator Myers, was "stopping immigration, or at least sharply restricting it." Speaking out against immigration in Montana, he cautioned, would be dangerous, but nevertheless he had "made twenty-four addresses only one or two of which were entirely public. I think you will understand me."[62] Immigrants and the political machines they supported would destroy America. Linderman, pondering a run for the US Senate, confided to a friend, "The Sinn Fein element would fight me to a stand still although I believe I could beat them."[63] His reference to Sinn Fein, the Irish nationalist movement, showed once again his revulsion for immigrants and the power they wielded in American politics. His assertion that he could defeat them turned out to be incorrect, as his narrow loss in the 1924 election showed.

Lummis and Linderman represented but two of the many who sought to protect true whiteness while also reserving a space for American Indians. Their efforts at contacting Indian peoples and learning about their cultures were part of a larger effort by ethnologists to understand Indian peoples and offer them up as paragons of a better, more authentic existence that differed from the increasing mechanization and alienation of modern society. As Americans entered the twentieth century with the frontier experience behind them, they turned increasingly to a mythological past and contact with a primitive, but less alienating and more invigorating and genuine, nature. Worried that future generations of Americans, men especially, would grow weak and morally bankrupt, reformers like Daniel Carter Beard and Ernest Thompson Seton sought to put children in touch with the natural world. They could thus learn skills like self-reliance, cooperation, and survival, which would create better, more confident Americans.

Beard turned to America's frontier past for inspiration, creating the Sons of Daniel Boone in 1905, while Seton created the Woodcraft Indians. For Beard, Indians were the antagonists, the obstacles Americans faced in taming the West, but Seton found in them avatars of a better existence. The historian Philip Deloria argues that Seton grasped the complicated and contradictory impulses of modernity better than did Beard. Beard advocated that young people emulate the pioneer experience and act like frontiersman, but such advice no longer seemed applicable in a modern Industrial Age. Seton, however, did not want people to reject modernity or live by outmoded methods. Instead, he wanted them to be modern by encountering the primitive. Deloria writes that this experience represented a "break not only historically [as in Beard's approach], but also racially, socially, and developmentally."[64] Indian peoples, unlike the frontiersman of Daniel Boone's era, still existed and, Seton hoped, remained largely unsullied by the evils of modernity. Ethnologists, by living with and observing Indian peoples, could then popularize supposedly authentic views of Indians, stressing their values and morals as examples for children to emulate and thereby enabling young Americans to engage this other world and emerge from the experience better and stronger people.

Similarly, the Camp Fire Girls used images of Indians to inculcate middle-class notions of gender into young women, stressing child care, cooking, and crafts. Children, unlike adults, could easily cross from modern society into primitive culture because they remained childlike and unaware of societal expectations and conventions, allowing them to play the role of noble savage. Playing Indian and dressing in Indian-inspired costumes helped open this world to them.[65] As with childhood itself, children could not remain in such a world forever. While the experience with the primitive and Indian culture would fade, the lessons would linger long after the children had become adults.

Playing Indian embodied many contradictory impulses. Having children dress and act like Indians to experience nature and the primitive so they could become good modern people is one example. Another contradiction came from acting like the people defeated by the United States to demonstrate loyalty to the United States. Indeed, playing Indian had long featured in American culture. As early as 1775, American colonists, by choosing to dress as Indians during the famous Boston Tea Party, asserted a uniquely American identity for themselves. Deloria writes, "As England became a them for colonists, Indians became an us."[66] Nearly a century and a half later, as writers like Lummis and Linderman denounced immigrants as indigestible and undesirable, immigrants themselves used Indian imagery to assert an American identity.[67]

These contradictions, between modern and primitive, savage and civilized, foreign and native, embodied the larger struggle to define the meaning of America in a radically changing world. Lummis and Linderman, like many Americans, used whiteness as the standard to judge other people. Lummis, for example, had slighted the rude Coloradans by writing that the only "white man" he'd found in the area was a kind and generous Italian immigrant.[68] Being white, in this case, meant treating others with respect and courtesy—something the settlers in Colorado refused to do, thinking that the roving newspaperman was a bandit perhaps. Nevertheless, the only hospitable person he found was an Italian immigrant, and, Lummis noted, the Italians as a group did not have the best reputation.

Linderman also used whiteness as shorthand for respectable and moral. Describing one of his trapping partners as a rough and dangerous man, prone to violent drinking binges, Linderman observed, "Though apt to be quarrel-some," the trapper "was always 'white' with me."[69] Similarly, in a discussion of labor problems in Butte-area mines in the wake of labor violence in the mines of Coeur d'Alene, Idaho, Linderman's boss at the Helena and Victor Mining Company, A. Sterne Blake, declared that sabotage would not happen in Butte because "there are some white men in our crew of miners, old-timers who would hang a dynamiter as quick as we would."[70] Being "white" meant being responsible, moral, intelligent, and, in the latter case, truly American.

Linderman went west in search of a vanishing world, a place where still-free Indians mingled with rough trappers in a beautiful landscape of open plains and towering peaks. Instead of these romantic scenes, however, the new industrial West was a place of toxic smelters and lawless, un-American rabble. Filled with nostalgia, he did what he could to preserve the past, writing books about "authentic" Indians who had not succumbed to the temptations and vices of the white man's civilization and doing his best to preserve Indian culture by helping to secure a reservation for the Rocky Boy Band of Cree and Chippewa Indians. Perhaps these efforts would never be completely successful, but Linderman felt it was worth a try. Charles Fletcher Lummis envisioned a slightly different world. In his world Hispanics, Indians, and even the Chinese could find a place in society, but that place was circumscribed. Certainly, Lummis proved more progressive on issues of race than Linderman, or nearly any of his contemporaries for that matter, but he, too, harbored romantic notions of genuine Indians and Hispanics. In addition, like Linderman, he sought to limit the power and influence of immigrants to the region, in large part because, unlike the Indians, Hispanics, and Chinese in California and the Southwest, European immigrants represented a direct threat to the culture Lummis desired to build. In the end, both men employed whiteness as a tool to shape the West in accordance with their visions.

Their efforts culminated a process of imagining the West as a refuge for Anglo-Americans. Taken as a whole, the West had undergone a reimagining throughout the nineteenth century. Early explorers questioned the compatibility of the arid, open, savage area for Anglo-American settlement. Later, some critics feared that the region was too pleasant for racial vigor, but by the end of the century westerners like Lummis argued that the region offered an ideal homeland for superior but increasingly beleaguered Anglo-Americans. The West, they argued, offered a last opportunity for a meaningful and authentic life, free from the alienating evils of industrial society. This imagining of the region provided a vision and intellectual basis that justified the real creation of the white man's West. Concomitant with this intellectual exercise was the process of physically transforming the West into the imagined refuge of Anglo-Americans. Western promoters and visionaries would employ the legal system, advertising, religious zeal, and finally violence in an effort to bring the white man's West into existence. While never complete, their vision would nonetheless become something of a reality.

NOTES

1. Rothman employed the term in his discussion of tourism, but the idea is appropriate, I believe, for the way people come to identify themselves as westerners. See Hal K. Rothman, *Devil's Bargains: Tourism in the Twentieth-Century American West* (Lawrence: University Press of Kansas, 1998).

2. G. Edward White, *The Eastern Establishment and the Western Experience* (Austin: University of Texas Press, 1989), 184.

3. Frank Bird Linderman, *Montana Adventure: The Recollections of Frank B. Linderman*, H. G. Merriam, ed. (Lincoln: University of Nebraska Press, 1968), 2.

4. Ibid.

5. A good secondary summary of Linderman's life is in Sherry L. Smith, *Reimagining Indians: Native Americans through Anglo Eyes, 1880–1940* (New York: Oxford University Press, 2000), 95–118.

6. Ibid., 95–96.

7. Linderman, *Montana Adventure*, 8.

8. Ibid.

9. Ibid., 183.

10. Ibid., 17.

11. Frank Bird Linderman, *Pretty-shield: Medicine Woman of the Crows* (Lincoln: University of Nebraska Press, 1972), 23.

12. Ibid.

13. Ibid., 9.

14. Charles [Fletcher] Lummis, *Letters from the Southwest*, James Byrkit, ed. (Tucson: University of Arizona Press, 1989), 20.

15. See Mark Thompson, *American Character: The Curious Life of Charles Fletcher Lummis and the Rediscovery of the Southwest* (New York: Arcade, 2001), especially chapters 8 and 11.

16. For an in-depth discussion of the Indian education system, see David Wallace Adams, *Education for Extinction: American Indians and the Boarding School Experience, 1875–1928* (Lawrence: University Press of Kansas, 1995).

17. Charles Fletcher Lummis, "My Brother's Keeper," part 1, *Land of Sunshine* 11, no. 3 (August 1899): 143.

18. Charles Fletcher Lummis to Theodore Roosevelt, May 11, 1902, MS.1.1.3805B, Charles Fletcher Lummis Papers, Braun Research Library, Southwest Museum, Autry National Center, Los Angeles, CA.

19. Charles Fletcher Lummis, *A Tramp across the Continent* (Lincoln: Bison Books, 1982), 94.

20. Ibid., 249–50.

21. Charles Fletcher Lummis to Theodore Roosevelt, November 21, 1902, MS.1.1.3805B, Charles Fletcher Lummis Papers, Braun Research Library, Southwest Museum, Autry National Center, Los Angeles, CA.

22. Lummis, *Letters from the Southwest*, 96.

23. Charles Fletcher Lummis, "Editorial," *Land of Sunshine* 2, no. 5 (April 1895): 91.

24. Works on the anti-Chinese movement in the West include George Anthony Peffer, *If They Don't Bring Their Women Here: Chinese Female Immigration before Exclusion* (Urbana: University of Illinois Press, 1999); Elmer C. Sandmeyer, *The Anti-Chinese Movement in California*, Illinois Studies in the Social Sciences Series 24, no. 3 (Urbana: University of Illinois Press, 1939); Najia Aarim-Heriot, *Chinese Immigrants, African Americans, and Racial Anxiety in the United States, 1848–1882* (Urbana: University of Illinois Press, 2003).

25. The only biography of Eaton is Annette White-Parks, *Sui Sin Far/Edith Maude Eaton: A Literary Biography* (Urbana: University of Illinois Press, 1995).

26. Charles Fletcher Lummis, *Land of Sunshine* 13, no. 6 (November 1900), 336.

27. Charles Fletcher Lummis, "In the Lion's Den," *Land of Sunshine* 13, no. 3 (August 1900), 182–88, quote is on 185.

28. Lummis, *Tramp across the Continent*, 74.

29. Charles Fletcher Lummis, "I Guess So," *Los Angeles Times*, September 30, 1917.

30. Charles Fletcher Lummis, "Editorial," *Land of Sunshine* 2, no. 2 (January 1895): 34.

31. Charles Fletcher Lummis, "Los Angeles: Metropolis of the Southwest," *Land of Sunshine* 3, no. 1 (June 1895): 43–48.

32. Charles Fletcher Lummis, "The Right Hand of the Continent, Part Six," *Out West* (November 1902): 527–55. The series ran from June through December 1902.

33. Lummis's defense of German immigrants as true Americans is best articulated in his weekly column in the *Los Angeles Times*, variously titled "Chile con Carnage," "I Know So," "I Guess So," and "I Wonder." The column became a victim of

wartime paper shortages (and perhaps of Lummis's outspoken opposition to the war); see Thompson, *American Character*, 293.

34. Lummis, *Letters from the Southwest*, 92.

35. Charles Fletcher Lummis, "In the Lion's Den," *Land of Sunshine* 9, no. 4 (September 1898): 200.

36. Ibid.

37. Charles Fletcher Lummis, "In the Lion's Den," *Land of Sunshine* 12, no. 3 (February 1900): 193.

38. Charles Fletcher Lummis to Theodore Roosevelt, January 15, 1904, MS.1.1.3805D, Braun Research Library, Southwest Museum, Autry National Center, Los Angeles, CA.

39. Tómas Almaguer, *Racial Fault Lines: The Historical Origins of White Supremacy in California* (Berkeley: University of California Press, 1994), 9–11.

40. Ibid., 7.

41. William Francis Deverell, *Whitewashed Adobe: The Rise of Los Angeles and the Remaking of Its Mexican Past* (Berkeley: University of California Press, 2004). Deverell traces the process of marginalizing Mexican Americans while simultaneously romanticizing them from the 1850s through the 1940s.

42. On Lummis's role in relocating the "Warner's Ranch" Indians, see Thompson, *American Character*, 213–44; Smith, *Reimagining Indians*, 119–44.

43. Senator Henry L. Myers to Frank Bird Linderman, February 1, 1916, Box 1, Folder 19, Frank Bird Linderman Collection, Museum of the Plains Indian, Browning, MT (hereafter FBLMPI).

44. Ibid.

45. Linderman, *Montana Adventure*, 140.

46. Frank Bird Linderman to Senator Henry L. Myers, February 8, 1916, Box 1, Folder 19, FBLMPI.

47. Ibid. The story is also recounted in Linderman, *Montana Adventure*, 141. In the published version Linderman does not name Oscar Lanstrum as the employer.

48. Charles M. Russell to Senator Henry L. Myers, January 11, 1913, Box 1, Folder 27, FBLMPI.

49. Linderman, *Montana Adventure*, 140–43, 157–60.

50. Frank Bird Linderman to John Collier, September 25, 1933, Box 1, Folder 5, FBLMPI.

51. John Evans to Frank Bird Linderman, June 10, 1925, Box 1, Folder 13, FBLMPI.

52. Linderman, *Montana Adventure*, 183.

53. Smith, *Reimagining Indians*, 115.

54. Linderman, *Montana Adventure*, 88.

55. Ibid., 88–89.

56. Ibid. See examples on 89, 92–93, 95–98.

57. Ibid., 109–10.

58. Ibid., 107.

59. Ibid., 109.

60. Frank Bird Linderman to Cato Sells, March 16, 1917, Box 1, Folder 28, FBLMPI.

61. Frank Bird Linderman to Mrs. Gertrude Atherton, March 9, 1922, Box 1, Folder 4, Series I, Frank Bird Linderman Collection (Mss. 7), K. Ross Toole Archive, Mansfield Library, University of Montana, Missoula (hereafter FBLML). Linderman was a fan of Grant's book because he apparently sent a copy to Senator Henry L. Myers. See Myers's response dated December 2, 1920, Box 3, Folder 19, Series II, FBLML.

62. Frank Bird Linderman to Senator Henry L. Myers, March 23, 1922, Box 3, Folder 19, FBLML.

63. Frank Bird Linderman to P. A. Morrison, April 29, 1922, Box 3, Folder 16, FBLML.

64. Philip J. Deloria, *Playing Indian* (New Haven, CT: Yale University Press, 1998), 105.

65. Ibid., 115–20.

66. Ibid., 22.

67. See Alan Trachenberg, *Shades of Hiawatha: Staging Indians, Making Americans, 1880–1930* (New York: Hill and Wang, 2004), for the story of the complex interaction between immigrants and Indian identity.

68. Lummis, *Letters from the Southwest*, 92.

69. Linderman, *Montana Adventure*, 35.

70. Ibid., 85.

PART II

CREATING AND DEFENDING
THE WHITE MAN'S WEST

5

THE POLITICS OF WHITENESS AND WESTERN EXPANSION, 1848–80

Anglo-Americans, from Thomas Jefferson at the beginning of the nineteenth century to Joseph Pomeroy Widney at the century's end, envisioned the West as more than an ordinary place. They dreamed of it as home to a rugged, independent, white population. For Jefferson, the West would be home to his ideal yeoman farmers, noble tillers of the soil and keepers of the sacred charge of freedom; for Widney, the Engle-Americans, as he called them, would complete the march to the setting sun that had begun on the steppes of Russia in a time before time. This geography of the imagination, these dreams of a whites'-only West, however, bumped up against a stubborn reality: the region remained racially diverse and could easily become even more so. Transforming it into the white man's West would require work. Creating a refuge for whites, in no small measure, meant encouraging the right people and discouraging those considered wrong. To do this, Anglo-American settlers would turn to the power of government.

Initially, governmental power had been considered a tool to remove undesirable and anomalous peoples, like free African Americans and eastern Indians,

DOI: 10.5876/9781607323969.c005

from the settled sections of the republic. While efforts to remove free blacks never came to fruition, the government did embark on a controversial and costly policy of Indian removal, and yet little more than a decade after moving eastern Indians to the Indian Territory—consigning them to the margins of society—the United States acquired California and the Southwest; the periphery had now become the center. The attempt to spatially segregate Indians and free African Americans had failed, but in its place developed the notion of the West as an ideal location for white Americans, especially those of Anglo ancestry. In a very real sense, this was the antithesis of the earlier idea of segregating undesirable racial groups in the West. Now the region should, as much as possible, be a reserve of real Anglo-American whites.

The introduction of slavery and free blacks, however, threatened this vision. By the 1850s the dual questions of where to expand and whether to allow slavery's extension into the West precipitated a crisis ultimately resolved at the cost of more than half a million American lives. Slavery would not take hold in the West, but neither would efforts to prevent blacks from settling in the region prove successful. Nevertheless, whiteness played a powerful, if inconclusive, role in preventing the arrival of both slaves and free blacks in the antebellum period, and, in the process, westerners tried to escape the cultural and political crisis that inexorably pulled the nation toward civil war.

The new Republican Party championed the exclusion of slavery from the western territories in the 1850s. In control of the North and the West under Republican president Abraham Lincoln, the United States set out to destroy slavery. Indeed, the Civil War and the passage of the 1862 Homestead Act during the war forever ended the question of slavery's expansion. It also meant that the western territories and states would have a tiny African American population, since these newly free peoples lacked the resources required to make a western journey and thus remained in the South after the war.

Yet the low numbers of African Americans in the West when compared with the South were not merely a result of the echoes of slavery. Westerners themselves had long sought ways of preventing African Americans from settling in the region. Taken together, therefore, the relative absence of blacks in the West resulted from economic and social concerns. Few blacks could afford to emigrate, and westerners did little to welcome them.

These issues, however, had surfaced long before the emergence of the Republican Party in the 1850s. Indeed, in the nation's very infancy, the character of future settlement in the trans-Appalachian West begged for some consideration. Expansion emerged as one of many pressing issues for the new nation, and one of the few successes of the nation's first government—the Articles of Confederation—was a land policy that effectively addressed the issue. The Northwest Ordinance outlined the process by which new states would be added to the nation and significantly forbade slavery north of the Ohio River.[1] Slaves did find their way into the Northwest Territory, often as vaguely defined servants, and legislatures in Indiana and Illinois tried unsuccessfully to legalize slavery in their respective states in the 1820s.[2] The Ohio River, however, held as a boundary between free and slave states and set a precedent for the confinement of slavery.

Crossing the Mississippi, however, changed the dynamics of expansion and the issue of slavery. Without the convenient North-South boundary of the Ohio River, no obvious line could be drawn between free and slave. This left the Louisiana Territory open for definition. What should be done with the territory's expansive lands? Would slavery be allowed anywhere, or would it be limited somehow by geographical boundary or political definition?

The admission of Missouri to the Union brought the issue of expansion and slavery into sharp relief and led to the first real debate over slavery's extension into the West. The Missouri Compromise of 1820 solved the issue of Missouri's admission to the Union, allowing it to enter as a slave state and creating Maine as a free state to preserve the delicate balance of power in the US Senate. In addition, a line extending west from the Arkansas-Missouri border (the 36-degree, 30-minute parallel) divided the Louisiana Territory into a free North and a slave South. The Senate debated the Missouri Compromise bill as one piece of legislation, attracting overwhelming northern and southern support. In the House, however, members treated each provision of the compromise separately. The Missouri Compromise line, forbidding slavery in the northern (and largest) part of the territory, drew strong support from northern congressmen but, somewhat surprisingly, was favored by a slim majority (39 to 37) of southern congressmen as well. Thus even southern congressmen, albeit by a slim majority, approved of banning slavery from the vast majority of the Louisiana Purchase.[3] Why they did so remains unclear, and a generation later southern politicians would decry the compromise line and vociferously oppose any effort to prevent the extension of slavery. The geographer Donald W. Meinig offers one explanation for southern support.

He argues that Americans still only vaguely understood the dimensions of the western territory in 1820, and southern politicians assumed that at least a few more slave states could be gleaned from the territory. Most important, they wanted to add Missouri to the Union as rapidly as possible, and the compromise accomplished that.[4]

The Missouri debate had temporarily inflamed passions on the issue of slavery, but the compromise cooled the rancor. The presence of two national, rather than sectional, political parties helped Congress arrive at a solution. As Martin Van Buren astutely observed in 1827, attachment to national political parties could furnish "a complete antidote to sectional prejudices by producing counteracting feelings."[5] Such had been the case even in the 1820 crisis. The annexation of Texas in the 1840s, though also hotly contested, similarly remained largely partisan and not sectional, with the Whigs opposed to its annexation and the Democrats mostly in favor. Typically, these national parties largely stayed away from the slavery issue, with both Whigs and Democrats focusing on local and sectional issues and coming together every four years for the presidential election when they would shift to issues of national importance. This invariably led northern Whigs and Democrats to commit to free soil, while their southern counterparts could remain in support of slavery. For a long time, this division worked.[6]

The Mexican-American War, however, brought the slavery debate into sharper focus. President James K. Polk, a Democrat, provoked a war with Mexico in 1846 with the hope not only of keeping Texas but of acquiring much of the Southwest and California as well. By starting the war with Mexico, historian Michael F. Holt declares, "Polk had pried open the lid on a Pandora's box."[7] Northerners saw the war as an effort to expand slavery, and the carefully created national parties buckled under the strain.

In August 1846, a few months after the commencement of hostilities, President Polk asked Congress to appropriate $2 million to pay Mexico for any land the United States might gain from the war. Northern Democrats, seeking to distance themselves from President Polk and his southern Democratic allies, promised to support the bill only if it included a provision to bar slavery from any territory conquered from Mexico. In this way they hoped to deflect the ire of northern free-soil voters in upcoming elections. David Wilmot, an obscure Democratic congressman from Pennsylvania, introduced the proviso that would forever bear his name. Echoing Jefferson's Northwest

Ordinance Wilmot wrote, "As an express and fundamental condition to the acquisition of any territory from the Republic of Mexico . . . neither slavery nor involuntary servitude shall ever exist in any part of said territory."[8] In the House, Wilmot's Proviso passed easily on a sectional vote of 134 to 91. All but four northern congressmen voted in favor of it and all southern represen-tatives, regardless of party, opposed it. The proviso would die at the hands of southerners in the evenly divided Senate, but it resurfaced continually in the next several sessions—much to the consternation of southern politicians. The Mexican-American War and the Wilmot Proviso split the Whigs and Democrats along sectional lines, propelling the nation toward a long-delayed reckoning with the "peculiar institution" of slavery.[9]

Although far removed from the center of the increasingly vociferous debates over slavery in the 1840s and 1850s, the turmoil nonetheless pulled the West into the growing controversy. Westerners hardly had monolithic views, and gauging them is difficult, but clearly many people opposed the extension of slavery into the West, and many also rejected the prospect of having free blacks in their midst. The debates over both slavery and the pres-ence of African Americans played out in the two Pacific Coast states that gained admittance to the Union before the Civil War: California and Oregon.

Debates over the future of California reflected Westerners' attitude toward both slavery and the presence of African Americans. Slaves had been brought into the newly acquired territory following the discovery of gold in 1848. Free blacks likewise journeyed to California in search of fortune. One correspondent for the *New York Tribune* claimed that in the goldfields "the Southern slaveholder [works] beside the swarthy African, now his equal."[10] The reporter no doubt exaggerated (or did not bother to ask either the southerner or the "swarthy" African their opinions), but clearly both enslaved and free blacks toiled in the goldfields alongside white, American Indian, and Asian miners. Indeed, Anglo-America miners appear to have deeply resented the presence of slaves in the goldfields. In the gold-laden streams of California, as individual miners worked against slave owners with several slaves at their command, the abstract debates over free labor versus slave labor became tangible. William Manney's four slaves, for example, panned an amazing $4,000 in gold in a single week.[11] Walter Colton declared that white miners "know they must dig themselves: they have come out here for that purpose, and they won't degrade their calling by associating it with slave labor." They cared little about "slavery in the abstract, or as it exists in other communities; not one in ten cares a button for its abolition, nor the Wilmot Proviso either: all they look at is their own position; they must themselves swing the pick, and they won't swing it by the side of negro slaves." Colton concluded that miners saw California as a "new world, where they have a right to shape and settle things in their own way. No mandate, unless it comes like a thunder-bolt straight out of heaven, is regarded."[12] Having slaves compete against free men seemed patently unfair.

The 1849 state constitution agreed with this view, its framers writing, "Neither slavery, nor involuntary servitude . . . shall ever be tolerated in this State." The state's suffrage requirements, however, conspicuously omitted African Americans. The law enfranchised all white males over twenty-one, as well as "every white male citizen of Mexico, who shall have elected to become a citizen of the United States." The constitution even allowed for the possibility of "admitting to the right of suffrage, Indians or the descen-dants of Indians, in such special cases as such proportion [a ⅔ majority] of the legislative body may deem just and proper."[13] Similarly, the law forbade blacks from serving as members of the state's militia. These restrictions, however, turned out to be far more moderate than many of the delegates wanted, and an effort to exclude blacks from California nearly found its way into the constitution.[14]

One delegate to the California Constitutional Convention, M. M. McCarver, offered a "negro exclusion clause" that drew a great deal of support. The amendment declared, "The Legislature shall, at its first session, pass such laws as will effectually prohibit free persons of color from immigrating to and settling in this State, and to effectually prevent the owners of slaves from bringing them into this State for the purpose of setting them free." Representative Oliver M. Wozencraft, in support of McCarver's amendment, declared that blacks' inherent inferiority and propensity for servitude would only degrade the value of free labor in the new state. Black exclusion would therefore protect the value of white labor. He declared, "If there is one part of the world possessing advantages over another where the family of Japhet [a son of Noah and considered by some the first European] may expect to attain a higher state of perfectibility than has ever been attained by Man, it is here in California. All nature proclaims this a favored land." The land would bless the efforts of whites, while blacks, Wozencraft asserted, would be better off living in the "boundless wastes" of Africa where God had first created them. Delegates withdrew the amendment out of fear that an exclusion clause might hurt efforts to get the state's constitution approved by the US Congress, but only on the promise that the legislature would take up the issue soon after statehood had been granted.[15]

California's first governor, Peter Burnett, introduced the issue of Negro exclusion soon after coming to office in 1849. During his inaugural speech on December 20, 1849, Burnett opened with a warning for his fellow Californians. Because of the state's natural advantages, most notably gold, California would "be either a very great or a very sordid and petty state." History, Burnett explained, showed that "in all those countries where rich and extensive mines of the precious metals have been heretofore discovered, the people have become indolent, careless, and stupid. This enervating influence operates silently, steadily, and continually, and requires counteracting causes, or great and continued energy of character in a people to successfully resist it."[16] Burnett hoped industrious Americans could resist the fate of lesser nations and maintain their vigor in the face of golden wealth.

Wise legislation, especially at the dawning moment of the state's admission to the Union, would forever determine the course of California's destiny, the governor warned. In Burnett's opinion, Californians needed to carefully select which groups would be allowed into the Golden State. Burnett warned about the dangers of Chinese immigration, noting that while hardworking and honest, they would never break their ties to the mother country. Further, their presence drove down wages for whites, accustomed as they were to surviving on next to nothing (a complaint that would be leveled repeatedly at the Chinese), and in time they could potentially overrun the state. "Were Chinamen permitted to settle in our country at their pleasure, and were they granted all the rights and privileges of whites, and the laws were impartially and efficiently administered, so that the two races would stand *precisely* and *practically* equal in *all* respects, in one century the Chinese would own all the property on this coast," Burnett claimed.[17] Far from banning the Chinese, however, Burnett would later argue for an amended treaty to replace the Burlingame Treaty that would ensure that Chinese immigrants stayed only temporarily, thereby giving California a much-needed labor force while still ensuring that the Chinese would not become permanent residents.

Burnett next turned his attention to the presence of free blacks, advocating strongly for Negro exclusion. Taken together, Burnett wished to maintain the dominance of Anglo-Americans in a state already the most diverse in the nation. The efforts of Burnett and others to limit the presence of blacks in California, however, came to little, as the legislature never acted to exclude blacks, who proved to be a statistically insignificant and therefore non-threatening group. After 1852, legislators instead turned to efforts to stymie the more worrisome Chinese immigration.[18] Legislating whiteness proved difficult, but nevertheless attempts to exclude blacks and the Chinese spoke volumes about the future Californians envisioned for their state.

Even in remote Oregon, the issue of slavery and black residence proved divisive. Slavery had been prohibited under an act of the 1844 provisional government and again in 1848 when the federal government created the Oregon Territory. By the 1850s, however, the issue had come to prominence, mirroring the national debate. Many Oregonians disliked the presence of African Americans, whether free or enslaved, in their territory and sought to exclude them.[19] Perhaps in this way, many believed they could avoid the evils of slavery and the presence of an inferior group of people as well.

Excluding children, most Oregonians had emigrated from older sections of the country—many from the Midwest. According to the 1860 census, 23 percent of Oregon's population hailed from the Old Northwest and another 17 percent from the border states of Missouri, Kentucky, and Tennessee. A full 43 percent were either foreign-born or children born in the West; the remainder were from the Deep South (5 percent), New England states (4 percent), and Mid-Atlantic states (8 percent). The majority of whites from Missouri, Kentucky, and Tennessee also owned no slaves. Thus, in a very real sense, Oregonians reflected the attitudes of midwesterners in their desire to prevent both slavery and the presence of blacks.[20]

The provisional government set the tone for Negro exclusion and the prohibition of slavery. The impetus for excluding blacks came after a dispute between James Saules, an African American settler, and a Wasco Indian named Comstock turned violent. After an exchange of bullets and arrows, Comstock lay dead. Local whites blamed Saules for the altercation and threatened his life. In response Saules, who had married an Indian woman, warned that he could turn the Indians against the whites. The Comstock affair seemed to prove that blacks, especially those who made alliances with

Indian peoples, posed potential danger and should be prevented from emigrating to Oregon.[21] Hailing from American culture like Anglo-Americans but embittered and envious of their social betters and willing to mix and fraternize with Indians, African Americans like Saules represented a dangerous group, Oregonians believed, that, as Saules claimed, could stir up trouble between the groups. Better, many felt, to limit their presence in the territory.

In June 1844 the provisional government took up the issue and outlawed slavery, giving slave owners three years to free their slaves. It ordered free blacks and mulattoes to leave the territory within two years or face periodic floggings. The flogging provision, however, proved too controversial, and in December the government changed the punishment to indentured servitude under a white man, a provision modeled on an 1819 Illinois act.

The Oregon act had been introduced by a Missourian named Peter Burnett—the same Burnett who would follow the Gold Rush to California and become that state's first governor. Burnett had come to dominate the legislative committee.[22] In a letter dated December 25, 1844, he explained that Oregon offered settlers an opportunity to right the failings of other societies. He bragged that Oregonians rarely engaged in drinking, quarreling, and gambling, and he declared that the exclusion of blacks would "keep clear of that most troublesome class of population. We are in a new world, under most favorable circumstances, and we wish to avoid most of those evils that have so much afflicted the United States and other countries. Availing ourselves of the peculiarities of our favored condition, we are determined, if we can, to improve upon the best systems that have existed, or now exist." The result, Burnett explained, was a vigorous white population "from various places; some from the commercial shores of Great Britain, some from the free pure air of the U. States, some from the cold region of Canada." He admitted that these disparate groups held different customs and views, "and yet we have the utmost harmony. National and sectional prejudices do not seem to exist."[23] That would not remain the case, however.

Burnett's exclusion law proved short-lived, and the following year, led by Jesse Applegate, a farmer recently removed from Missouri, the legislature repealed the act. In September 1849 the issue resurfaced when legislators passed a new bill to prohibit free blacks and mulattoes from settling in Oregon. The justification for the act reiterated the alleged cause of the

Comstock affair, arguing that "it would be highly dangerous to allow free Negroes and mulattoes to reside in the Territory, or to intermix with Indians, instilling into their mind feelings of hostility toward the white race."[24] Given relations between whites and Indians in the Northwest, Indians certainly did not need blacks to instill feelings of hostility in them, but Oregonians feared the feasibility of an alliance between the two non-white groups. However, excepting James Saules, little proof exists that African Americans held any sway over native peoples whatsoever. More likely, Oregonians, like Burnett, sought to ensure the "utmost harmony" in the state's population by keeping it as white as possible.

As the venom of the slave issue spread through the body politic in the 1840s and 1850s, even far-off Oregon was not immune. Efforts to organize it into a territory foundered over the issue. It took nearly a year and a half for Congress to finally create a bill to organize the Oregon Territory—usually a fairly sedate and mundane task—but in the tense climate of the Mexican-American War and slavery's expansion the task became anything but mundane. Northerners hoped to explicitly exclude slavery in the territory, believing it an essential precedent for future territories and states in the West. David Wilmot, for example, asserted that if slavery stretched to the Pacific Ocean, it would ensure "the ultimate subjugation of the whole southern half of this Continent and its dominion."[25] Similarly, Julius Rockwell, a congressman from Massachusetts, argued during the 1848 debates in favor of creating the Oregon Territory with an explicit prohibition of slavery. He explained, "The Territory of Oregon, by reason of its high northern latitude, may be justly thought to stand upon different grounds in relation to slavery from the other Territories [acquired following the Mexican-American War]. But none of these free Territories, I wish it distinctly understood, shall ever, so far as my vote is concerned, be organized without this restriction."[26]

Fear of such a precedent, however, worried southern congressmen. The stakes of the debate really had little to do with Oregon, which few people thought suitable for slavery, and everything to do with the settlement of the vast territory soon to be taken from Mexico. Finally, in 1848 the bill creating the Oregon Territory, a bill that implicitly banned slavery, passed the House and Senate by a narrow margin.[27]

Even some northern lawmakers felt the West should be free not only of slavery but also of the presence of blacks. During debates on western expansion in the 30th Congress, John Adams Dix, a senator from New York, addressed the issue of slavery and the future of the West in a long speech on June 26, 1848. After a lengthy legal analysis of whether Congress had the authority to specifically bar slavery from newly acquired territories, Dix spoke about a grand vision of the West as a land destined to be settled by whites. He argued that those who maintained that spreading slavery would not increase the number of blacks grossly underestimated the power of human beings to reproduce and that in a climate as good as Oregon's, it was inevitable that a substantial black population would increase dramatically. Dix claimed to "foresee in our political organization the foundations of an empire increasing more rapidly, and destined to expand to broader limits, than the Roman Republic; not an empire, like the latter, founded on brute force; but an empire founded on peace, and extending itself by industry, enterprise, and the arts of civilization." Dix thought it was America's mission to accept "the surplus of the over-peopled and over-governed countries of Europe" and "instruct them in the arts of peace, and to accelerate the march of civilization across the continent." America would continue to grow, Dix predicted, reaching at least 100 million people by 1900.[28]

Yet, Dix asked, what would be the racial makeup of that population? The "earth is peopled . . . [by] four grand divisions—the Asiatic, the Caucasian, the Ethiopian, and the Indian. The whole surface of Europe, with some inconsiderable exceptions, is occupied by the Caucasian race . . . [which] laid the foundations of nearly all the civilization the world contains." Ultimately, Dix argued, Europeans roughly equaled each other in talent and intellect, and God wanted them to settle the West and transform the United States into a powerful nation: "It is in the vast and fertile spaces of the West that our own descendants, as well as the oppressed and needy multitudes of the Old World, must find the food they require, and the rewards for labor which are necessary to give them the spirit and independence of freemen. I hold it to be our sacred duty to consecrate these spaces to the multiplication of the white race."[29]

Speaking in the House the day following Dix's speech, Congressman Julius Rockwell argued that exporting slavery would inevitably lead to the development of a free black population in the far West. He noted that slave owners, including those in Congress, held up the allegedly degraded condition of free blacks as proof that they qualified only for slavery. "It is said with great force,"

Rockwell began, "that slavery in the slave States must not be interfered with, because, among other reasons, the white and black races in numbers so nearly equal can never exist together in a state of freedom; because the emancipation of the black race implies destruction to one race or the other." If such became reality, Rockwell continued, "What do you propose to do? You propose to put that institution into these free Territories, and forever subject them to that condition of things; to plant an institution there which must exist forever, because it can never safely be removed."[30] Once established in the West, he warned, slavery could never be destroyed, since the two races could not coexist. Barring slavery, therefore, would also prevent large numbers of free blacks from ever living in Oregon and would prevent the same conditions that many argued made emancipation impossible in the South.

During the 1850s Oregonians continued to reject both slavery and the presence of blacks. Samuel Thurston, Oregon's territorial delegate to Congress, spoke out against an Ohio congressman's proposal to open the Oregon Territory to African American settlement during debates over passage of the 1850 Oregon Donation Land Law. Asahel Bush, a newspaperman and friend of Thurston's, quoted the delegate as saying, "The people of Oregon were not pro-slavery men, nor were they pro-negro men; there were but few negroes in the territory and he hoped there never would be more; the people themselves had excluded them and he trusted that Congress would not introduce them in violation of their wishes."[31]

In 1853 the Oregon territorial supreme court ruled that Nathaniel Ford, a migrant from Missouri who had brought several slaves with him, must free his slaves. In 1854 and again the following year, the territorial legislature entertained bills to exclude blacks and mulattoes from the territory in an effort to ensure that Oregon remained for whites only. One member of the territorial house declared: "Niggers . . . should never be allowed to mingle with the whites . . . If niggers are allowed to come among us and mingle with the whites, it will cause a perfect state of pollution . . . I don't see that we should equalize ourselves with them by letting them come among us."[32] Oregonians, by and large, endorsed the principle of "popular sovereignty" as outlined in Stephen Douglas's 1854 Kansas-Nebraska Act, seeing it as an avenue for giving them increased control over their own affairs. Many, like Delazon Smith, a territorial representative from Linn County, argued that Oregonians could support the concept of popular sovereignty and still remain opposed to slavery.[33]

Finally, in 1857 Oregonians voted overwhelmingly in favor of organizing a state government and applying to Congress for statehood. This step led to a final reckoning with the issue of slavery in the Oregon country. The national situation had grown more divisive with the election of the pro-slavery Democrat James Buchanan to the presidency, bloodshed over popular sovereignty in Kansas, and the US Supreme Court's decision in the Dred Scott case. As Oregon politicians jockeyed for position ahead of the necessary constitutional convention, these national events focused Oregonians' attention on the issue of slavery.

While Oregon had a vocal group of pro-slavery advocates (perhaps one-third of the state's population, according to anti-slavery editor William L. Adams of the *Oregon Argus*, a number almost certainly exaggerated) and some strongly anti-slavery agitators, in general, Oregonians rejected both slavery and the presence of free African Americans. Asahel Bush, who founded the Democratic *Oregon Statesman* (with Thurston's covert financial backing), argued that Oregonians, a practical lot, cared little for the debate over the morality of the institution.[34] As one letter opined in the *Statesman*, Oregon's cool and wet climate was not conducive to slave labor.

George H. Williams, the territory's chief justice and a leading Democrat, wrote an influential and widely circulated letter in which he argued that slavery could not flourish in Oregon's climate. He noted, for example, "New York, Pennsylvania, Massachusetts, Connecticut, Rhode Island, New Jersey, and New Hampshire ascertained by actual trial that slavery was detrimental to their interests, and therefore abolished it"—states with cool climates like Oregon's where labor-intensive cotton and similar crops could not be grown.[35] Williams claimed that slaves did not work hard since no incentive motivated them to do so, and they cost far more than it cost to hire free laborers for a few months during the growing season. Further, Williams asserted, the climate might actually be hazardous to African American slaves, since their ancestors originated in hot and sunny Africa. One winter's work in Oregon's cold rain could very well kill them.[36]

Controlling slaves would also be a problem, Williams warned, since they could easily flee the state and take refuge in the free state of California, in Canada, or among Indian tribes, just as fugitive slaves had once taken shelter among the Seminole of Florida. Even worse, Williams argued, census numbers revealed that settlers to the Midwest preferred to settle in free territories.

Emigrants rarely came as men of means, but they were men "whose limbs are made sinewy by hard work; who go to new countries to get land and homes and who expect to depend chiefly upon their own labor. Slave states are objectionable to such men."[37] Oregon needed these hardworking, independent, and ambitious men, but such men would not compete with slavery. Similarly, foreign immigrants looking to escape poverty and oppression in Europe could be expected to find homes in Oregon. These immigrants tirelessly built farms, canals, and railroads—developing every place they settled—but they would not deign to work beside slaves. Establish slavery in Oregon, Williams cautioned, and "you will turn aside that tide of free white labor which has poured itself like a fertilizing flood" on the free states and territories.[38] Worse yet, laboring whites and enslaved blacks would invariably mix, and each would learn the bad habits of the other. "Taking everything into consideration," Williams concluded, "I ask if it is not the true policy of Oregon to keep as clear as possible of negroes, and all the exciting questions of negro servitude. Situated away here on the Pacific, as a free state, we are not likely to be troubled much with free negroes or fugitive slaves."[39] Williams argued that Oregon therefore should be reserved for whites.

Similarly, the *Oregon Statesman* in August 1857, with the constitutional convention looming, argued that slavery fit in the South and that southerners should keep the black and white races separate through slavery because "the wisdom of man has not yet devised a system under which the negro is as well off as he is under that of American slavery. Still, we think that our climate, soil, situation, population, etc., render it, to any *useful* extent, an *impossible* situation for Oregon."[40]

Those in favor of slavery certainly had supporters, including Democrats Joseph Lane (Oregon's territorial delegate following Thurston's death in 1851) and Matthew P. Deady, like Williams a territorial supreme court justice.[41] Their argument rested on the belief that slavery would prevent the chronic labor shortages plaguing the region, especially when news of a gold strike somewhere caused many hired hands to flee to the goldfields. Further, some claimed, Oregon's climate did not differ markedly from that of Virginia, Kentucky, or Missouri—all places with slaves (a markedly different interpretation of Oregon's climate than that of Williams).

Oregon's constitutional convention convened on August 17, 1857. The territory's prominent Democrats led the convention, including Deady, who was chosen president. The presence of blacks, whether free or enslaved, occupied a great deal of attention in the sessions. Thomas Dryer, the Whig editor of the *Oregonian* and a convention delegate, declared that he would "vote to exclude Negroes, Chinamen, Kanakas [Hawaiians], and even Indians" from Oregon.[42] Indeed, delegates drafted articles of the constitution intended to deny citizenship to blacks, mulattoes, and the Chinese, as well as to prevent Chinese immigrants from purchasing real estate. These issues and that of slavery, however, threatened to derail the convention. The delegates therefore decided not to address the issues of slavery and the presence of free blacks and instead to send them directly to the people.

In November 1857 Oregonians weighed in on the constitution, the issue of slavery, and the presence of blacks. They voted overwhelmingly for statehood and in favor of excluding slavery, by 7,227 votes to 2,645 votes. Oregonians also prohibited free blacks from settling in the fledgling state by a stunning margin of 8,640 to 1,081.[43] Statehood, though, waited for more than a year, as Congress bickered about admitting Oregon in a time of acrimonious debate, but the results of the election on Oregon's fate showed, perhaps better than any other measure, how Oregonians felt about the institution of slavery and the presence of blacks in their midst. Oregon would strive to be a free state but also a white state.

Peter Burnett, reflecting late in life on his prominent role in debates over Negro exclusion in both Oregon and California, explained that he always staunchly opposed slavery. From the vantage point of the 1880s and advanced age, he justified exclusion as part of a belief that the West would be different from and better than the older regions of the country and that racial purity would be a key part of that superiority. He noted, "One of the objects I had in view of coming to this coast was to aid in building a great American community on the Pacific; and, in the enthusiasm of my nature, I was anxious to aid in founding a State superior in several respects to those east of the Rocky Mountains. I therefore labored to avoid the evils of intoxication [by supporting prohibition efforts], and of mixed-races, one of which was disfranchised."[44] Being staunchly anti-slavery, however, was only half of the equation, a fact that Burnett carefully left out of his reminiscences, for he, like many other westerners, attempted to use whiteness to create a uniform society.

As Oregon and California worked to prevent the presence of both slavery and free blacks, national leaders continued their march toward war. As late as

1850 cooperation remained possible, but it had become increasingly difficult, as the motley provisions that composed the California Compromise of 1850 demonstrated. Lacking a new slave state to offset California's admission to the Union as a free state, northerners offered several provisions, including efforts to strengthen the fugitive slave law, to win enough support to pass the legislation.

By the mid-1850s such forced cooperation became impossible as the debate over slavery grew increasingly hostile. Most northerners came out against the expansion of slavery, while their southern counterparts remained in favor of expansion. Southern partisans believed slave owners had the right to take their slaves anywhere, since the legal system recognized them as private property. Navigating this split proved to be fraught with difficulty. Illinois senator Stephen Douglas, seeking to address the issue and propel himself into the national spotlight, offered the Kansas-Nebraska Act in 1854. Essentially, the act created two separate territories, Kansas in the south and Nebraska to the north. He advocated a system called popular sovereignty in which the voters would decide for themselves whether to allow slavery. He assumed that Kansas (directly west of the slave state Missouri) would endorse slavery and that the Nebraska Territory would not, sustaining a tee-tering balance for a bit longer. Opposition to this act (and to the broader 1857 Dred Scott decision by the US Supreme Court, which effectively allowed slav-ery anywhere) gave birth to the Republican Party, whose issues and support were sectional, not national. As popular sovereignty in Kansas demonstrated, however, not even the voters could solve this problem.

Facing its second presidential election campaign in 1860, the Republican Party chose Abraham Lincoln as its candidate. While Lincoln stressed that he would not interfere with slavery where it already existed, he nevertheless advo-cated for the territories in the West to be preserved as "free soil" and free of the institution of slavery. Southerners feared as well that Lincoln's triumph in the 1860 election repudiated their rights and standing as equal members of the Union. A bare majority of northern voters had overridden their values, beliefs, and key economic institutions; and the constitution, they contended, included protection of minority views from such a tyrannical majority. This new presi-dent and his party, southern secessionists claimed, desired their subjugation and the destruction of the southern economy and way of life. As one Mississippi newspaper editor claimed, "The domination of Black Republicanism is wholly inconsistent with every idea of a free or beneficent government." As for Lincoln he asked, "Can a man be said to.be [a] constitutionally elected president, the very object of whose election is to *destroy* the Constitution?" Southern fire-eaters argued that dissolving the Union and seceding was the only logical way to preserve the fundamental principles of the revolution on which the nation was founded.[45] During the first six months of 1861, the nation tore itself in two.

Ironically perhaps, secession sealed the fate of the West as free soil. Issues, such as the Homestead Act and location of the transcontinental railroad, long mired in sectional politics, could now be easily resolved since the West remained firmly in the hands of the federal government and the United States. Northerners rather than southerners determined the course of the new western empire, championing both free labor and whiteness in the process.

The Homestead Act in particular had been a long time coming. Northern politicians before and during the Civil War offered a vision of the West as populated by Jefferson's yeoman farmers, whose own strong hands provided their only source of labor. This would be a free West, where no person received an unfair advantage by drawing off the labor of slaves. Assumptions about free labor drove the creation of a homestead law. In the past, the prospect of a homestead law had been supported by both northerners and southerners, but a law had never come to fruition. Indeed, Democrats had long advocated a policy of allowing settlers to claim sections of the public domain. Southern politicians like Thomas Hart Benton of Missouri, James Walker of Mississippi, and, later, Tennessee's Andrew Johnson argued in the 1830s and 1840s for a policy that would help settlers procure farms in the West. Opposition to a homestead policy in those years came not from the pro-slavery South but rather from the Northeast.[46]

The dynamics behind a homestead law changed when homesteading by yeoman farmers became equated with "free labor." The belief that the West should be reserved as "free soil" helped destroy the second-party system, creating a split in political views along sectional lines, a split personified by the rise of the Republican Party. The Republicans' support of free soil turned the Old Northwest away from the Democrats and, in turn, forced the Old Southwest, long a supporter of homesteading, into an alliance with the Southeast.[47] This realignment doomed the passage of the act until the Civil War.

In their attacks on slavery and its extension, it became almost axiomatic for northern critics of slavery to denounce the institution as an evil not only for slaves but also for whites. Slavery degraded and debased labor in areas where it thrived, and few whites of any social class would work, they claimed. Republicans like William H. Seward and Frederick Law Olmsted invariably denounced southerners as lazy, shiftless, and eager to make their slaves work. Northerners pointed to that reluctance to work as a major cause of the South's alleged economic backwardness. Olmsted in particular made something of a cottage industry out of touring the South and denouncing it as inferior to northern society.[48] He rejected the common belief that beneficent climates would cause white racial deterioration and instead pointed an accusing finger at slavery in his 1857 Texas travelogue *A Journey through Texas*.

Like much of the Southwest, Texas had both a warm climate and a multiracial society. Touring the state in 1853–54, Olmsted marveled at its fertility, declaring, "The labor of one man in Texas will more easily produce adequate sustenance and shelter for a family . . . than that of two anywhere in the Free States."[49] Labor in Texas, however, did not always mean merely subsistence for small families, the northern abolitionist stressed. Many Texans engaged in cotton production, and cotton, with few exceptions, meant slavery. Some thought the heat and humidity of Texas, like elsewhere in the South, weakened and exhausted whites. Supposedly, only peoples of African descent could endure it. Southerners therefore considered slavery an economic and environmental necessity.[50] Olmsted dismissed this argument, writing, "Nor did we . . . have reason to retain the common opinion . . . that the health of white people, or their ability to labor, was less in the greater part of Texas than in the new Free States."[51] Whites, he observed, could be seen in the cotton fields alongside slaves, and their health did not seem adversely affected.

Yet Texas, Olmsted asserted, was underdeveloped even by the meager standards of the frontier. He described fertile fields that lay fallow, homes of rude and haphazard construction, neglected livestock, and a poor, backward, uncouth, anti-intellectual white citizenry—all typical effects associated with climatic degeneration, or so conventional wisdom asserted.[52] Such striking poverty in a land of abundance did seem to make a case for climate-induced, white racial degeneration, but Olmsted differed with the "common opinion" and concluded that climate did not account for the inferior quality of Texas's white population. The pernicious influence of slavery, however, did. Olmsted described the son of a northerner who had settled in Texas as being "without care, thoughtless, with an unoccupied mind." He dwelled in a hovel on

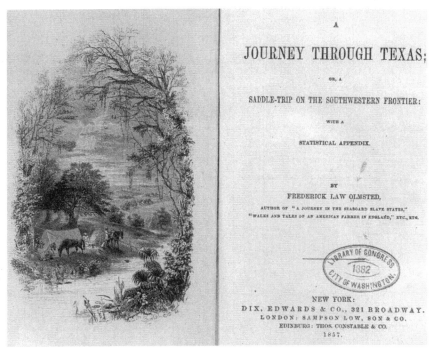

A

JOURNEY THROUGH TEXAS;

OR, A

SADDLE-TRIP ON THE SOUTHWESTERN FRONTIER:

WITH A

STATISTICAL APPENDIX.

BY

FREDERICK LAW OLMSTED,

AUTHOR OF "A JOURNEY IN THE SEABOARD SLAVE STATES,"
"WALKS AND TALKS OF AN AMERICAN FARMER IN ENGLAND," ETC., ETC.

NEW YORK:
DIX, EDWARDS & CO., 321 BROADWAY.
LONDON: SAMPSON LOW, SON & CO.
EDINBURG: THOS. CONSTABLE & CO.
1857.

FIGURE 5.1. Frederick Law Olmsted, before earning fame as a landscape architect, spent much of his youth touring Europe and the United States. His 1857 travelogue, *A Journey through Texas*, discounted the common belief that beneficent climates would lead to white racial degeneration and blamed slavery for the lack of development in Texas. Frontispiece to Frederick Law Olmsted's *A Journey through Texas*. *Courtesy,* Library of Congress, Washington, DC.

a neglected farm, living a pointless and wretched existence. "Educate him where you please," Olmsted continued, "in any country not subject to the influence of slavery, how different would have been his disposition, how much higher . . . his hopes, aims, and life."[53] Slave owners relied on their slaves for everything, and those without slaves saw no reason to try to compete against the slaveholders, thus making all classes lazy. Unfortunately, this inferior condition prevailed among most Texans, Olmsted concluded.

Recent European immigrants contrasted starkly with the downtrodden, lazy whites. Olmsted marveled at the progress made by German immigrants in Texas, who, he felt, embodied the transformative power of free labor and hard work. At a typically neat and ordered homestead, Olmsted met a farmer who proudly exclaimed that upon finishing the day's fieldwork, he still had the time and energy to construct a home made from native stone. Olmsted deadpanned, "I could not see that the climate was to be accused of having in any degree paralyzed his ambition or his strength."[54] The quality of the homes and farms of German immigrants so impressed him that he titled his chapter on their settlement at Neu Branfels "An Evening Away from Texas."[55]

Instead of a land of plenty, frontier Texas exemplified a wasteland where American vigor—the hallmark of the nation's development—had fallen victim to the evils of slavery. Expanding slavery, Olmsted warned, meant creating more places like frontier Texas, but, contrary to popular opinion, climate could not account for Texas's arrested development.

In contrast to the degenerate South, the Republican Party offered free labor as ideal for the continuation of American democracy and the settlement of the West. Coupled with cheap western land, free labor would transform the West from a wilderness into a landscape of settled, orderly towns, providing economic growth and upward mobility for working-class Americans. In contrast, Republicans countered, the South persisted as an economically stagnant expanse dominated by wealthy slave owners who ruled at the expense of degraded poor whites and uneducated slaves.[56] For the ultimate success of the nation and the continuation of democracy, therefore, new territories in the West had to be populated by free men and not slaves.

The influential newspaper editor Horace Greeley, like Olmsted, sought a future West populated by free white yeoman farmers, unencumbered by unfair competition from slavery. He wrote, "The public lands are the great regulator of the relations of Labor and Capital, the safety valve of our industrial and social engine." He advised the poor and unemployed to leave the crowded, filthy cities and "go straight into the country—go at once."[57] Republicans, including Greeley, felt that the settlement of western lands by free yeoman farmers would effectively contain slavery.[58] Such advice, although seemingly prosaic, had calculated political undertones and unforeseen ramifications for the racial makeup of the region.

The Civil War rendered debates over slavery like those in California and Oregon, as well as the tension between free labor and slave labor in the territories, moot. The sectional deadlock that had long prevented Congress from acting on critical western issues disappeared. Having seceded, the South essentially forfeited the ability to shape the West. With little opposition, northern Republicans set about passing legislation designed to integrate the West into the nation. While they did not promote whiteness per se, they certainly promoted free labor.

Two fundamentally important acts spurred the first transcontinental railroad, on a route through northern territory, and the settlement of the West's land. The Homestead Act, signed into law in May 1862, opened the public domain to any citizen or immigrant "who shall have filed his declaration of intention to become [a citizen] as required by the naturalization laws of the United States."[59] This law, therefore, applied to native-born whites, immigrants from European nations, Hispanics (granted citizenship under the Treaty of Guadalupe Hidalgo), and African Americans after ratification of the Fourteenth Amendment. It also expressly forbade Confederates or anyone who had ever "borne arms against the United States Government or given aid and comfort to its enemies" from acquiring land under the act.

To claim the 160 acres promised under the act, settlers were required to pay a small filing fee and then to reside on and improve the land for five years. Alternatively, settlers could buy the land for $1.25 an acre after six months of residence. To be sure, several problems plagued the system, and settlers found that much of the best land had already been awarded to the states or railroad companies, but it did offer the possibility of owning a farm of one's own, a prospect that at the time defined the American dream. Given the generous terms required to claim land under the act, many people decided to go West.[60]

Go they did. From the 1870s through the early decades of the 1900s, western states exploded in population. Between 1862 and 1913, over 2.4 million people filed claims under the Homestead Act.[61] The throngs of emigrants included a considerable number of African Americans. For them, earning their freedom during the Civil War signified only the first step in achieving a better life. Following the Civil War, southern African Americans desired a chance for economic as well as political freedom, but as the federal government lost the will to enforce its policies of reconstruction, which gave free blacks some semblance of social and economic power, segregation began to take hold. African Americans sought ways of protecting their rights and of fostering a sense of community, and they could do so by leaving the South for friendlier regions. According to the historian Steven Hahn, an "interest in emigration arose as one of several strategies designed to create or reconstitute freed communities on a stable foundation."[62] Emigration sentiment grew strongest in the Deep South, especially areas "where freedpeople labored on cotton plantations, had made major efforts . . . to organize themselves into stable communities, but then suffered, or were threatened by serious reversals" because of the rise of so-called white Redemption in the South.[63] As the members of the Colonization Council, an African American colonization organization, explained in an appeal to President Ulysses S. Grant, they wanted "to be removed to a territory where they could live."[64] The African nation of Liberia, created in the antebellum period by American blacks and the American Colonization Society, attracted some, but the distance and expense proved prohibitive. Emigration therefore took on a more regional tint.

Many western states experienced an increase in the number of African Americans in the 1870s and 1880s. California, for example, had 6,018 "colored" residents in 1880, but by 1900 the population had grown to 82,326. Colorado's black population in 1880 stood at 2,435, and by 1900 it had grown nearly five-fold, to over 10,000. Oregon's black population grew from a mere 487 in 1880 to nearly 19,000 by 1900. Impressive increases, but they were minuscule compared with the numbers of African Americans in the South. In 1900 Alabama's black population numbered over 800,000, Mississippi's was nearly 1 million, and Georgia had over a million blacks.[65] Nevertheless, African Americans headed West in greater and greater numbers.

African Americans founded all-black towns from Oklahoma to California, but Kansas in particular attracted thousands because of its proximity to the Deep South and reputation for tolerance.[66] As is the case for all immigrants, push and pull factors propelled them in search of new homes. Increasing disfranchisement, segregation, and violence in the South pushed African Americans; and the expectation of owning farms and building communities where they could govern themselves and live relatively free from the problems found in the states of the former Confederacy pulled them. "Kansas," in the words of historian Quintard Taylor, "became to the freeperson what the United States was to the European immigrant: a refuge from tyranny and oppression."[67] The so-called Exodusters (nicknamed that because they resembled the Israelites in Exodus who left slavery in search of the promised land) began arriving in the Sunflower State in the late 1870s, and the first wave included many with the means and ability to pay their way. Stories and rumors, however, built Kansas into an almost biblical land of milk and honey, and the small movement of African Americans into the state grew to a crescendo in 1879–80. The throng of emigrants—totaling perhaps 30,000—was largely destitute, and they overwhelmed the cities of Kansas.[68]

Promoters and developers, as in all such rushes, played a large role in attracting African Americans to Kansas, but railroad promoters remained conspicuously absent from efforts to recruit them. Two black ministers from Tennessee, William Smith and Thomas Harris, along with W. R. Hill, a white Kansas land speculator, founded the all-black community of Nicodemus in central Kansas. Hill's ambitions kept him busy, and he laid out the mostly white town of Hill City in 1878, a year after founding Nicodemus.

Nicodemus became a symbol of hope for many southern blacks, and stories of the place as a utopian society soon emerged, but the town struggled like other frontier communities. Willianna Hickman, a Kentucky woman who emigrated to Nicodemus with her family, found most of the town's residents living in dugouts. Approaching the rough town, she began to cry.[69] Nicodemus would grow for several years, but by the mid-1880s blizzards, crop failures, and the Union Pacific Railroad's decision to bypass the town doomed it to irrelevance.[70]

Similarly, Benjamin "Pap" Singleton, the so-called Black Moses, recruited "Exodusters" throughout the South, establishing colonies in Kansas and Colorado.[71] Edwin McCabe, a former resident of Nicodemus, created the all-black town of Langston in Oklahoma.[72] These towns owed their beginnings largely to the work of local speculators and African Americans leaders who hoped to improve the condition of their race. Powerful railroads, which were heavily promoting their lines to European immigrants, played no role in erecting black towns.

In ways both conscious and unconscious, westerners clearly shaped the character of the western population. Efforts in Oregon and California, for example, to exclude African Americans reflected white attempts to legislate whiteness, but less obvious if no less real were efforts by railroads and promoters to ignore tens of thousands of southern blacks. Following the Civil War, the black population of the West grew in real and appreciable ways, but that augmentation would certainly have been greater had westerners been willing to embrace more black emigrants.

Opposition to black settlement in the 1840s and beyond illustrated a remarkable transformation in Anglo-Americans' views of the West. The early, negative assessments of the region by Zebulon Pike and Washington Irving had given way to a belief in the West as destined to be free of Peter Burnett's "troublesome class of population." Many Anglo-Americans now saw the West as an ideal location in which to settle, a region free from undesirable immigration and the taint of slavery. How this transformation occurred, however, how the West came to be seen as a refuge from the aftermath of slavery and the dangers of non-Anglo immigration, constitutes a story in itself.

NOTES

1. Donald W. Meinig, *The Shaping of America: A Geographical Perspective on 500 Years of History,* vol. 2: *Continental America, 1800–1867* (New Haven, CT: Yale University Press, 1993), 432–35, 450

2. For a discussion of the slavery issue in the Old Northwest, see Eugene H. Berwanger, *The Frontier against Slavery: Western Anti-Negro Prejudice and the Slavery Extension Controversy* (Urbana: University of Illinois Press, 1967), 7–29.

3. Michael F. Holt, *The Fate of Their Country: Politicians, Slavery Extension, and the Coming of the Civil War* (New York: Hill and Wang, 2004), 6.

4. Meinig, *Shaping of America,* 453–54.

5. Quoted in Holt, *Fate of Their Country,* 7.

6. Ibid., 7–9.

7. Ibid., 18.

8. Ibid., 20.

9. Ibid., 19–35.

10. Quoted in Rudolph M. Lapp, *Blacks in Gold Rush California* (New Haven, CT: Yale University Press, 1977), 18.

11. Berwanger, *Frontier against Slavery,* 61.

12. Walter Colton, *Three Years in California* (New York: S. A. Rollo, 1859), 374–75.

13. "Constitution of the State of California, 1849," Archives, California Secretary of State, http://www.sos.ca.gov/archives/collections/constitutions/1849/full-text.htm (accessed July 12, 2012).

14. Berwanger, *Frontier against Slavery,* 60.

15. J. Ross Browne, *Report of the Debates in the Convention of California on the Formation of the State Constitution in September and October, 1849* (Washington, DC: John T. Towers, 1850), 47–50, Archives, California Secretary of State, http://www.archives.cdn.sos.ca.gov/1849/pdf/convention-debates-reports.pdf (accessed July 12, 2012). On the belief that Europeans are descendants of Noah's son Japhet,

see Colin Kidd, *British Identities before Nationalism: Ethnicity and Nationhood in the Atlantic World, 1600–1800* (New York: Cambridge University Press, 1999), 28–30, 52.

16. Peter H. Burnett, *Recollections and Opinions of an Old Pioneer* (New York: D. Appleton, 1880), 351–52.

17. Ibid., 354–55; italics in original.

18. Berwanger, *Frontier against Slavery*, 60.

19. Ibid., 78; Quintard Taylor, "Slaves and Free Men: Blacks in the Oregon Country, 1840–1860," *Oregon Historical Quarterly* 83, no. 2 (Summer 1982): 153–70.

20. Berwanger, *Frontier against Slavery*, 78.

21. Taylor, "Slaves and Free Men," 153–70.

22. Ibid.

23. Peter Burnett, "Letter from Peter Burnett," dated December 25, 1844, *Jefferson* [Missouri] *Inquirer*, October 23, 1845.

24. Taylor, "Slaves and Free Men," 153–70, quote on 157.

25. Quoted in Berwanger, *Frontier against Slavery*, 81.

26. *Congressional Globe*, 30th Congress, Session 1, Appendix, 793, Library of Congress, http://memory.loc.gov/ammem/amlaw/lwcglink.html#top (accessed July 12, 2012).

27. Robert W. Johannsen, *Frontier Politics and the Sectional Conflict: The Pacific Northwest on the Eve of the Civil War* (Seattle: University of Washington Press, 1955), 17–19.

28. *Congressional Globe*, 30th Congress, Session 1, Appendix, 865.

29. Ibid., 866.

30. Ibid., 792.

31. Barbara Mahoney, "Oregon Voices, Oregon Democracy: Asahel Bush, Slavery, and the Statehood Debate," *Oregon Historical Quarterly* 110, no. 2 (Summer 2009): 202–27.

32. Quoted in Johannsen, *Frontier Politics and the Sectional Conflict*, 23. Original quote from Portland *Weekly Oregonian*, January 6, 1853.

33. Johannsen, *Frontier Politics*, 24–30.

34. On Bush's career, see Mahoney, "Oregon Voices."

35. George H. Williams, "The Free State Letter of Judge George H. Williams," *Oregon Historical Quarterly* 9, no. 3 (September 1908): 258.

36. Ibid.

37. Ibid., 265.

38. Ibid., 265–66.

39. Ibid., 272.

40. Johannsen, *Frontier Politics*, 32–38; italics in original.

41. Mahoney, "Oregon Voices."

42. Quoted in ibid, 222.

43. Williams, "Free State Letter of Judge George H. Williams."

44. Burnett, *Recollections and Opinions of an Old Pioneer*, 221–22.

45. Quoted in Michael A. Morrison, *Slavery and the American West: The Eclipse of Manifest Destiny and the Coming of the Civil War* (Chapel Hill: University of North Carolina Press, 1997), 255–62, quotes 258–59; italics in original.

46. Henry Nash Smith, *Virgin Land: The American West as Symbol and Myth* (Cambridge, MA: Harvard University Press, 1970), 168–69.

47. Ibid.

48. Eric Foner, *Free Soil, Free Labor, Free Men: The Ideology of the Republican Party before the Civil War* (New York: Oxford University Press, 1995), 41–48.

49. Frederick Law Olmsted, *A Journey through Texas, or, A Saddle-Trip on the Southwestern Frontier* (New York: Mason Bros., 1857), xiii.

50. See Conevery Bolton Valenčius, *The Health of the Country: How American Settlers Understood Themselves and Their Land* (New York: Perseus Books Group, 2002), 237.

51. Olmsted, *Journey through Texas*, xiii.

52. The belief that lower-class, rural whites were lazy, stupid, and inferior to their social betters has a long history. See Matt Wray, *Not Quite White: White Trash and the Boundaries of Whiteness* (Durham, NC: Duke University Press, 2006).

53. Olmsted, *Journey through Texas*, 122–23.

54. Ibid., 279.

55. Ibid., 142.

56. Foner, *Free Soil, Free Labor, Free Men*, 40.

57. Quoted in ibid., 27. On Greeley's advocacy of the West as a safety valve, see Smith, *Virgin Land*, 201; Coy F. Cross, *Go West Young Man! Horace Greeley's Vision for America* (Albuquerque: University of New Mexico Press, 1995), 3–12.

58. Cross, *Go West Young Man*, 28.

59. "Homestead Act," Avalon Project, Yale University, New Haven, CT, http://avalon.law.yale.edu/19th_century/homestead_act.asp (accessed July 12, 2012).

60. Richard White, *It's Your Misfortune and None of My Own: A New History of the American West* (Norman: University of Oklahoma Press, 1991), 143.

61. Walter Nugent, *Into the West: The Story of Its People* (New York: Alfred A. Knopf, 1999), 131.

62. Steven Hahn, *A Nation under Our Feet: Black Political Struggles in the Rural South from Slavery to the Great Migration* (Cambridge, MA: Belknap, 2003), 322.

63. Ibid., 331.

64. Quoted in ibid., 320.

65. "Historical Census Browser," University of Virginia Library, Charlottesville, http://mapserver.lib.virginia.edu/index.html (accessed July 12, 2012).

66. For a discussion of African American settlement in the trans-Mississippi West, see Quintard Taylor, *In Search of the Racial Frontier: African Americans in the American West, 1528–1990* (New York: W. W. Norton, 1998), especially 134–63. Longer works on the Exodusters are Robert G. Athearn, *In Search of Canaan: Black Migration to Kansas, 1879–1880* (Lawrence: Regents Press of Kansas, 1978); Norman L. Crockett, *The Black Towns* (Lawrence: Regents Press of Kansas, 1979); Nell Irvin Painter, *Exodusters: Black Migration to Kansas after Reconstruction* (New York: Alfred A. Knopf, 1977).

67. Taylor, *In Search of the Racial Frontier*, 137.

68. Athearn, *In Search of Canaan*, 3–6.

69. Crockett, *Black Towns*, 1–8.

70. Taylor, *In Search of the Racial Frontier*, 139–41.

71. Ibid., 137–38; Roy Garvin, "Benjamin, or 'Pap,' Singleton and His Followers," *Journal of Negro History* 33, no. 1 (January 1948): 7–23.

72. Crockett, *Black Towns*, 16–26; Taylor, *In Search of the Racial Frontier*, 140–46.

6

"OUR CLIMATE AND SOIL IS COMPLETELY ADAPTED TO THEIR CUSTOMS"

Whiteness, Railroad Promotion, and the Settlement of the Great Plains

Dr. William A. Bell, a transplanted English physician and promoter for the Denver and Rio Grande Western Railway, observed in his 1869 book *New Tracks in North America* that the West offered unlimited potential for creating prosperous new towns and generating profits for discerning investors, but its development would require men of vision, courage, and capital to make dreams a reality. The West stood forth as a vast region "where continuous settlement is impossible, where, instead of navigable rivers, we find arid deserts, but where, nevertheless, spots of great fertility and the richest prizes of the mineral kingdom tempt men onward into those vast regions." In this environment, he continued, "Railways become almost a necessity of existence—certainly of development; and the locomotive has to lead instead of follow the tide of population."[1] This fact put the western railroads in a difficult position. Instead of simply building a line to tap an existing market, connecting smaller established towns to larger established cities, railroads in the West had the unenviable task of laying thousands of miles of expensive track in the hope of creating a market; the supply,

DOI: 10.5876/9781607323969.c006

in many cases, preceded the demand in a strange inversion of capitalism's most sacrosanct principle.

Railroad construction, therefore, carried a great deal of risk, and many failed. An acerbic newspaperman and critic of the bankrupt Northern Pacific Railroad put the railroad's weakness in a different perspective, remarking in 1873—the year the company's collapse helped bring down the financial house of Jay Cooke and propel the nation into an unprecedented economic depression—that the line's failure surprised few, as it amounted to "a wild scheme to build a railroad from Nowhere, through No-man's Land, to No Place."[2] Such criticism had substance, for indeed many of the West's cities and towns existed as evanescent dreams, living only in the imaginations and on the maps of railroad developers like Bell. These towns would only come to be if the railroads themselves actively recruited settlers to emigrate, but this also gave railroads an opportunity to shape the population of western cities and towns. It was with a sense of urgency that railroads set out to find settlers, and, without exception, the settlers they recruited were descended from old-stock Americans or Northern Europeans. When railroad promoters dreamed of settlers for their lines, they dreamed only in white.

Railroad executives, like most other nineteenth-century Americans, made numerous distinctions between ethnic and racial groups. Certainly, they saw racial divisions between whites and African Americans or Native Americans, but they also discriminated between the ethnic groups of Europe, or as many preferred to call them, the "races" of Europe.[3] "Real" whites, usually defined as those of Northern European ancestry, rated as the most desirable potential citizens. Believed to be hardworking, independent, and intelligent, they allegedly made ideal settlers. Thomas Jefferson eloquently celebrated them as "the chosen people of God, if ever he had a chosen people, whose breasts he has made his peculiar deposit for substantial and genuine virtue."[4]

A key part of the agrarian myth maintained that white farmers, as virtuous republicans, possessed the temperament to tame a savage wilderness and construct new communities. The settling of new lands, the historian Henry Nash Smith argued, reflected a "collective representation, a poetic idea . . . that defined the promise of American life" and encapsulated a variety of meanings, including "fecundity, growth, increase, and blissful labor in the earth."[5] Railroad developers therefore reflected deeply held American views of desirability when they set out to recruit settlers.

to advertise to these groups, railroads actively shaped the racial and ethnic makeup of the towns along their lines. Although less important than farming experience, race and ethnicity clearly factored into the railroads' advertising campaigns—this is what the NP's land committee had no doubt implied when mentioning the character of its would-be settlers.

By the 1870s, immigration to America had become decidedly multinational. People from England, Scotland, Ireland, Northern, Southern, and Eastern Europe, and even China immigrated to America. The Chinese famously labored to carve the Central Pacific Railroad from the stubborn granite of the Sierra, but when they finished their work, they did not reap the rewards. All of these groups sought work eagerly, and many dreamed of owning their own land in the United States. As the major western lines began colonization campaigns in the 1870s, they naturally looked to nationalities already migrating to the United States in substantial numbers. The largest group of immigrants coming into the United States in the 1870s was the Germans (718,182, or 25 percent), then the Irish (436,871, or 15 percent), and Scandinavians, including Swedes, Norwegians, and Danes (243,016, or less than 10 percent of the total). The Irish and Germans in 1860 accounted for nearly 70 percent of the nation's foreign-born citizens and in 1900 still represented 40 percent.[12] Railroad campaigns, however, consciously targeted Germans, Scandinavians, and Englishmen to a much greater degree than the Irish, and when groups like the Italians passed Germans in numbers in the 1890s, the focus remained on the latter.[13]

These campaigns, especially the Northern Pacific's efforts in the Dakotas and Minnesota, left a profound mark. Counting immigrants and their American-born children, the West had the highest foreign-born population in America in the nineteenth century. According to the historian Frederick C. Luebke, "North Dakota's immigrant percentage, an astounding 71.3 percent [in 1900], ranked highest in the country. South Dakota, Nebraska, Montana, Wyoming, Colorado, Utah, Nevada, Washington, and California all exceeded the national average of 32.1 percent in 1900."[14] In terms of specific ethnic groups, census data revealed a bias toward Northern Europeans in areas where railroads had heavily colonized. Germans, English (including English-speaking Canadians), Norwegians, Swedes, Russians (most of them actually native German speakers, such as the Mennonites), and Danes collectively accounted for 59.1 percent of North Dakota's population in 1900.

The Irish, Welsh, Italians, and Eastern Europeans combined for just over another 10 percent, less than half of the 22.6 percent for the Norwegians alone in the state. The number of Irish (3.6%) was low in North Dakota, while the number of Norwegians was excessively high, a marked contrast to most other western states where the Irish ranked first or second and the Norwegians were statistically insignificant. Percentages of Irish attained their highest levels in mining states, such as Montana (11.3% of the population), California (10.2%), and Nevada (10.0%)—all higher than the national average. In Kansas, with a much lower immigrant population of 25.8 percent, the numbers of desirable European colonists were no less apparent. The largest group by far was the Germans (8.9%, or 131,563 people), followed by the Irish (3.3%), English (3.1%), Swedes (2.4%), and Russians at 1.7 percent (essentially Mennonite colonists).[15] This dominance of Northern Europeans resulted in no small measure from the colonization campaigns of the Northern Pacific and the Atchison, Topeka and Santa Fe Railroads.

Clearly, the West symbolized opportunity for many, but only certain groups received the specific support of the railroads. Eager to attract Northern Europeans, many lines set up immigration agencies in European nations, provided free or subsidized transport to the United States, shipped immigrants' baggage at no charge, and set up offices along their lines to help immigrants select their new homes. The writer Helen Hunt Jackson, touring Oregon in the 1870s, stopped in Portland and visited the office of the Bureau of Immigration of the Northern Pacific Railroad, describing it as "one of the most interesting places in town." The office showcased grains grown in Oregon and Washington, especially on the farmlands east of the Cascades. "Swedes, Norwegians, Germans, [and] Irish," she wrote, jammed into the office. Watching the patient Norwegian land officer answer these immigrants' questions did "more in an hour to make one realize what the present tide of immigration to the New Northwest really is than reading of statistics could do in a year." The land officer was, in fact, the most pleasant surprise for the immigrants. "It was touching," Jackson wrote, "to see the brightened faces of his countrymen, as their broken English was answered by him in the familiar words of their own tongue."[16] This was indeed a warm welcome for immigrants who had traveled thousands of miles. Given the amount of control railroads had over their grants, the ethnic and racial makeup of the Great Plains resulted from no accident, and the composition

FIGURE 6.1. Attracted by climate and promises of cheap land, thousands of Northern European immigrants, like this group of Norwegian immigrants in front of a sod house near Madison, South Dakota, came to America for a better life. Railroads coveted and competed for these groups, believing their experience as farmers and their unquestionably white race made them ideal Americans. *Courtesy*, Minnesota Historical Society, St. Paul.

of this population represented a massive and largely successful effort at social engineering.

Nearly twenty years before the transcontinental lines, the Illinois Central Railroad, a north-south line running through Illinois, received the first government land grant in 1850 and soon launched the first immigration campaign.[17] Building the line and populating the lands along it became the major concerns of the Illinois Central. During construction of the road in the early 1850s, the company employed between 6,000 and 10,000 workers, almost all of whom were foreign immigrants. These laborers, David Neal, the vice president of the Illinois Central, declared, would likely remain in the state after settlement and increase "the population of the country."[18] Initially, the company employed Irish laborers, but the reputation of the Irish came with them. Reports of drinking and violence made them unpopular with Illinois farmers, forcing the company to prefer married men and especially married German men as laborers, although many Irish remained in the company's employ. According to the historian Paul Wallace Gates, the owners of the Illinois Central felt the Germans "were less hardy and less suited to the rugged work required than the Irish, [but] they were steadier and more docile, and in the long run better adapted to the work." In other words, the company, though worried that the Germans lacked the strength of the Irish, employed them with the hope that they would settle and become ideal citizens. Recruiting German laborers became a top priority of the line, and, as Neal predicted, many remained in the region after its completion in 1856.[19] In addition to their hard-drinking reputation, the Irish, unlike the mostly Protestant Germans, came from a Catholic background; in addition, as many Americans believed at the time, they were of a different race than Englishmen and other Northern European groups.[20] This bias against the Irish as settlers remained long after the completion of the Illinois Central.

The Illinois Central's executives also sought to find more desirable immigrants, and they pioneered the organized colonization campaign in 1852. Following their success in attracting Germans as first workers and then settlers, the Illinois Central set out to actively recruit Scandinavians. The company hired Oscar Malmborg, a Swedish immigrant and Mexican-American War veteran, as its chief immigration agent. For the next decade, Malmborg flooded Norway and Sweden with pamphlets and personally visited hundreds of villages. Malmborg promised his employer that he could effectively monitor the ports from which these immigrants would depart. He chose the cities carefully, avoiding Southern Europe and Ireland and focusing on "Liverpool, Hamburg, Bremen, Gothenburg, and Christiania." He included Antwerp and Harve, noting that he spoke French well enough to "attend even to those places if You desire."[21]

Malmborg considered Norway and Sweden fertile ground for potential colonists, as many experienced farmers there eagerly wished to relocate. In Sweden, Malmborg explained, the rise of tenancy was behind the impulse to leave as small farmers gradually lost control of their lands to larger landholders. In an 1861 letter to an Illinois Central executive, he explained that farmers in Norway stood in a decidedly better position because, unlike Sweden, Norway "enjoys the advantage of having neither a hereditary nor a so called landed aristocracy." In Sweden, "It is the object of the large gentleman farmer to annex the small farms in his vicinity to his estate. Of the three classes of actual farmers—the peasants—it is the poorest who are gradually being reduced from being owners to become mere laborers." These peasant farmers "cannot in the long run, after the heavy taxes are paid, support an increasing family." Yet if the peasants could be encouraged to sell and move before being reduced to tenants, they would "have more than sufficient to establish themselves independently on at least a 40 acre lot of the Company's lands." As for the Norwegians, spared the humiliation of tenancy, their mountainous nation lacked much arable land, and, invariably, they too could be convinced to immigrate.[22]

If economic changes at home pushed Scandinavians out of their homelands, then Illinois's climate pulled them toward the "Prairie State": "The Scandinavian immigrants, a great majority of which choose the state of Illinois for their future homes, being accustomed to a colder climate, seem to prefer the central and northern part of the state; while those from the more temperate Germany, find it easier to acclimatise [sic] in any portion of the state."[23] Other factors as well nudged Scandinavians toward the United States. Norway's population, for example, nearly doubled between 1801 and 1865, growing from 900,000 to 1.7 million. This rapid growth overburdened an agricultural system that could not modernize fast enough to feed such a population. Immigration or famine seemed the most likely outcomes of this scenario. Not surprisingly, those who could chose immigration. The first shipload of Norwegians left for the United States in 1825. Seventy-eight thousand claimed the United States as their home in 1865. By 1925 over 800,000 Norwegians had left the old country, almost all of them settling in the United States.[24]

The state of Minnesota also sought to attract Scandinavians. By the 1870s state representatives had been working for almost two decades to convince Scandinavian settlers that the "North Star State" could become a new Scandinavia. Fredricka Bremer, a Swedish writer and feminist, toured the states of Illinois and Wisconsin and the territory of Minnesota in 1850, when the latter had only 4,000 non-Indian residents.[25] When she saw Minnesota she declared, "What a glorious new Scandinavia might not Minnesota become!" Its familiarity would certainly make immigrants feel at home: "The climate, the situation, the character of scenery agrees with our people better than that of any other of the American states."[26] At the time of her pronouncement, few Scandinavians lived in the territory, but that would soon change.

The St. Paul and Pacific Railroad (SP&P), Minnesota's first railroad, acting in concert with the Minnesota Board of Immigration, set out to advance the cause of Scandinavian settlement in the late 1860s. The board printed advertising pamphlets in Dano-Norwegian, Swedish, German, and Welsh, the latter the only non-Scandinavian language included. "The predominance of Norwegian and other Scandinavian settlers in western Minnesota was thus a deliberate policy enacted by the railroad company and also by the state government," according to the historian Odd S. Lovoll.[27]

Building off the efforts of the SP&P and the state of Minnesota, the Northern Pacific became one of the most aggressive lines in attracting settlers. Congress chartered the NP in 1864, but construction did not begin until 1870 when financial backing came from the banking firm of Jay Cooke. In 1871 the Northern Pacific created a land department charged with bringing settlers to its lands. Workers completed the easternmost portion of the line, through Minnesota, by mid-1871, making the state suitable for large-scale immigration. Projected to pass from Minnesota through the territories of Dakota, Montana, Idaho, and finally Washington, this northernmost transcontinental line crossed a landscape that many critics asserted would be unsuitable for farming. The NP therefore spent a great deal of time convincing would-be settlers that the climate suited them and, in the case of the Scandinavian immigrants they coveted, was reminiscent of Northern Europe.

The land department of the Northern Pacific extolled the virtues of Minnesota and its "bracing" climate. In the September 1872 edition, *Land and Emigration* (the NP's London-based emigration newspaper) described Minnesota's climate as like a physician who "first cleanses the blood and rouses the liver, then gives the patient what is known as the 'Minnesota appetite,' and prompts him to action in the open air, and he is soon on the highway to robust health."[28] In a circular addressed to soldiers and sailors, the land department attributed to Minnesota a "climate [that] is unusually healthful, with cold, dry winters, total exemption from fever and ague, and a rapid growing season of ample length."[29] It never made clear, however, just how cold those cold, dry winters could be.

The NP used the similarity of the climate of Minnesota and the Dakotas to that of Scandinavia as one selling point to attract people, but the company had long sought to attract Scandinavians, first as laborers and then as settlers, for the simple reason that Americans considered them desirable, hardworking, and white. The NP hired the Scandinavian Emigrant Agency to furnish the line with laborers, a necessity since no local labor force existed to build the road. In a January 22, 1870, letter, the agency promised to deliver 100 laborers to the construction site within three weeks of receiving the request. The initial hundred "will be of different nationalities, but are railroad laborers." In the future, however, "when European Emigration begins, say from the first of April, we shall be able to furnish Germans and Scandinavians entirely." Johnson and Peterson, the heads of the agency, explained that these were not unattached bachelors but hardworking family men: "The Lake Superior and Mississippi RR Co. prefers these people to any others, and one thing is certain, that they are all strong and healthy, accostomed [*sic*] to as hard labor as any people, [and are] industrious and honest." Most important, many laborers would buy land and become permanent residents. All the railroad companies, they concluded, longed to obtain "this Class of Emigration to settle along the line of their roads."[30]

With track through Minnesota by 1871, NP headquarters charged the land committee with bringing permanent Northern European settlers. The committee, created in 1871 with Frederick Billings as its head, quickly set about organizing the colonization strategy for the line. It selected John S. Loomis, president of the National Land Company—an organization that worked with the Kansas Pacific Railroad on colonization in Kansas and Colorado—as the head of the new land department. Loomis outlined a plan for how to operate the line's land company in a February 1871 letter to Billings. Advertising material would be printed in several European languages, and relationships with leading citizens and religious figures in European countries would be cultivated so that they, too, would promote immigration. Offices would be set up in England, Holland, Germany, and the Scandinavian countries to spread the word about immigration.[31]

In 1872 the company hired George Sheppard as the agent in the London office to oversee operations in Europe. Sheppard, an Englishman who had lived a large part of his life in the United States, was a perfect choice to head the European side of the railroad colonization campaign. He had led a colony of English immigrants to Iowa in 1850 and was thus acquainted with the numerous problems and pitfalls that plagued immigrants. George Hibbard, the NP's superintendent of immigration, marveled at his work. In mid-1872 Hibbard declared, "We are sending forward a good stream of first class settlers and I am happy to report that the tide has commenced flowing from Europe every day bringing us a few good emigrants from Mr. Sheppard who seems to have got things thoroughly organized on the other side [of the Atlantic]."[32] By the end of the year, everything appeared to be in place for successful colonization. Hibbard wrote to Sheppard thanking him for "the apparently successful efforts which you are making in Europe to promote immigration to our rich and fertile lands. I have spent the last five months on the line of our road in Minnesota and Dakota, and have met with all of the parties sent out by you during the summer and can congratulate you upon the success of your labor in awakening an interest in so good a class of farmers, and others, and think we can confidently expect a good harvest from the seeds sown this season."[33] In addition to permanent agents, the company also employed prominent immigrants, among them Dr. J. P. Tustin, a Scandinavian minister who traveled throughout Sweden, Norway, and Denmark. In meetings with church officials and in lectures, Tustin worked to convince emigrants to choose the Northern Pacific over the other lines competing for them.[34]

Piecemeal settlement of lands by individual families, however, would be too slow and less profitable. The solution, as the Illinois Central discovered, should be colony settlement. The NP's land department targeted two groups in its advertising campaigns: Union Army veterans and Northern Europeans. Following the Civil War, Congress amended the Homestead Act to make it easier and more affordable for former soldiers and sailors to purchase land in the West. The 1870 and 1872 amendments to the 1862 Homestead Act allowed veterans to file 160-acre claims on the alternating sections of government land within the limits of railroad land grants—double the acreage allowed to non-veterans inside railroad holdings. In Minnesota the NP owned twenty miles of land on either side of its line, and in the territories farther west it owned fifty miles on either side. The proximity to the railroad made the land (including the alternate sections of government land) inside the NP's grant worth more than land outside the railroad holdings. The Northern Pacific's circular for soldiers explained, "Settlers will find it to their advantage to go in groups or colonies. Fifty or one hundred persons combining may secure, on favorable terms, all the land held by the Railroad Company in a township." These colonies would be instant towns, with all the necessary occupations already in place, and the isolation and hardship of the frontier period would be bypassed. Civilization, shipped en masse at affordable rates, would appear in the form of "good government, good neighbors, morality, security to property, comfort and prosperity."[35] For soldiers, these colonies could be composed of the numerous veterans' organizations that appeared after the war, such as the Society of the Army of the Cumberland and the Grand Army of the Republic, both of which, along with the Northern Pacific Railroad, proved instrumental in getting Congress to approve the amendments to the Homestead Act.[36]

Similarly, small farming communities in Europe could be induced to settle in large numbers. The circular listed the names of five colonies that had already settled (or were prepared to settle) on the company's lands. All of these colonies constituted either former Union soldiers or foreigners, but often little difference existed between them. The heavily Norwegian western part of Minnesota included both Union veterans and immigrants. "So many earlier soldiers were among the first settlers in the Park Region [of western Minnesota] that a list of them looks like a roll call of the [Norwegian] Fifteenth Wisconsin Regiment," writes the historian Hjalmar Rued Holand.[37]

The NP also eagerly targeted the Mennonites, a group that would eventually settle in several places along the NP's lines. Although many of the Mennonites would not settle in the Northwest until the 1880s and 1890s, the vanguard began to relocate in the 1870s. Ethnically German, the Mennonites had settled on the southern Russian steppe to avoid military service, a prohibition based on a fundamental tenet of their religion. They had played a tremendously important role in developing Russia, but Czar Alexander II decided to force the pacific religious sect to submit to military service. Beginning in 1883, therefore, all Mennonites would have to participate in the draft. This decision prompted many to search for another nation to call home.

George Hibbard, eager to convince this group to settle along the NP's lines, brought everything he could to his campaign, including introducing them to the famous financier Jay Cooke. In a May 19, 1873, letter to Cooke, Hibbard outlined the importance of these colonists. He explained that a party of 5 Mennonites had arrived on an inspection tour of the line's land. As many as 40,000 Mennonite families would follow to avoid mandatory military service in Russia. "I need not say to you," Hibbard wrote, "that it is of the utmost importance to our Company that we secure the location of this body of men and I hope no stone will be left unturned to accomplish this object." Although the Canadian government and other rail lines also courted the Mennonites, Hibbard felt the NP could win since "our climate and soil is completely adapted to their habits and customs." Although of a religious persuasion unfamiliar to most Americans, they were "the best class of settlers we could possibly secure for our rich and fertile lands."[38]

One of the NP's chief competitors for the German Mennonites was the Atchison, Topeka and Santa Fe (AT&SF). The AT&SF in the early 1870s had been busy surveying its landholdings in an effort to attract colonists. Although less extensive than the NP's massive grant, the Santa Fe line nevertheless controlled 3 million acres in Kansas, an area larger than the state of Connecticut.

By 1870 the AT&SF had begun to actively survey its Kansas landholdings under the direction of its land commissioner, D. L. Lakin. Lakin resigned in 1872 and A. E. Touzalin assumed control. Touzalin set out to recruit immigrants to the lands that were surveyed and ready for settlement. He aggressively courted the Mennonites, assigning a German-speaking agent, Carl Schmidt, to guide the Mennonite's representative, Cornelius Jansen, around the Santa Fe's lands in the summer of 1873. Jansen, a Mennonite and Prussian consul to the Russian government, was instrumental in convincing the Mennonites to leave Russia before they lost their privileges in 1883. Schmidt continued his efforts for most of the next decade, visiting Prussia and Russia and recruiting settlers from both nations. Schmidt's efforts largely succeeded, and by 1883 an estimated 15,000 Mennonites (from Russia as well as Germany, Prussia, and Switzerland) had settled on lands along the Santa Fe's line. By 1905 nearly 60,000 had settled in Kansas, Oklahoma, and Colorado.[39] Like the NP, the AT&SF was eager to attract them because of their extensive experience as dryland farmers on the Russian plains, and indeed they proved to be excellent and innovative farmers, introducing the new Red Turkish wheat that helped transform Kansas into the nation's top wheat producer. Reflecting on their success, the historian Glenn Danford Bradley observed in 1920, "These people have proved their worth as farmers, colonizers, and citizens of the highest type . . . They have contributed much to the wealth and higher morale of Kansas. They are ideal citizens."[40] They indeed embodied such American values as thriftiness, temperance, and hard work and therefore made ideal citizens.

Even smaller lines looked to Northern Europe for desirable settlers. The Denver and Rio Grande Western (D&RGW), a Colorado-based railroad with standard-gauge and narrow-gauge track (the latter designed for navigating through tight mountain corridors), made most of its money servicing mining towns.[41] Yet it, too, had aspirations of attracting farmers to Colorado's plains and mountain valleys. William Jackson Palmer, an ambitious thirty-five-year-old Civil War veteran and former Kansas Pacific employee, founded the D&RGW. Palmer worked to secure the Kansas Pacific's connection to Denver, but he had a much grander plan to leave and start his own railroad. In January 1870 Palmer launched his scheme for a north-south railroad running along the Front Range of Colorado's Rocky Mountains. He wrote to Mary Lincoln Mellen, his fiancé, of his plans: "How fine it would be to have a little railroad a few hundred miles in length, all under one's own control with one's friends . . . to be able to carry out unimpeded and harmoniously one's views in regard to what ought and ought not to be done."[42] Palmer imagined Colorado's Front Range as his own personal kingdom, a perfect society free of the problems of the East.

Palmer's new mother-in-law, however, worried about her daughter, a wealthy eastern girl, being transported to the rough-and-tumble Colorado frontier. Palmer laughed off her concerns in an 1871 letter to his young bride. "It is more dangerous," he explained, "to live in proximity of a great city such as New York than it would be amongst the Indians on the Plains." Instead of fearing the move to the West, the Mellen family should be glad to leave the East behind. Emigration to the young states and territories would create "a new and better civilization in the far West." The East, conversely, forced people to live in close and unsuitable conditions: "We [the Anglo-Americans] will surrender that briny border [of the Eastern Seaboard] as a sort of extensive Castle Garden to receive and filter the foreign swarms and prepare them by a gradual process for coming to the inner temple of Americanism out in Colorado, where Republican institutions will be maintained in pristine purity."[43] Castle Garden in New York predated the more famous Ellis Island as the major port of entry for thousands of immigrants, and Palmer, like others, hoped to keep the meanest (in both senses of the word) of these immigrants far from Colorado.

Individuals like Palmer, men with grand plans and visions for this supposedly unpeopled frontier, populated the West. Unlike many visionaries, Palmer actually brought his vision to life. The D&RGW, however, did not receive a grant of lands, like most of the other western lines, but with the help of his friends Alexander C. Hunt—for a time Colorado's territorial governor—F. Z. Salomon, and Irving Howbert, Palmer quietly set up a railroad company and began to purchase the nearly worthless land along the imaginary line. He purchased, among other acquisitions, 9,312 acres for the "Fountain Colony," soon to be called Colorado Springs.[44]

The job of attracting people to this colony fell to Palmer's enthusiastic and articulate friend Dr. William A. Bell. Bell had befriended Palmer when the two worked on the 1867 surveying party that laid out the Kansas Pacific line. He and Palmer became lifelong friends and business partners. Bell, a native Englishman, felt his homeland, with its masses of urban poor, was the perfect place from which to draw settlers.

England had a surplus population and a lack of land. Poverty and despair, he noted, made it susceptible to radical notions like Marxism. In England, he wrote, "we require depletion [of our population]. The abject poverty which now stares us in the face is becoming unendurable. How can our destitute artisans educate their children when they are clothed with rags? Or what do starving parents care for school reform? Equilibrium between the demand and the supply o[f] labour must be attained; and wholesale emigration is the only means by which this can be accomplished."[45] He concluded, "If we, as a nation, persist in keeping down labour by feeding millions of unproductive paupers at home, instead of helping them to find employment elsewhere, we shall richly deserve to be overpowered by that rabble form of democracy which aristocratic England dreads so much."[46] Thus immigration to America could provide a kind of safety valve for England, siphoning off a substantial portion of the population and undercutting the desperation that fed extremist ideologies.

Why not, therefore, relocate the surplus population in a region conducive to its settlement. Bell observed, "Though [the West] is almost without tillage or inhabitants, it is not like Africa, Central Asia, or even South America, in being far removed from the present limits of Anglo-Saxon occupation." Instead, as an outpost of Anglo-Saxon civilization, it "contain[ed] cradles for nations which are destined to spring from our own hardy and prolific stock."[47] Later, Bell returned to the theme of America, the West particularly, as an Anglo-Saxon stronghold: "The United States being a foreign country ought not to affect the question [of English immigration] in the least. Canada, Australia, New Zealand, all or any one of our colonies may soon become independent of the mother country; and perhaps it is better for both that they should before long dissolve partnership. It is, however, our desire, and also greatly to our advantage, to remain on the best terms with our American neighbours." Only the Irish of all the peoples in the United States hated England, and if they came to form the dominant population in America, then war would soon follow. For that reason, Bell claimed, "the ascendancy of the Saxon and Teutonic elements in the States" must be cultivated.[48]

Dr. Bell, having returned to England after the Kansas Pacific survey, set out to raise interest in Palmer's railroad scheme. He massaged investment money from his father's wealthy friends but also tirelessly promoted immigration to D&RGW lands. Bell expected his colony to be composed of British workers and artisans who would desire to relocate to a village in the temperate and healthful climate along Colorado's Front Range.[49] Bell's vision, though never fully implemented, became the town of Colorado Springs. The company's pamphlets, perhaps with help from Bell, convinced so many English immigrants to settle there that promoters soon dubbed the town "Little London."[50] The arrival of the railroad in the colony town (also owned by Palmer and his investors) in the fall of 1871 marked the completion of the railroad's first sixty miles. From nothing, Colorado Springs had grown to 800 people by the spring of 1872, and by year's end Palmer claimed a population of 1,500.[51]

The colonization enterprise chiefly concerned itself with attracting Northern European farmers. Alexander C. Hunt wrote to Palmer in 1872 complaining that while Colorado Springs was indeed growing, its settlers were "suited only as denizens of towns, the smallest sprinkling of whom being hardy husbandmen or Tillers of the soil, which, are the ones most needed—Every one cannot be a Shopkeeper; there must be some to buy, indeed, there should be One Hundred buyers to every seller." With tens of thousands of acres at their disposal, they needed to "secure emigration of a character to make these lands remunerative, and, at the same time, stimulate business upon the line of our road." Hunt proposed a campaign to target Scottish, Swiss, French, German, and Scandinavian communities: "Instruct [the company's agents] to go into rural districts, alone; (keeping clear of towns) hold public meetings; explain fully and fairly the advantages our country offers; recruit none, save those, able to pay their own passages, and have something left on arriving here." These settlers could then be sold, on credit if necessary, 40-acre tracts that would support their families and generate enough of a surplus to provide produce that would travel over the company's lines, and in time the area might be able to export wheat and meat all the way to the "Extreme East."[52]

Hunt noted that the Mormons had been experiencing tremendous success targeting these groups of people: "This plan I believe to be exactly the one adopted by the Mormons." Discounting the possibility that these immigrants were true believers, he noted, "The question of the Mormon Religion has little or nothing to do with the Yearly influx of the Laboring classes into the Salt Lake basin. It is the Material need, of this class of people, that is appealed to, rather than their Spiritual wants or prejudices. Half fare tickets, Cheap lands on arrival, Healthy Salubrious climate, Rich soil, and [a] number of Old friends to settle together, are the chief inducements, that assume success to the Mormon Elders who go abroad to recruit for the Church of the Latter-day Saints." With an active recruiting campaign, Hunt asserted, "many of these same people might choose to locate upon leased lands along the Fountain, and the Arkansas valles, while the Merchants that might come along, would find ready employment in the Towns and Cities."[53]

Although some farmers would settle, especially in the Arkansas River valley, the residents near Colorado Springs remained "denizens of towns." Dr. Bell seemed particularly eager to recruit among them. Bell, as the line's public relations officer, exploited the Little London idea, describing the area in florid prose in the pages of English newspapers, but the arrival of Charles Kingsley, the canon of Westminster Abbey, in 1874 provided a wealth of publicity. Kingsley had fallen ill while visiting San Francisco, and doctors recommended he convalesce in the drier air of Colorado Springs. Bell used the canon's month-long stay to showcase to Englishmen Colorado Springs's cultural and climatic suitability for all of the nation's social classes. Young Englishmen like himself could acquire large estates, complete with herds of cattle and sheep, while tenant farmers and artisans could also establish themselves in the colony. Ironically, Kingsley hated the town and wanted to move on as soon as his health improved. Bell left that fact out of the advertisements.[54]

Dr. Bell, in an 1874 pamphlet that was characteristic of his advertising strategy, outlined the numerous advantages of Colorado Springs for English immigrants. Members of all of England's social classes would find opportunity and betterment on the Front Range. The small farmer, struggling in a nation of insufficient land, could be transplanted to Colorado and "would come up again in prosperity without a shadow of a doubt, unless something inherent in the individual himself prevented him from doing so." Farmers would benefit from Colorado's growing population and relative isolation. Distances from settled farming areas in the East were so great that Colorado offered the opportunity to create a home market that precluded competition from other regions. Farmers could therefore expect to turn a tidy profit feeding miners and urban dwellers. Tradesmen and middle-class businessmen would similarly find ample opportunity in Colorado, and even England's upper class, facing tremendous changes and feeling the social problems caused by a shortage of land, could find a home in Colorado. Bell wrote, "I refer to the sons of men of more or less wealth, who, being obliged to make a living for themselves in these days of large expenditures and many wants, have not, unfortunately for themselves, had the opportunity of acquiring business habits, or any knowledge capable of being turned to practical account." These wealthy men made ideal settlers: "A selected few of such men could, I am convinced, make their way as colonists. With more capital than the average of colonists at his command, with intelligence and common sense, such a man could easily find in the young community many channels for turning his abilities and money to very profitable account, and, becoming wiser by experience, could in a few years gather up a competency." He finished by reminding his readers that Colorado abounded "in natural resources, [and was being settled] by an energetic and hard-working community of Anglo-Saxons."[55]

Even the Englishman Edward Money, whose criticism of western immigration and railroad agents was caustic, found much to appreciate in Colorado Springs and the surrounding area. Money, in fact, purchased a ranch near the town, hoping to settle there with his sons and have land enough for all of them (if Americans viewed the West in Jeffersonian yeoman farmer terms, Englishmen seemed prone to imagine themselves as feudal barons—and, indeed, in many ways men like Money and Bell imagined the West as a place out of time, an anti-modern refuge for traditional English values). He soon returned to England, however, because pioneer life did not suit him, lamenting, "The want of intellectual pursuits, the absence of society, the lack of a woman's influence, and the many charms connected therewith, wearied me sadly. In two words I found I was too old for the life, and, that I could not, at my age, adapt myself to such great and violent changes."[56]

Money did think Colorado Springs had potential, offering English immigrants an opportunity at a better life. He quoted extensively in his *The Truth about America* from the English authors of *Colorado Springs and Manitou*, a book that outlined the many advantages the area's health resorts offered to

English health seekers and settlers. Mrs. Simeon Dunbar, one of the book's authors, observed, "The society is the very best; people of culture and refinement, and many possessing much wealth, have been attracted here by the climate and surroundings, and these have drawn others of like taste and habits, till [sic] on this little mesa where the mountains and the plains meet, there was grown up in a few short years a city of nearly six thousand people 'the cream of eastern society.'" She explained that while many of these wealthy were invalids, many healthy men also settled in the area. They included "men of means from the East owning large herds of cattle and sheep that roam over the great western plains from Montana to Mexico," and "others interested in the mineral wealth of the Rocky Mountains . . . have also settled here."

Mrs. Dunbar especially approved of Colorado Springs's population: "Unlike many of the towns and cities of the West, Colorado Springs is not cosmopolitan; it has scarcely any French, German, or Irish element[s]. The people are from the older states of the Union, and from Canada, England, and Scotland; hence an entirely English-speaking community. The people as a whole are probably better educated and possess more wealth than those of an eastern town of the same size. It is more New-England–like in the general makeup of its social, religious, and educational characteristics than any town west of the Mississippi." The community was composed of Anglos, and even "the poorer people are a respectable class who have received some social and educational advantages; none but enterprising or well-to-do people would ever cross the plains to establish a new home in the West."[57] The homes of Colorado Springs, another writer observed, were the finest in the state because "many cultured people have come hither for their health and . . . the colony organization has done much to improve and adorn the town."[58]

Here then emanated familiar tropes: a town with potential, a small but desirable population, far enough from larger cities with their inferior populations, and all waiting for vigorous Anglo-Saxon settlers. Colorado Springs may have boasted a wealthy and elite population, but in all other respects it sounded like any of the scores of other small towns heavily promoted by railroads, and implicit in this promotion were notions of racial and ethnic desirability.

At the same time lines like the Northern Pacific, AT&SF, and D&RGW competed to lure European settlers onto their lands, tens of thousands of African Americans set out for the West, but no lines sent agents into southern states to convince them to do so. Despite this fact, tens of thousands of African

Americans headed to Kansas in the 1870s, creating such towns as Nicodemus, but they received a chilly reception. Kansas governor John Pierce St. John worried, "Indications are that we will be over run with them [African Americans]."[59]

Cain Sartain, an African American from Louisiana, wrote to the governor in 1879 about the prospect of emigration. He asked if "life and property is [sic] secure" and if "the right of franchise is respected." Given the imposition of Jim Crow laws and southern "Redemption," these were not minor concerns. Sartain explained, "There is [sic] a great number of my race of people in my state [who] are determined to leave it . . . They are a poor people but a hard working class of people, and anything like a half a showing and they will prosper."[60] Governor St. John showed some sympathy for the plight of the Exodusters, and emigrants inundated his office with letters discussing the deplorable conditions they endured. He therefore tried hard to dissuade these emigrants, warning that Kansas did not live up to the promoters' rhetoric as a promised land. In a reply to Roseline Cunningham's letter, the governor warned that Kansas did not have an office of emigration and could not provide any aid to would-be emigrants: "I am informed that parties have represented to the colored peoples in your state that by coming to Kansas they would receive 40 acres of land [and] a mule." Indeed, since the end of the Civil War, this hope had taken on mythic proportions. "All such representations," he continued, "are without any foundations whatsoever in fact, and are intended to deceive the colored people." He explained that all settlers had the right to purchase lands in the state, which ranged from $2.25 to $10.00 per acre. These lands, he warned, remained unimproved and would require a team of horses and sufficient capital to improve them. Certainly, many black emigrants had managed to establish themselves in Kansas, but "I would advise, however, the colored people not to come to any of the Northern States entirely destitute." Should Cunningham and others decide to emigrate to Kansas, the governor promised them fair treatment and freedom, but unless they could locate a desirable tract of land and pay their own way to get started, it would be better for them not to come.[61]

The Kansas Pacific even sent potential black emigrants a form letter explaining that all the good farmland had been settled, that laborers could not find work, that the weather tended to be capricious, and that would-be emigrants needed at least $500 to get started. The writer Ian Frazier has wryly observed, "It was probably the only time in history that a railroad ever told the truth of the situation to a prospective settler."[62] Such discouraging pro-nouncements attempted to dissuade potential black settlers, and, indeed, in only one instance did a railroad actively recruit African Americans.

In Mississippi a new scheme for African American settlers owed its exis-tence to the Louisville, New Orleans and Texas Railroad (LNO&T), owned by Collis P. Huntington (of Central Pacific fame) and R. T. Wilson. George McGinnis, the land commissioner for the LNO&T, hoped to attract white settlers to the company's lands, but whites proved reluctant to settle the swampy, malaria-prone lands in the Mississippi Delta. Believing that blacks could endure the heat and malaria and eager to find someone willing to set-tle the lands, McGinnis approached Isaiah T. Montgomery. Montgomery, a former slave on Joseph Davis's (brother of Jefferson Davis) plantation, had become a businessman and leader of the black community in Vicksburg. He agreed to lead the colony, and in 1886 Montgomery and the rest of the col-ony members carved out the town of Mound Bayou. The town grew to 400 residents and 2,500 farmers in the surrounding countryside by 1904, but by 1915, following the closing of the bank and sawmill, Mound Bayou entered a period of slow decline.

Yet its very existence provided a rare case of a railroad actively promoting its land to black farmers.[63] It was telling, perhaps, that this happened in the Mississippi Delta, where African Americans had long been a presence; where notions of climate and race made the land appear suited only for blacks, sup-posedly able to endure malarial climates; and where whites did not try to com-pete with them for the land. In the West, by contrast, railroads did not actively recruit African Americans as settlers. Explaining why western railroads refrained from advertising to southern blacks is difficult because railroad land companies do not seem to have even entertained the notion—with the excep-tion of the Kansas Pacific's letter clearly intended to dissuade potential black settlers. Several explanations, however, are probable. First, western railroads wanted settlers with experience in similar climates. The Mennonites, who had settled the Russian steppe, made ideal farmers for the Great Plains, and several rail lines courted them. Second, railroads desired settlers who could, for the most part, pay their own way and who had enough capital to begin the process of farm building. Third, the black towns in Kansas and elsewhere encountered a chilly reception from local whites. In Oklahoma, for exam-ple, whites expressed open hostility, worried about plans to convert the state into a black stronghold.[64] Finally, railroads wanted "desirable" emigrants, and, whether consciously or not, they believed settlers should be white. Whatever the causes, the transcontinental lines—desperate for settlers to populate their extensive land grants—ignored a numerous, nearby, and willing group of immigrants in favor of those on the other side of the Atlantic.

The last third of the nineteenth century saw a tremendous influx of new immigrants into the United States. Millions of people left their homes in Europe and Asia and set out for America. Asians faced tremendous discrimination and found entrance into America barred through acts like the 1882 Chinese Exclusion Act. Desirable immigrants would be European. Yet most Americans further divided European immigrants into desirable and less desirable groups. Without exception, western promoters rated Northern Europeans as the most desirable. The English, Scots, Welsh, Norwegians, Germans, Swedes, and Russo-German Mennonites were all groups Americans felt could enter the country and be productive citizens.

Railroads, by actively recruiting these groups, indelibly shaped the ethnic landscape of the West. Railroads stressed most of all that they desired experienced farmers for their lines, but in practice they limited their search for experienced farmers to Northern Europeans, ignoring Southern Europeans, Asians, and African Americans—all of whom likewise faced dislocation from their homelands. Although the railroads do not appear to have overtly discriminated against these groups, by sending agents to England, Scandinavia, Prussia (and Germany after unification), and the Russian steppe, they nevertheless created territories dominated by supposedly desirable ethnic groups. The railroads wanted to tie the nation together and gain a tidy profit, but by attracting Northern Europeans they also created, especially on the central and northern plains, societies that were rural, Protestant, and white.

The *Great West*, a promotional pamphlet of the Chicago, Rock Island, and Pacific Railroad (CRI&P), described the land along its lines as "a land of Goshen, literally flowing with milk and honey." The CRI&P had created a land of peace and harmony, populated by people from

> every corner of the habitable globe . . . The exiled sons of Erin here cultivate their own lands in peace, the economic Highlander no longer grieves for the heather clad barrenness of his Scottish moors . . . the wearied workers from English mines and looms, the laborer from his ill rewarded toil, gladly nestles

with his family upon these teeming lands and becomes independent; the hardy Norsemen, the Swede, the Dane, the Bohemian, the ever industrious German, the toiling sons of far off lands, all gather together, in undivided harmony, bound in a golden link of brotherhood by mutual usefulness and an equal prosperity.[65]

As the origins of these ideal settlers indicated, however, this brotherhood proved anything but colorblind.

NOTES

1. William A. Bell, *New Tracks in North America: A Journal of Travel and Adventure Whilst Engaged in the Survey for a Southern Railroad to the Pacific Ocean during 1867–68* (London: Chapman and Hall, 1870), xxiv–xxv.

2. Quoted in Gordon L. Iseminger, "*Land and Emigration*: A Northern Pacific Railroad Company Newspaper," *North Dakota Quarterly* 48, no. 2 (Summer 1981): 70–92, quote on 70.

3. For examples of how white ethnic groups struggled to claim whiteness, see David R. Roediger, *The Wages of Whiteness: Race and the Making of the American Working Class* (New York: Verso, 1991); Noel Ignatiev, *How the Irish Became White* (New York: Routledge, 1995); Matthew Frye Jacobson, *Whiteness of a Different Color: European Immigrants and the Alchemy of Race* (Cambridge, MA: Harvard University Press, 1998).

4. Thomas Jefferson, *Notes on the State of Virginia* in *The Complete Jefferson, Containing His Major Writings, Published and Unpublished, Except His Letters*, Saul K. Padover, ed. (New York: Tudor, 1943), 678–79.

5. The agrarian myth is recounted in Henry Nash Smith, *Virgin Land: The American West as Symbol and Myth* (Cambridge, MA: Harvard University Press, 1970), 123.

6. Elliott West, *The Last Indian War* (New York: Oxford University Press, 2009), xviii–xxiii.

7. John Bell Rae, *The Development of Railway Land Subsidy Policy in the United States* (New York: Arno, 1979), 126.

8. James Blaine Hedges, "The Colonization Work of the Northern Pacific Railroad," *Mississippi Valley Historical Review* 13, no. 3 (December 1926): 311–42.

9. "Land Committee Minutes for May 11, 1871," Northern Pacific Railway Company Land Department Records, microfilm, roll 37, Minnesota Historical Society, St. Paul.

10. Ibid.

11. Claire Strom's *Profiting from the Plains: The Great Northern Railway and Corporate Development of the American West* (Seattle: University of Washington Press, 2003)

looks at the efforts of the Great Northern to encourage agriculture along its lines and the environmental results of its attempts.

12. Roger Daniels, *Coming to America: A History of Immigration and Ethnicity in American Life* (New York: Harper Perennial, 1990), 129, 146, 165.

13. Ibid., 146, 189.

14. Frederick C. Luebke, "Introduction," in Frederick C. Luebke, ed., *European Immigrants in the American West: Community Histories* (Albuquerque: University of New Mexico Press, 1998), xi.

15. Statistics drawn from ibid.

16. Helen Hunt Jackson, *Glimpses of Three Coasts* (Boston: Roberts Brothers, 1890), 135–36.

17. Paul Wallace Gates, *The Illinois Central Railroad and Its Colonization Work* (Cambridge, MA: Harvard University Press, 1934), 21–43; John F. Stover, *History of the Illinois Central Railroad* (New York: Macmillan, 1975), 15–30.

18. Gates, *The Illinois Central Railroad and Its Colonization Work*, 96.

19. Ibid., 96–98.

20. This is the focus of Ignatiev, *How the Irish Became White*.

21. Oscar Malmborg to D. A. Neal, May 28, 1854, "Letters of an Early Illinois Central Emigration Agent," *Swedish-American Historical Bulletin* 3, no. 2 (June 1930): 7–52.

22. Oscar Malmborg to Thomas Walker, March 9, 1861, in ibid.

23. Oscar Malmborg to D. A. Neal, May 28, 1854, in ibid.

24. Odd S. Lovoll, *Norwegians on the Prairie: Ethnicity and the Development of the Country Town* (St. Paul: Minnesota Historical Society Press, 2006), 26–28.

25. Ibid., 15.

26. Quoted in ibid., 24.

27. Ibid., 40.

28. *Land and Emigration* (September 1872), quoted in Iseminger, "*Land and Emigration*: A Northern Pacific Railroad Company Newspaper," 88.

29. George B. Hibbard, *Land Department of the Northern Pacific Railroad Company: Bureau of Immigration for Soldiers and Sailors* (N.p.: Northern Pacific Railroad, 1873), Western Americana microfilm, reel 393, no. 3936, 10, Beinecke Library, Yale University, New Haven, CT.

30. Johnson and Peterson to J. Gregory Smith, January 22, 1870, Northern Pacific Railway Company Land Department Records, microfilm, roll 1, Minnesota Historical Society, St. Paul.

31. John S. Loomis to Frederick Billings, February 20, 1871, Northern Pacific Railway Company Land Department Records, microfilm, roll 9, Minnesota Historical Society, St. Paul.

32. George Hibbard to the General, May 19, 1872, Northern Pacific Railway Company Land Department Records, microfilm, roll 24, Minnesota Historical Society, St. Paul.

33. George Hibbard to George Sheppard, November 16, 1872, Northern Pacific Railway Company Land Department Records, microfilm, roll 24, Minnesota Historical Society, St. Paul.

34. Hedges, "Colonization Work of the Northern Pacific Railroad," 311–42.

35. Hibbard, *Land Department of the Northern Pacific Railroad Company*, 9.

36. Ibid., 9.

37. Quoted in ibid., 43.

38. George Hibbard to Jay Cooke, May 19, 1873, Northern Pacific Railway Company Land Department Records, microfilm, roll 20, Minnesota Historical Society, St. Paul.

39. Glenn Danford Bradley, *The Story of the Santa Fe* (Boston: Richard G. Badger, 1920), 107–38.

40. Ibid., 138.

41. See Robert G. Athearn, *Rebel of the Rockies: A History of the Denver and Rio Grande Western Railroad*, Yale Western Americana Series (New Haven, CT: Yale University Press, 1962).

42. Quoted in ibid., 8.

43. Quoted in John S. Fisher, *A Builder of the West: The Life of General William Jackson Palmer* (Caldwell, ID: Caxton, 1939), 202–3.

44. Marshall Sprague, *Newport in the Rockies: The Life and Good Times of Colorado Springs* (Denver: Sage Books, 1961), 28–29.

45. Bell, *New Tracks in North America*, 513.

46. Ibid., 516–17.

47. Ibid., viii.

48. Ibid., 513.

49. Athearn, *Rebel of the Rockies*, 13.

50. Ibid., 20.

51. Ibid., 21.

52. Alexander C. Hunt to William Jackson Palmer, November 9, 1872, FF1, no. 5, William A. Bell Collection, Mss. #49, Colorado Historical Society, Denver.

53. Ibid.

54. Sprague, *Newport in the Rockies*, 80–82.

55. William A. Bell, *A Paper on the Colonies of Colorado in Their Relation to English Enterprise and Settlement* (London: Chapman and Hall, 1874), 69–70.

56. Edward Money, *The Truth about America* (London: Sampson, Lowe, Marston, Searle and Rivington, 1886), 144–45.

57. Quoted in ibid., 172–73.

58. A. A. Hayes, "Vacation Aspects of Colorado," *Harper's New Monthly Magazine* 60 (March 1880): 548.

59. Quoted in Ian Frazier, *Great Plains* (New York: Penguin Books, 1989), 166–69.

60. Cain Sartain to His Excellency the Governor of the State of Kansas, March 30, 1879, Governor's Office, John St. John, Correspondence Received–Subject File, Kansas Historical Society, Topeka, at Kansas Memory, http://www.kansasmemory.org /item/210296/page/1 (accessed July 12, 2012).

61. Governor John Pierce St. John to Roseline Cunningham, June 24, 1879, Governor's Office, John St. John, Correspondence Received–Subject File, Kansas Historical Society, Topeka, at Kansas Memory, http://www.kansasmemory.org/item /210547/page/1 (accessed July 12, 2012).

62. Frazier, *Great Plains*, 166–69.

63. Crockett, *Black Towns*, 8–15, 158–65.

64. Ibid., 21–24.

65. Chicago, Rock Island, and Pacific Railroad, *The Great West* (Chicago: Rollings, 1880), 6.

7

UNWELCOME SAINTS

Whiteness, Mormons, and the Limits of Success

Whiteness influenced the Church of Jesus Christ of Latter-day Saints in two important ways. First, the Mormons attempted to convert souls across the globe with little blatant regard for issues of race and ethnicity. Yet invisible boundaries of language, culture, and religion limited their success. At times they saw great harvests of new believers, particularly in Protestant Northern Europe. Other times, especially in Southern Europe and the Middle East, their proselytizing fell on deaf ears. Occasionally, they found success in places like the Polynesian islands that surprised even them.

Initially, Mormon theology preached that all believers should congregate on the New Jerusalem the Mormons carved from the Utah desert, but such a pronouncement proved impractical, despite Mormons' best efforts to finance passage for fellow believers. Pacific Islanders, for example, remained in their native lands, but many European converts eventually made the journey across the ocean and the Great Plains. The result of these forces was the creation of a new homeland between the towering Wasatch Front and the Great Salt Lake, a homeland where the entire population was composed of Anglo-Americans

DOI: 10.5876/9781607323969.c007

and Northern European converts. Utah's racial makeup, therefore, was not a conscious effort to promote one racial or ethnic group over another (indeed, with the exception of their feelings regarding Africans, Mormons were no more discriminatory than the average American toward non-whites) but rather a by-product of successful conversion efforts among Northern Europeans. It would long remain one of the whitest places in the nation and a stronghold of peoples of Northern European ancestry, but Utah's overwhelming whiteness had arisen largely by accident.

Whiteness influenced Mormons in another, more negative way. The sect, as it grew in the middle decades of the nineteenth century, fascinated and repelled non-Mormon Americans for its creative and scandalous interpretations of Christianity, its invention of a newer testament to the life of Jesus after his crucifixion, the alleged direct revelation from God that its leaders received, and especially the practice of polygamy. Harriet Beecher Stowe, the author of *Uncle Tom's Cabin*, for example, declared polygamy "a slavery which debases and degrades womanhood, motherhood, and family." While such denunciations said more about non-Mormon values than about those of Mormons, they nevertheless helped marshal a near-universal dislike for the practice and for Mormons more generally.[1]

Most converts to Mormonism in the nineteenth century hailed from the nations of Northern Europe: England, Scotland, Germany, and the Scandinavian countries. These converts could therefore be counted among the most desirable potential immigrants, the very hardworking and often rural people railroads in particular coveted. Yet critics asserted that any person, regardless of race, who submitted to the authoritarian and polygamous church could not be truly white because whiteness implied independence and free will. By converting to Mormonism, these converts essentially forfeited their whiteness, becoming almost slaves to the leaders of the church.

Mormons therefore dealt with derision from outsiders and limitations of culture that stymied their efforts to spread the gospel. Both would indelibly shape this community of believers. Despite these obstacles, the church appealed to those who sought something new and more meaningful in their lives, and it grew rapidly. Jules Remy, a French traveler, discussed the success of Mormon missionaries in his 1861 travelogue, *A Journey to Great Salt Lake City*. Barely thirty years had passed since the advent of Mormonism, but the sect had established an impressive census of followers. He wrote, "The success of the [Mormon] missionaries is far from being the same in every part of the world where they preach their doctrine. Their finest harvests have been reaped in Great Britain, in the north of Europe, particularly Denmark. In Oceania they cite with pride the Sandwich Islands as the spot in which their labours have had great and rapid success." Conversely, he claimed that comparatively few converts came from the native-born American population and were "almost exclusively [from] the class of the newly-arrived emigrants. This significant fact is the most decisive proof that it is not liberty, but ignorance, which delivers up men [to Mormonism]." Finally, he claimed that virtually no immigrants came from the Catholic world and that Mormonism could flourish only where Protestantism had already taken root: "Up to this day the sects which admit the Bible as the fundamental and indeed only rule of their faith, are precisely those which furnish the largest contingent to the Church of Joseph Smith. In Catholic countries, where the Bible is of course a revered book, but only possessed of secondary importance, the number of neophytes who join the Mormons is comparatively insignificant, as if the authority to which they submit rendered them less susceptible of being led away by innovation."[2]

Remy provided a rough census of Mormon believers in 1859. Most American Saints, as the Mormons called themselves, lived in Utah (80,000) and Joseph Smith's home state of New York (10,000). Overseas, England and Scotland had perhaps 32,000, the Sandwich and Society Islands counted 7,000, and 5,000 lived in Sweden, Norway, and Denmark as compared with 500 in France and perhaps 50 in Italy.[3] While Remy, like most outsiders, ridiculed Mormonism, his census numbers probably reflected reality. The Mormons indeed had far more success in Northern Europe than in Southern Europe, as well as among Pacific Islanders. Very specific reasons accounted for success at winning converts to the doctrines of the Latter-day Saints (LDS), reasons, as Remy suggested, that had much to do with the cultural environments in which Mormon missionaries found themselves.

Mormon conversion efforts flowed from their theology, especially the belief that hidden among all the world's races lived a few chosen people who, in fact, had descended from the ancient Israelites. Africans and African Americans were the only exceptions to this belief, as they were allegedly descendants of Cain and carried that mark of unforgivable sin with them for all time. Christianity, of course, begat Mormonism, and so the LDS drew off of mainstream Christian theology, but members broke with the Pauline belief that anyone could convert to the gospel and instead endorsed the Old Testament idea of a chosen people of God. Christianity derived from both the Old Testament (the story of the founding of Israel and the special place Jews occupied as a chosen people of God) and the New Testament, which told of the coming of Jesus, the Messiah, who would redeem humanity. The former stressed a blood relationship—only God's chosen people, the Jews, could expect to receive God's love—while the latter offered everyone the opportunity to convert to Christianity and be redeemed.

Early Mormonism, however, stressed that believers were blood descendants of the tribes of Israel. As these tribes scattered around the globe, they proliferated and passed their blood on to their descendants. These blood descendants could therefore be found among any group of people or any nation, including non-white groups like American Indians and Pacific Islanders. In practice, however, their theology allowed for the conversion of almost anyone because these lost children of Israel dwelled among larger ethnic and racial groups. The proof for Mormons that a person had the blood of ancient Israel in his or her veins was whether the individual accepted Mormonism. This therefore allowed for wide proselytizing while maintaining the belief in a special individual and group identity. In some ways these doctrines proved to be ethnically and racially blind, and Mormon missionaries did not explicitly promote whiteness.

The belief that Mormons belonged to a special group that had the blood of ancient Israel flowing through their veins helped make sense of their place in the world and enabled them to endure the trials and tribulations they faced. Harried and persecuted by non-believers, Mormons could look to the story of the Israelites, who also faced hardship and persecution, for solace. Not surprisingly, Mormons eagerly sought to reach out to Jews, who obviously had a blood connection to ancient Israel, but their attempts were rejected.

Like other Christian denominations, the Mormons hoped to win converts among supposedly savage peoples, but Mormons believed American Indians had a special destiny to fulfill in the building of their church. Given that no European had heard of the Americas before 1492, it took a good deal of explaining to show that Indians constituted one of the lost tribes of Israel, but Joseph Smith stressed that fact in the *Book of Mormon*. Unlike other denominations that sought to introduce Christianity to the Indians, the Mormons believed they were, in fact, bringing Christianity back to the Indians centuries after the word of God had been lost.

Mormons considered Native Americans to be descendants of Laman, the prodigal son of Lehi, a prophet and patriarch in the *Book of Mormon*. Lehi migrated from Jerusalem to the Western Hemisphere, according to Mormon doctrine, around 600 BC. Breaking with his father and younger brother, Nephi, Laman and his followers became a separate group of darker-skinned peoples. The appearance of Jesus Christ in the New World (after his crucifixion in the Old World) led to a temporary reconciliation between the two groups. In AD 231, however, a war between the Lamanites and the Nephites ended in the extermination of the Nephites and ultimately the loss of the gospel of Jesus in the New World. The winners of this war became modern Native Americans, according to Mormon theology. The history of this lost tribe of Israel and the story of Jesus coming to the Indians was, Joseph Smith claimed, hidden away on golden tablets—the tablets he discovered and then translated and published as the *Book of Mormon*. Smith intended his discovery of these tablets to go beyond simply resurrecting this lost religious history. He hoped to bring the gospel back to the Indians and get their help in building the New Jerusalem, as foretold in the *Book of Mormon*. Lamanite participation in Mormonism therefore promised to be a key component of its ultimate success.[4]

These religious beliefs led to a concerted effort to proselytize among the Indians from the earliest days of Mormonism's nineteenth-century founding. Indeed, the title page of the *Book of Mormon* describes it as the "record of the people of Nephi, and also of the Lamanites—Written to the Lamanites, who are a remnant of the house of Israel."[5] In 1830, the same year as the publication of the *Book of Mormon,* the church called a group of LDS elders (including the influential Parley P. Pratt) to preach to Native Americans, founding what came to be called the Lamanite mission. The missionaries arrived in Independence, Missouri, in January 1831 and proceeded from there to Delaware settlements in modern Kansas.

Converting the Lamanites proved difficult, however, and despite a century of missionary activities, Indian peoples were largely indifferent to missionary efforts.[6] The few who did convert, according to scholars who criticize the Lamanite mission, occupied subservient positions in Mormon society.[7] Yet other dark-skinned tribal peoples seemed willing to embrace Mormonism, including Polynesian Islanders, and the LDS church soon expanded its definition of Lamanites to include them. This boundary expansion, the sociologist Armand Mauss observes, came about because of increasing missionary success in Polynesia as well as Central and South America a bit later.[8] Mormon theological evolution therefore followed Mormon missionary success.

The establishment of the Mormon church in the Pacific began on May 11, 1843, when Joseph Smith called Addison Pratt to lead a mission into the Pacific. Pratt was chosen because he had been a sailor in the Pacific and had spent time in Hawaii.[9] Fellow missionaries Benjamin Franklin Grouard, Noah Rogers, and Knowlton F. Hanks accompanied Pratt. They probably intended to sail for Hawaii, but finding no ship heading there from San Francisco, they instead sailed for French Polynesia. Hanks died from tuberculosis only a month into the journey, but the other three missionaries successfully landed on the island of Tubuai in April 1844. Missionaries from the London Missionary School (LMS) had already been active on the island, and the natives had acquired some familiarity with the basics tenets of Christianity. This undoubtedly helped Pratt in his efforts (although the LMS missionaries were not pleased to see the Mormons arrive). So, too, did the presence of several white settlers, mostly former sailors who had taken wives from among the native population. Pratt won his first converts from these white settlers. By the end of 1844 Pratt had converted a third of the tiny island's population, including all but one white resident.[10] While small in number, these converts' enthusiasm encouraged continued efforts.

Elders Rogers and Grouard, meanwhile, left Pratt on Tubuai and headed from the much larger island of Tahiti. The French had established control over the island only the year before, following a protracted dispute with the British, and in the process had instituted a policy of religious freedom that made it easy for the Mormons to espouse their beliefs. Nevertheless, the LMS missionaries denounced the Mormons and tried to convince the native population to stay clear of these new arrivals from the United States. As a result, for months they converted only a few Europeans and Americans.[11]

The mission ended in 1852 when the French government, worried about the Mormons' strange doctrines, expelled them, but the missionaries claimed to have converted an estimated 2,000 French Polynesians. The missionary effort spread through the Pacific to Hawaii in 1850, New Zealand in 1854, Samoa in 1888, and Tonga in 1891.[12] Hawaii would prove the most fertile ground, however.

George O. Cannon, a member of the first group of missionaries to Hawaii in 1850, pioneered efforts to convert the native peoples. Approximately ten missionaries set out from Honolulu to bring the gospel to the white population, the group they assumed to be the target of their efforts. To their dismay, they found very few whites on the island, most of whom dismissed their message. After a few weeks without success, the elders decided to approach the native Hawaiians. Cannon wrote, "The question arose directly, 'Shall we confine our labors to the white people?'" "For my part," Cannon explained, "I felt it to be my duty to warn all men, white and red; and no sooner did I learn the condition of the population than I made up my mind to acquire the language, preach the gospel to the natives and to the whites whenever I could obtain an opportunity, and thus fill my mission."[13]

Cannon received a revelation from God telling him to convert the native Hawaiians, which greatly augmented his resolve. The Hawaiians, according to his revelation, were descended from a branch of the people of Israel through the prophet Lehi, thus making them another group of Lamanites.[14] Following this revelation, Cannon and the other Mormon missionaries began to focus their efforts on the native Hawaiians, despite the language barriers. The going proved difficult, and half of the missionaries left within the first few months. Cannon and Hiram Clark remained, however, and began to convert the native Hawaiians, seeing their first success in February 1851. By 1853 they had converted over 3,000 Hawaiians and, to escape the acrimony of competing Protestant and Catholic missionaries, they moved the church to the small island of Lanai.[15]

Within a decade of Cannon's revelation, church leaders began to echo the belief that Hawaiians were a remnant of the house of Israel.[16] Brigham Young, in a letter to King Kamehameha the Fifth in 1865, outlined the Mormon belief in Pacific Islanders as Lamanites. Young stressed that the Mormon missionaries would obey all laws and work in conjunction with the king, and he promised that both the spiritual and cultural tutoring of the missionaries would benefit the natives by arresting "their decrease and [thus] enable them to perpetuate their race. There is no reason why they should perish and their lands become the property of the stranger." Here Young espoused a commonly held belief that primitive, tribal peoples were doomed once they came into contact with Western civilization. However, this dismal outcome need not come to pass, since God had secretly made a covenant with the Lamanites to return to them the word of God. Revealing this hidden covenant had been the work of missionaries. Mormon-Indian relations had long been good, Young explained, because Mormons believed "that the aborigines of this Continent are of Israel." Indeed, Young claimed, "They look upon us as fathers." As for Hawaiians, he wrote, "We have not a doubt in our minds but that your Majesty and the people of your Majesty's nation . . . are a Branch of this same great family."[17] If they accepted the help of the missionaries, then Hawaiians would receive not only the gospel but also vital skills for surviving in a changing world. Through this offer, Young and the missionaries hoped to enlist the king's support of their efforts.

The success of these Pacific missions had been largely serendipitous, and Mormon theology had adapted to accept the islanders as members of the church. Although early Mormonism stressed a gathering of believers in Utah, by the end of the nineteenth century this had become impractical, and nearly all Polynesian converts remained in the Pacific. As such, they existed as believers in faraway lands, while the Saints in Utah remained overwhelmingly white.

Although concerned about attracting Lamanites, Mormon missionaries also focused on winning converts of Northern European ancestry. Heber C. Kimball and Orson Hyde were the first Mormons to establish an overseas mission, focusing their efforts on England in 1837. The previous year Joseph Smith commanded that all parts of Israel be gathered from around the world. It would be the job of missionaries to find these hidden members of Israel, baptize them, and arrange for their transportation to Zion. Sending converts to the capital of Mormonism (first Navoo, Illinois, and later Salt Lake City) would animate missionary efforts until well into the twentieth century.

Kimball and Hyde found instant success, baptizing 1,500 people into the church. They drew heavily from textile workers in the Ribble Valley and Lancashire. Following their success, Smith ordered a larger effort in 1839, and nine members of the Quorum of the Twelve Apostles journeyed to England, including Brigham Young, who had become a senior member of the quorum the previous year. Smith desired to test these men and to keep them from questioning his authority, and thus he received a revelation from God that they should be sent overseas. Under Young's direction these apostles fanned out across the British Isles. Despite opposition from local clergy, the missionaries continued to be successful. By 1841 an additional 4,000 Englishmen, Scots, and Irishmen had converted to Mormonism. Equally important, however, Young and his followers established England as the base of operations for missions throughout Europe, as well as a collection point for converts en route to Zion. Liverpool in particular became the headquarters of what would become a very large operation.[18]

As Mormon missionaries spread across the globe, they took their beliefs (religious, political, and racial) with them. Like most Americans, they saw a plurality of races among both Europeans and non-Europeans. By the mid-nineteenth century, as Mormons became active in proselytizing in Europe, Germans had come to be seen as among the most desirable Mormon converts. The *Millennial Star*, the most influential Mormon missionary and emigration publication, routinely included articles about the culture and history of target groups. The paper published a short article titled "The Germans" in the March 8, 1856, issue. The author described the Germans as stern believers in patriarchy, with the father having nearly total authority over his wife and family (something the Mormons also believed in), but the article admitted that polygamy had never proliferated among them. Physically, however, the Germans epitomized manhood: "The physical form of the ancient Germans . . . was all the same. They had mild blue eyes, reddish hair, and strong muscular bodies."[19] Only in comparatively recent times had the independent and freedom-loving Germans been victimized by corrupt governments—undoubtedly making them perfect potential converts and emigrants to Utah, since these natural democrats would not long tolerate such deplorable conditions.[20]

German-speaking converts, including those from the areas that composed the modern German nation-state, as well as Austria and Switzerland, constituted the third-largest group of Mormon converts, trailing only the English and Scandinavian nations (with the exception of Finland, which had only a few dozen converts in the nineteenth century in the face of local opposition).[21] The LDS established a German mission in the early 1840s. Orson Hyde's tract *Ein Ruf aus der Wuste* (A Call from the Desert), published in 1842, became the first Mormon publication in German, and John Taylor followed with a German-French version of the *Book of Mormon* in 1852. Local authorities, however, worried about the presence of these strange believers, with their odd gospel and scandalous customs. Authorities arrested missionaries in Hamburg and Berlin and threatened them with long prison sentences. Troubled by run-ins with law enforcement, the missionaries fled these large cities in the 1850s.[22]

Switzerland, with its tradition of religious tolerance, proved an easier place for the missionaries to proselytize, and from the 1850s through the 1880s Switzerland sent the largest number of German-speaking converts to Utah. Nevertheless, Mormon missionaries faced harassment and intimidation from local authorities. George Mayer, in an 1854 letter to his superiors, wrote, "I went to a lawyer, and he drew up a writing against their [the Zurich police] proceedings and I handed it to the council of Zurich, and there it lies yet. They find their law cannot take hold of me, as there is religious liberty here by law, but they thought they could scare me out of Zurich."[23]

Mormons eagerly proselytized wherever they could, but a border would soon be drawn between Northern and Southern Europe. This invisible border, one of culture and ethnicity, would profoundly shape Mormonism. Lorenzo Snow, an apostle of the church (and much later its president) led a mission to Italy in 1850, following orders Brigham Young had given him the previous year.[24] In his book on the experience, he noted that he would have preferred to stay near his family, but "as a servant of Jesus Christ, I was going to oppose 'one who exalteth himself against all that is called God,' and held an usurped authority over many nations. Italy appeared a death-wrapt land, where the errors of ages were ready to combat my attempt with gigantic powers."[25] The errors of ages were the allegedly corrupt practices of Catholicism.

Snow's mission began in the fall of 1849 from his home in Salt Lake City with a crossing back over the plains. With a heavy heart he left behind "the gardens and fields around our beloved city . . . for the vast wilderness which lay spread out before us for a thousand miles." The often hazardous crossing of the plains marked only the beginning of Snow's journey, but by the spring of 1850 Snow and his companion Joseph Toronto, a native Sicilian and early Mormon convert, had reached England, where Snow had previously worked as a missionary in 1842. He found many people he had baptized preaching the Mormon gospel, and the church appeared to be growing and prosperous. He likened England to a green oasis in the desert but lamented "before me is a land of strangers, whose tongues soon will sound in my ears like the jargon of Babel."[26] In England he met T.B.H. Stenhouse, the president of the Southampton Conference, and Jabez Woodard. Stenhouse impressed Snow with his energy and zeal, while Woodard had been studying the Bible in Italian. His language skills would prove essential to the mission. This quartet—Snow, Toronto, Stenhouse, and Woodard—formed the core of the Italian mission.[27]

Upon arriving in Genoa in June 1850, Snow sent Toronto and Stenhouse to Torre Pellice, the largest community of the Waldenses in the Italian Alps, to ascertain the level of interest in Mormonism there. The daunting task of converting Italians soon became apparent, and Snow felt dejected at the limited prospects for new church members in Italy. In a letter to Franklin D. Richards—the highest-ranking leader of the church in Europe and the man who organized the transportation of Mormon converts from Europe to Utah—Snow complained, "I am alone and a stranger in this vast city [Genoa], eight thousand miles from my beloved family, surrounded by a people [with] whose manners and peculiarities I am unacquainted. I am come to enlighten their minds, and instruct them in principles of righteousness; but I see no possible means of accomplishing this object. All is darkness in the prospect." Snow soon grew disenchanted with Genoa. He did attempt to convert a religious Englishman he met in his travels, but the man's interest evaporated as soon as he discovered Smith's membership in the Church of Jesus Christ of Latter-day Saints.[28] It is also telling that this was the only real attempt he made to convert anyone, or at least the only one he thought worthy of mentioning to Richards. Italian apathy toward his message and his lack of language skills undermined his efforts, and he shuddered to think what stern judgment would soon befall these wayward souls. In despair and disappointment he asked God, "Hast thou not some chosen ones among this people to whom I have been sent? Lead me unto such, and Thy name shall have the glory through Jesus Thy Son."[29]

The situation soon improved, however, as Snow learned that Stenhouse and Toronto were having more success in the city-states of northern Italy (Italy would not become a unified nation until the early 1870s).[30] Snow soon decided to make this the focus of his missionary efforts. He wrote:

I have felt an intense desire to know the state of that province to which I had given them an appointment, as I felt assured it would be the field of my mission. Now, with a heart full of gratitude, I find that an opening is presented in the valleys of the Piedmont, when all others parts of Italy are closed against our efforts. I believe that the Lord has there hidden up a people amid the Alpine mountains, and it is [with] the voice of the Spirit that I shall commence something of importance in that part of this dark nation.[31]

In a letter to Brigham Young, Snow explained the decision to head to the Piedmont: "As I contemplated the condition of Italy, with deep solicitude to know the mind of the Spirit as to where I should commence my labours, I found that all was dark in Sicily, and hostile laws would exclude our efforts. No opening appeared in the cities of Italy: but the history of the Waldenses attracted my attention."[32] For centuries, the people of the Waldenses had struggled against the authority of the Catholic Church, often targets of religious persecution from 1198 onward. This tradition of resistance, Snow hoped, would make them amenable to hear the Mormon gospel. Brimming with optimism he explained to Young, "I was soon convinced that this people were worthy to receive the first proclamation of the Gospel in Italy."[33]

Snow felt at home among the Waldenses and in the mountains. He declared that the health of his small band of missionaries improved in the mountains, especially that of Toronto, and they felt welcomed by the poor people of the region. Indeed, he described their existence as one of extreme labor and poverty as they tried to eke out a living from the mountainous soil and short growing seasons—but unlike Catholic Italians, whose poverty made them largely undesirable converts, the Waldenses struggled with poverty because of the difficult environment and not from lack of effort. Hard work, an attribute that typified whiteness, made these Alpine peoples truly desirable converts. He saw in them kindred spirits. Like the Mormons, the Waldenses had been victims of religious bigotry and persecution, and also like the Mormons, they had retreated to the refuge of mountains, as far away from their persecutors as possible. There were also theological similarities, for both groups had doctrines that stressed a return to primitive Christianity, emphasized a willingness to revolt against established beliefs, and believed Catholicism was a false religion.[34]

He informed Young, "I felt assured that the Lord had directed us to a branch of the House of Israel; and I was rejoiced to behold many countenances that reminded me of those with whom I had been associated in the valleys of the West."[35] His choice of words is important here. By countenances, he could simply be referring to a feeling of camaraderie that reminded him of home, or he could mean that they literally looked like people he knew back home in terms of their physical and ethnic appearance. More than likely, he meant both. Clearly, these hardscrabble mountain people made worthy converts, and Snow and his fellow missionaries set out to make friends with as many people as possible. At first, they limited discussion of their religious views. Snow also had a small book on the life of Joseph Smith called the *Voice of Joseph* published in French (a language understood by many in the region, given the close proximity of France).

The mission seemed to be going well, and Snow claimed the miraculous healing of their innkeeper's three-year-old son was proof of their religious powers. Indeed, the boy's family would eventually convert. By the fall of 1850 Snow, Toronto, Stenhouse, and Woodard formally established the LDS church in Italy on the summit of a mountain they renamed Mount Brigham. They christened a prominent spire connecting to the summit "the Rock of Prophesy" because Snow predicted great things for the mission.[36]

This optimism found its way into the *Millennial Star*. An editorial in the March 15, 1851, edition praised the successes of the "French, Italian and Danish missions [for] . . . moving forward with a degree of prosperity which is truly cheering." The article singled out Snow's efforts for special praise: "This [Italian] mission has been attended with much care and solicitude; many have felt that labors bestowed in that country would prove futile and unavailing, that doctrines of present revelation would not be able to obtain credence with that people" given the long history of Catholicism. The editorial continued, noting that the publication of the *Book of Mormon* in "the Danish, Italian, French, and German languages" would help the people learn the gospel "in their own tongues in which they were born."[37]

The Mormons presented their religious beliefs at various meetings in the region. Following one three-hour meeting in October 1850, "One man, at least, retired with the conviction that we were the servants of the Lord." In his letter to Young, Snow continued, "On the 27th of October, this person presented himself as a candidate for baptism." This man, Jean Bose, was their first convert.[38]

Bosc, however, would prove to be one of the few successful converts, for the road before them soon became more difficult. Snow complained that local authorities barely tolerated their presence, but ultimately the greatest impediments, Snow claimed, were the people themselves. He complained to Young, "We have to preach, on the one hand, to a people nominally Protestants; but who have been, from time immemorial, in a church where any organized dissent has been unknown. The people regard any innovation as an attempt to drag them from the banner of their martyred ancestry." Indeed, the very reasons the missionaries had targeted these mountain people now worked against them: having fought so hard to carve out a place for their beliefs, they proved unwilling to give them up so easily. "On the other hand," Snow continued, "we have the Catholics, with their proud pretensions to a priesthood of apostolic origin." Despite concerted effort on the part of Snow and the other missionaries, he concluded that the Waldenses remained backward and largely irredeemable. He ended his letter to Young on a pessimistic note: "Popery, ignorance, and superstition form a three-fold barrier to our attempts. Strange customs, laws, and languages surround us on every side. In a word, we feel that we are in Italy—the polluted fountain which has overspread the earth with her defiling waters."[39]

Soon after he wrote his pessimistic letter to Young, Snow left for England to supervise the translation of the *Book of Mormon* into Italian. In his absence, Woodard continued the work until he was replaced by Samuel Francis in October 1854. Filled with trepidation, Francis nevertheless prepared to embark on his mission to Italy. He wrote in his journal on October 5, "[My] mission to Italy, without a knowledge of the French or Italian languages, weighed upon my mind and caused much reflection. I had heard many deplorable tales of Italy. A land covered in corruption, whose unholy fountains had corrupted nearly the whole earth." Tormented and filled with doubt, he slept little that night. Francis realized that these doubts were the work of Satan, and he "knew the mission was not man's and knowing that God had sent me I felt his omnipotence would support me as well as preserve me."[40]

Arriving in Turin, the large city at the foot of the Alps, Francis made contact with Elder John Jacques Ruban, a Mormon convert who had been proselytizing in Italy. Though neither could speak the other's language, there was an instant kinship. Ruban led Francis up to the mountains where they stayed with John D. Malan and family. The Malan family had converted shortly after Snow's departure and would prove to be devout followers.[41] Francis worked tirelessly at learning French and within a few months was able to converse a little bit.

Like Snow and Woodard before him, Francis found the going difficult. Local authorities proved hostile to the Mormons, often deriding them for their beliefs. In a debate with a local schoolmaster, Francis noted that the man "manifested great ignorance and soon left the house with a bad spirit." Also, it soon became apparent that Brother Ruban's interest was focused not on the gospel but rather on Malan's teenage daughters. Although he eventually repented for his lascivious behavior, a year later Francis caught him literally with his pants down in the company of one of the girls. Shortly thereafter, Rubans fled to Geneva.[42]

The effort teetered on the verge of collapse, prompting President Franklin D. Richards to visit with the missionaries in September 1855. Richards came to both encourage them in their efforts and exhort them to work harder. The missionaries ascended Mount Brigham and the nearby "Rock of Prophesy," and there Richards began to prophesize on the fate of the enterprise. Daniel Tyler, one of the missionaries, recorded Richards as chiding, "No man not even Brigham [Young] can preach the gospel without faith and confidence in God as the ancient apostles and prophets did, if he be supported with means from other sources; but on the other hand, if he goes between God and the people the Lord will open his way before him and bless his labors." He instructed Samuel Francis to redouble his effort and "predicted that if Brother Francis [would] go to Turin his way shall be opened to do a good work in the name of the Lord and gather out the Israel of God from that city." Elder Francis thanked Richards and promised to focus on the large city of Turin. Richards ended by declaring that the truth of Mormonism would ultimately prevail, and "many would be gathered out" of Italy.[43]

Richards's exhortations proved cold comfort for Francis, who found it almost impossible to proselytize in the city. Local authorities refused to let the Mormons preach in public, and Turin's Protestant congregations ignored them. By 1857, Francis had grown despondent, and on a spectacular July evening, as crowds strolled through the city, he could only see tragedy for the people of Turin:

> All was life and gaiety[;] bands were playing, the people dancing, the Café's were crammed also the Theatres; Il Geordion . . . and other promenades were thronged. Every one was apparently happy. None among all the people were thinking of Eternity, their only object was to make the present sweet. Oh!, how my soul wept in looking upon that people. I was unhappy, yes, I could have sat down and cried for them. The spirit of my mission was upon me and I felt the burden of their sins. I wished I had the liberty to preach in the streets. I wished I could declare the Gospel to them in their own language, but I was bound on every side, and I returned to my room sick of the scenes I had witnessed.[44]

By the late 1850s their efforts had netted only 92 converts, almost all of them from the Waldenses, despite some tentative efforts to recruit in other areas. Between 1850 and 1860, 170 people from Italy converted to Mormonism. Seventy-three would eventually immigrate to Utah, while an equal number would be excommunicated for a variety of reasons. By 1867 only 6 converts remained in Italy. The mission had, in short, been a failure.[45] Language and religious barriers proved difficult to surmount, and even among the supposedly Protestant Waldenses, the message found few listeners. The failure had little to do with ethnic considerations and everything to do with culture, but this cultural line was also an ethnic line. Early Mormonism would not extend in Europe beyond the line of Protestantism. The European Saints would remain of Northern European stock.

Brigham Young voiced his disappointment with the results of the Italian mission in a December 3, 1854, address to the tabernacle. Young argued that the focus of the conversion effort should instead be on the Lamanites and other people who had not heard the Gospel of Jesus. He declared, "If you can find an Island upon which a portion of the people who were scattered from the Tower of Babel found a resting place, and whose inhabitants were never visited by any of the ancient Apostles and Prophets, and where Jesus Christ did not visit, and who have not received any knowledge of the Father, nor the Son, from the days of the confusion, there is the spot the Elders will reap the fruits of their labor more than anywhere else."[46]

Missionaries, he asserted, would have better results among these people than among people who had heard the Gospel and rejected it, namely, Christians and Jews. Indeed, Young claimed, these groups would be among the last people to convert to Mormonism. For elders futilely working among these peoples Young asserted, "LEAVE THEM AND COME HOME, THE LORD DOES NOT REQUIRE YOU TO STAY THERE, FOR THEY MUST SUFFER AND BE DAMNED."[47] This statement, in many ways both contradictory and stunning, ignored the successful conversion efforts occurring in many parts of Europe. Perhaps Young had been influenced by the rather negative report on the Italian mission by Jabez Woodard, for a few passages earlier he noted that the peoples of the Waldenses, often held up as ideal Protestants by other groups, had shown little interest in Mormon gospel. Young attributed this failure to these peoples' ignorance and superstition and to the fact that they were "a mixed race, and are the descendants of those who heard, and most of whom rejected the Gospel." Like Catholics, they had been misled and victimized by corrupt church leaders. Less intelligent and inquisitive than the ethnic groups of Northern Europe, the Waldenses and other Southern Europeans would dwell in darkness and ignorance. "Do you think," he asked, "they as a people will receive the Gospel? No. A few of them will."[48] Young here gave vent to his own frustrations, but those frustrations took on an ethnic cast, reinforcing beliefs that he and most other Mormons certainly already held about the desirability of potential converts. Their hard work, Francis had believed, made them appear to be ideal white converts, but following the failure of the mission, Young accused them of being a mixed race and therefore not worthy converts in the first place.

Mormons' racial and ethnic views also surfaced in the letters of a group of Mormon tourists to Europe and the Holy Land. The tourists—Lorenzo Snow, his sister Eliza, George A. Smith, and Paul A. Schettler—wrote letters to friends like Brigham Young and for publication in Mormon newspapers and periodicals. These letters discussed various aspects of the exotic and distant locations that few, if any, Mormons had ever seen. In general, the tourists found Northern Europeans to be superior, while finding Southern Europeans downtrodden, ignorant, and saddled with superstitions and an inferior religion. They also saw little of worth in the peoples of the Holy Land. Like most tourists, these intrepid Mormon travelers invariably judged the peoples with whom they came in contact by their own standards and values.

Despite the failure of the Italian mission, Brigham Young still sought opportunities for conversion among peoples in both Southern Europe and the Holy Land. In a letter (written with Daniel Wells) to George A. Smith, Young wrote, "We desire that you observe closely what openings now exist, or where they may be effected, for the introduction of the Gospel into the various countries you shall visit." They continued, "We pray that you . . . may be abundantly blessed with words of wisdom and free utterance in all your conversations pertaining to the Holy Gospel, dispelling prejudice, and sowing seeds of righteousness among the people."[49] Young would be disappointed once again in the reports sent back by the Palestine tourists.

Northern Europeans, of course, possessed many desirable qualities, and the tourists discussed them in their correspondence. Eliza Snow, in a letter to *Woman's Exponent* magazine, praised the hard work, thrift, and cleanliness of the Dutch:

Cleanliness seems to be a characteristic with hotels in Holland; and, admitting industry to be promotive of neatness, it must also be a national characteristic. No sensible, candid person can visit this country without according to the people the credit of industry, and indomitable perseverance. Most people think they do well to cultivate the ground after it is made, but the Hollanders make much of the ground they cultivate, and when made and cultivated, it requires constant labor and expense to protect it from inundation. They must, as a matter of course, be honest, they have not time to be otherwise.[50]

Conflating cleanliness with hard work, thrift, and honesty said much about the personal views of Snow and her fellow travelers. Snow mentioned cleanliness in another letter, but there it appeared rather as a strange contradiction to the rest of her surroundings in the Levant. Again to *Woman's Exponent* she wrote, "Considering the outside appearance of the den-like houses of the Arab Mahommedans [Muslims], it is very surprising to see how neat they look. Many, both men and women, dress in white, and *really* white; their religion enjoins cleanliness."[51] Muslims, though a clearly degraded and degenerate lot, practiced cleanliness, which Snow considered a desirable trait, but in this case it did not signify any other positive attributes as it did among the Dutch. Cleanliness stood out as a by-product of their peculiar religious beliefs and even as a contradiction to their other practices. This ambivalence characterized the tour through the Holy Land.

As the only woman among the Mormon tourists, Eliza Snow, not surprisingly, paid closer attention to the status of women in the various nations they visited than did her male counterparts. "The Grecian women," she claimed, "are, many of them at least, 'beasts of burden.' I never saw such gigantic bundles carried by human beings as the poor women carry on their heads."[52] Lorenzo Snow noticed the state of women in Italy as well, writing in a letter to the *Salt Lake Herald*, "We saw here, and in many other parts of Italy, the women engaged in this laborious employment—in one instance we noticed a company of women repairing a break in the railroad, by carrying gravel upon their heads in baskets."[53] For the Snows, the treatment of women reflected the state of degeneracy of the various cultures they visited, and their observations, though reflective of their culture, were somewhat ironic given that the status of Mormon women under polygamy had long been a weapon Mormonism's critics had wielded against them.

Italy, Greece, and the Holy Land—the founts of Western civilization—appeared to the quartet of travelers as backward and degenerate, largely because of their religious traditions. George A. Smith, writing to Brigham Young, noted, "Twenty-five hundred years ago these islands [of Greece] contained 'the most learned and highly advanced nation of antiquity'; but now their appearance does not justify the rule of progress, only in the backward way. The Greek church has been the religion here for 1,400 years."[54] Similarly, Eliza Snow observed the New Year's Day mass in Milan in 1873. She found herself both amazed at the beauty of the cathedral and appalled at the pomp and trappings of the Catholic Church. She described the members of the congregation as idolaters, bowing and supplicating themselves before the golden crucifix and the archbishop. The sight moved her to lament, "How long, O Lord, shall these, thy children, be bound in the dwarfing chains of traditional superstition and ignorance? It is true the powers of earth are shaking, but at present I can see no hope for millions of people under the training of the 'Mother of Harlots' [Catholic Church], and the influence of priestcraft."[55]

The Holy Land had also seen a marked decline in the quality of its civilization. A group of Bedouins encamped near the Palestine tourists, and regaled them with songs and dancing in exchange for money. Lorenzo Snow wrote, "Recollecting several robberies and murders which had occurred in the vicinity, we paid them for this wretched entertainment, constantly adding more, until we excited their admiration." What an odd contradiction, he felt, between the biblical history of the Holy Land and its current state. Snow continued, "We retired to our tents, reflecting on the strange difference between the present occupants of this locality and those who inhabited it when prophets converted bitter springs into sweet fountains, and smote impetuous streams, piling up their waters on either side and walked through on dry ground."[56] The prophets and holy men had long ago vanished, Snow felt, and murderers and thieves now occupied the land.

Eliza Snow, like many educated Victorian Americans, fancied herself something of a poet and penned a delightfully awful poem on the state of Jerusalem. The poem began by celebrating Jerusalem's past:

> Thou City with a cherished name,
> A name in garlands drest
> Adorned with ancient sacred fame,

As city of the blest.
Thy rulers once, were mighty men,
Thy sons renowned in war:
Thy smiles were sought and courted then
By people from Afar.

Then came the fall:

Degraded, and on every hand,
From wisdom all estranged;
Thy glory has departed, and
All, but thy name is changed!
From God withdrawn—by Him forsook—
To all intents depraved;
Beneath the Turkish iron yoke,
Thou long hast been enslaved.

The poem, however, ends on something of a hopeful note:

Thy children—seed of Israel,
Of God's 'peculiar care'
On whom the weight of judgment fell,
Are scattered everywhere."

And the final stanza:

"Thy sun has not forever set—
God has a great design,
and will fulfill His purpose yet,
concerning Palestine.[57]

Snow's poem illustrated the way these Mormon tourists viewed the world around them. Their denunciation of Catholics, Greek Orthodox believers, and Muslims fit with the narrative of the Mormons as the new chosen people of God. Indeed, Snow says as much when she writes that the people of Israel "are scattered everywhere," because Mormon doctrine held that the blood of ancient Israel had been scattered throughout the nations of the earth and that God intended Mormonism to once again bring these chosen people together. Thus the optimistic conclusion comes from the belief that God is working through the Mormons to redeem humanity. The reality of conversion, however, stood in marked contrast to her lyrical rhapsodizing.

The only real attempt the Palestine tourists made to spread their religion occurred on a steamship crossing between the Greek island of Corfu and Alexandria, Egypt. George A. Smith, in a February 8, 1873, letter to Brigham Young, described the steamship passengers as including many Americans and Englishmen: "They were much surprised to find live specimens from 'Mormondom'; and, as they would keep talking to us, we preached to them nearly the whole voyage. They were a class of people that would not go to our meetings, but by this means heard something of the gospel."[58] Smith doubted that any of them took the message seriously but hoped that perhaps some good had been done. Their efforts resembled those of Lorenzo Snow when he first entered Italy two decades earlier in that the only people they attempted to convert already spoke English. To be fair, the Palestine tourists spent their time sightseeing and trying to establish a personal connection to the land of Jesus and the prophets rather than attempting to win converts among the peoples they encountered. Nevertheless, they clearly saw no reason even to try, since the peoples of the Holy Land seemed of such poor character.

Language barriers, race, and culture circumscribed Mormon conversion efforts (with the marked and important exception of the Pacific Islanders). Thus converts were largely composed of Northern European whites, ethnic groups like the English, Welsh, Scandinavians, and Germans, or, in short, the most desirable potential immigrants in the eyes of most Americans. This should have been a cause for celebration, but their religious views made them suspect.

Nineteenth-century critics of Mormonism—and there were many—often pointed out how supposedly degenerate the European converts seemed when compared with non-Mormon immigrants from the same countries. Poor, stupid, and easily manipulated, these converts seemed anything but desirable, critics contended. Mormon belief, in short, had stripped these desirable immigrants of their whiteness.

Hard work had long been considered a chief attribute of a successful American and of a desirable immigrant. While Americans praised the work Mormons had done in transforming the Utah desert into productive farmland, they denounced them as apostates and polygamists and condemned their society as immoral. Mark Twain, in his classic travelogue *Roughing It*, described Salt Lake City as an orderly "city of fifteen thousand inhabitants with no loafers perceptible in it; and no visible drunkards or noisy people." He continued, "And everywhere were workshops, factories, and all manner of industries; and intent faces and busy hands were to be seen wherever one looked; in one's ears was the ceaseless clink of hammers, the buzz of trade and the contented hum of drums and flywheels."[59] This was the sound of productivity, of hard work, a sound familiar to most Americans. Twain noted that his home state of Missouri featured a crest with two bears holding a cask between them, apparently in the act of imbibing an alcoholic beverage (or at least that was Twain's interpretation), but in contrast the Mormon crest "was simple, unostentatious [sic], and fitted like a glove. It was a representation of a Golden Beehive with the bees all at work!"[60] In Twain's typical deadpan style, he made several shrewd observations about both Americans and the Mormons of Utah. The Mormons were abstemious, hardworking, and communal—all traits held in great regard in American society (unlike drunken Missourians and their ursine stand-ins) and that should have brought praise to the Mormons. Yet others, while acknowledging the Mormons' hardworking character, nevertheless found much to criticize.

James Rusling, in a comment typically praising the thrift of Mormons, wrote of first meeting Mormon settlements in the Weber Valley: "Fine little farms dotted the valley everywhere, and the settlements indeed were so numerous, that much of the valley resembled rather a scattered village. The little Weber River passes down the valley, on its way to Great Salt Lake, and its waters had everywhere been diverted, and made to irrigate nearly every possible acre of ground. Fine crops of barley, oats, wheat, potatoes, etc., appeared to have been gathered, and cattle and sheep were grazing on all sides." As for the people, Rusling observed that they "looked like a hardy, industrious, thrifty race, well fitted to their stern struggle with the wilderness. Everybody was apparently well-fed and well-clad, though the women had a worn and tired look, as if they led a dull life and lacked sympathy."[61] He found Salt Lake City even more impressive than the Weber Valley: "Without doubt, it must be said of the people of Utah, that they are an industrious, frugal, and thrifty race. By their wonderful system of irrigation, they have converted the desert there into a garden, and literally made the wilderness, 'bloom and blossom as the rose.' "[62]

Yet Rusling, like many others, attacked Mormonism as an abomination that aided the powerful and preyed on the powerless. Women, subject to the practice of polygamy, appeared tired and no doubt suffered under its inhumane sway. Mormon leaders also preyed on the new arrivals. Rusling asserted that the foreign-born Mormon converts came from among the "very lowest and poorest classes" and ended up in a quasi-feudal relationship with American Mormon leaders. Rusling accused the Latter-day Saints of being less a religion than a highly effective immigration scheme: "Indeed, to sum it up in one word, the whole institution of Mormonism—polygamy and all—apart from its theological aspects, impresses you rather as a gigantic organization for collecting and consolidating a population, and thus settling up a Territory rapidly, whatever else it may be; and its success, in this respect, has certainly been notable and great."[63]

The Mormon practice of polygamy, however, would lead the Latter-day Saints into racial degeneration, he believed. Rusling discussed the situation with a federal judge and opponent of the Mormon leadership in Utah. The judge confided that the city cemetery was a "perfect Golgotha of infant graves." The children of the Mormons' polygamous marriages were "inferior, of course, in many ways . . . as the fruits of such a practice always are, and must be." Rusling, playing something of the devil's advocate, countered that the children he had seen appeared spry and healthy. The judge responded, "No doubt. It is a good climate, and there has not been time enough yet." A few generations of wretched polygamy, however, would leave the children "feeble and tainted . . . in constitution" and erase the benefits of Utah's benefi-cent climate. If degeneration did not result from polygamy, the judge argued, then "all History is false, and Science a slander."[64] Mormon Utah, Rusling and his wisely anonymous judge asserted, provided an example of white racial degeneration in the West, degeneration that resulted not from climate but rather from the supposedly debauched practices of the Latter-day Saints.

Rusling's condemnation of the Mormons appeared nearly measured compared with that of John Hanson Beadle. A gentile (as Mormons called non-Mormons) newspaperman in Utah for a time, he became a vocal oppo-nent of Mormonism. Beadle wrote *The Undeveloped West*, a fairly typical travelogue designed to encourage settlement, in the 1870s. He declared the Scandinavian immigrants he encountered in Iowa and Minnesota as "among the wealthiest people in the country; their national industry has raised them from poverty to opulence." In contrast, he wrote, "I saw people of the same races in Utah, by the most exhaustive labor a *little* better off than they had been at home, and heard them boasting what great things 'the Lord and Brother Brigham had done for them.' These in Iowa had no Prophet, and consequently made a good selection for their homes, and prospered without being tithed."[65] Discounting the environmental suitability of arid Utah and the territory's still-developing society as causes, Beadle instead attributed the material difference between the two groups to religious belief. Without the suffocating authority of the Mormon church, the immigrants in Iowa and Minnesota prospered while those in Utah suffered under the yoke of Mormon domination. The former embraced the values of independence, hard work, and self-reliance, making them truly desirable white yeoman farmers; but the latter, despite their hard work, had exchanged their freedom and self-reliance for obedience to a false religion and thus could not truly be said to have the privileges of whiteness.

Upon meeting the Mormons later, Beadle again noted that their immigrants were of a decidedly poor quality. In the smaller settlements away from Salt Lake and the railroad, he declared, the traveler would "find a degree of poverty and ignorance he would scarcely have credited among the peasantry of Europe. And there he will find the simon-pure, straight-out and fanatical Mormons—a race of simple shepherds, with reason scarce above the sheep they drive. There the unhappy traveler, if compelled to seek shelter in winter, will find it in a Swedish 'dug out' or a half-mud hut, tenanted equally by dogs, Danes, fleas, and other undesirables."[66] Beadle declared that gentiles could not compete on equal footing in Utah because Mormon immigrants could live with a state of poverty Americans would not tolerate: "No American could go into the country and compete with the foreign-born Mormons, who worked little five[-] and ten-acre patches, and thought themselves in affluence if they had a hundred dollars' worth of surplus produce."[67] Filled with ignorant, poverty-stricken fanatics, the Utah Territory offered little opportunity for other Americans. Though composed of thrifty, hardworking Anglo-Americans and Northern European immigrants, Beadle nevertheless labeled the Mormons an undesirable group. His comments, curiously, echoed the rhetoric of the opponents of Chinese immigration, and by using the language of race, he effectively marginalized the Mormons as a lesser and inferior "race of simple shepherds" whose presence as "undesirables" made them incompatible with the larger nation. By sinking to the level of the poorest and most ignorant immigrants, these servile Mormons had exchanged their whiteness for a false religion.

The US government agreed with the poor condition of Mormon converts and sought ways to limit this immigration. In 1879 the US chargé d'affaires, M. J. Hoppin, asked the British government to help restrain Mormon immigration. Mormonism, he explained, preyed on "the ignorant classes who are easily influenced by the double appeal to their passions and their poverty held out in the flattering picture of a home in the fertile and prosperous regions where Mormonism has established its material seal." These converts, however, existed to feed the Mormons' need for plural wives, and "these so called 'marriages' are pronounced by the Laws of the United States to be crimes against the statutes of the country and punishable as such." Hoppin, however, noted that "the bands and organizations to which are got together in foreign lands as recruits cannot be regarded as otherwise than a deliberate and systematic attempt to bring persons to the United States with the intent of violating their Laws and Committing Crimes expressly punishable under the Statutes." He hoped the British government would do everything within its legal authority to "check the organization of these Criminal enterprises by agents who are thus operating beyond the reach of the Law of the United States and to prevent the departure of those proposing to go thither."[68] In short, he wanted a government crackdown on Mormon immigration efforts.

Hoppin's request made its way through the channels of the British government, finally reaching the office of police magistrate J. Vaughn. Vaughn, while sympathetic to the American desire to prevent Mormon immigration and the spread of polygamy, asserted, "This Government is powerless to prevent the private adoption of those doctrines, or, to restrain the believers in them from quitting Great Britain and emigrating to any other country."[69]

The official response from Britain's secretary of state for foreign affairs, the Marquis of Salisbury, echoed Vaughn's opinion that, regretfully, the British government could do nothing to stop the emigration of Mormon converts to the United States, but his office did promise to print "a notice to be inserted into the newspapers cautioning persons against being deceived by Mormonite Emmisaries and making generally known the Law of the United States affecting polygamy and the penalties attaching to infringement thereof which he hopes will have the desired effect."[70]

Mormon immigration remained a concern for the US government, but, curiously, American law could do little to prevent Mormon immigrants from coming into the country—after all, they were considered white and they hailed from highly desirable nations. Nevertheless, there remained a bias against the Mormons. The historian Douglas Dexter Alder observes, for example, that an 1891 revision of the exclusion list added "persons suffering from loathsome and contagious diseases, persons convicted of moral turpitude, polygamists, [and] aliens assisted by others" as among those undesirable elements that should be refused admission to the United States. Alder writes that this is an odd inclusion, since in 1890 the church officially outlawed polygamy as a condition of statehood. He asserts that the government had earlier prevented those who professed a belief in polygamy (essentially all Mormons) from voting, serving jury duty, or holding public office; and such a policy could have easily been implemented to prevent Mormon immigration, but the US government never did so.[71]

US immigration law, however, did draw distinctions among racial and ethnic groups, first with the Chinese and then with virtually all groups after the implementation of the 1924 Immigration Act. This law had little effect on Mormon immigration, though, since nearly all converts came from Northern European nations that were not subject to quota restrictions. Further, Alder observes, "The church might have been vitally concerned with this law if it were not already in the middle of a policy change which resulted in discouraging immigration." This policy change marginalized the importance of all converts moving to Utah to build the new Zion and instead commanded them to spread the gospel in their native communities. In this way, Mormon leaders felt, these converts could do more good by staying in their home countries. The language barrier, which had long frustrated missionary enterprises, would no longer be a problem. According to Alder, "The 1924 law actually came as a welcome guest to Mormon officials and the mission presidents quickly adopted as one of their arguments for remaining in Europe the increased difficulty of gaining entrance into the United States."[72] Indeed, by 1924 Mormonism had grown and changed. While far from mainstream, the faith had matured to the point where it boasted of believers scattered around the globe. Too many converts would overwhelm Utah, which could not support them economically, and the cost of transportation, especially since most converts lacked the financial resources necessary to undertake the journey, proved prohibitive.

Race and culture, as much as religion, shaped the Mormons and their new Zion. Despite the best, sincere efforts of missionaries, Mormon converts were mostly found among Protestant Northern Europeans. The Saints would remain white for some time to come.[73] Non-Mormon Americans, however, often used the rhetoric of racial desirability to attack the Mormons as somehow less than white. Their religious practices allegedly led believers into a state of racial decline, not unlike other undesirable groups, and no peoples who gave up freedom for subservience could truly be white. For decades to come, the Mormons would continue to be seen as an anomaly, an other, and they would work hard to demonstrate their patriotism, loyalty, and status as equal, white citizens.

NOTES

1. Julie Roy Jeffrey, *Frontier Women* (New York: Hill and Wang, 1998), 179, 213, quote on 181.

2. Jules Remy, *A Journey to Great Salt Lake City*, vol. 2 (London: W. Jeffs, 1861), 211–12.

3. Ibid.

4. Daniel H. Ludlow, ed., *Encyclopedia of Mormonism* (New York: Macmillan, 1992), 2:801–5, 3:981–85.

5. Joseph Smith, *The Book of Mormon: Another Testament of Jesus Christ* (Salt Lake City: Church of Jesus Christ of Latter-day Saints, 1981), ii.

6. Armand L. Mauss, *All Abraham's Children: Changing Mormon Conceptions of Race and Lineage* (Urbana: University of Illinois Press, 2003), 10.

7. Elise Boxer, " 'To Become White and Delightsome': American Indians and Mormon Identity," PhD dissertation, Arizona State University, Tempe, 2009; Thomas W. Murphy, "Imagining Lamanites: Native Americans and the Book of Mormon," PhD dissertation, University of Washington, Seattle, 2003.

8. Mauss, *All Abraham's Children*, 11. Maus recounts the contradictory and complicated history of Mormon-Indian relations in chapters 3, 4, and 5, pp. 41–156.

9. R. Lanier Britsch, *Unto the Islands of the Sea: A History of the Latter-day Saints in the Pacific* (Salt Lake City: Deseret Book, 1986), 3.

10. Ibid., 5–6.

11. Ibid., 7–9.

12. "The Church in Oceania," in Ludlow, *Encyclopedia of Mormonism*, 3:1022–26. See also Britsch, *Unto the Islands of the Sea*.

13. Quoted in Britsch, *Unto the Islands of the Sea*, 97.

14. Ibid., 97–99.

15. Ibid., 111–15.

16. Ibid., xiv.

17. Brigham Young to King L. Kamehameha the Fifth, March 24, 1865, Brigham Young Papers, Mss. B 93, Utah State Historical Society, Salt Lake City.

18. "Missions of the Twelve to the British Isles," in Ludlow, *Encyclopedia of Mormonism*, 3:920–22.

19. W. B., "The Germans," *Millennial Star* 18, no. 10 (March 8, 1856), http://contentdm.lib.byu.edu/cdm4/browse.php?CISOROOT=%2FMStar (accessed July 12, 2012).

20. Nell Irvin Painter, *The History of White People* (New York: W. W. Norton, 2010), 248–50.

21. On the Mormon experience in Finland, see Kim B. Östman, "Mormons, Civil Authorities and Lutheran Clergy in Finland, 1875–1889," *Scandinavian Journal of History* 35, no. 3 (September 2010): 268–89.

22. Douglas Dexter Alder, "German Speaking Immigration to Utah, 1850–1950," MA thesis, University of Utah, Salt Lake City, 1959, vi, 5–9.

23. Quoted in ibid., 10.

24. Michael Homer, "The Italian Mission, 1850–1867," *Sunstone* 7, no. 3 (May–June 1982): 16–21.

25. Lorenzo Snow, *The Italian Mission* (London: W. Aubrey, 1851), 3.

26. Ibid., 7.

27. Homer, "Italian Mission."

28. Snow, *Italian Mission*, 9.

29. Ibid., 10.

30. Homer, "Italian Mission."

31. Snow, *Italian Mission*, 10.

32. Ibid.

33. Ibid., 11.

34. Homer, "Italian Mission."

35. Snow, *Italian Mission*, 11.

36. Homer, "Italian Mission." The mountain, Michael Homer believes, is most likely Monte Vandalino.

37. "Glad Tidings of Great Joy," *Millennial Star* 13, no. 6 (March 15, 1851): 88–89.

38. Snow, *Italian Mission*, 17.

39. Ibid., 18.

40. Samuel Francis, *Journal Containing the Most Important Items of My Life and Ministry, 1850–57*, Mss. 3268, Folder 2, L. Tom Perry Special Collections, Harold B. Lee Library, Brigham Young University, Provo, UT.

41. Homer, "Italian Mission."

42. Francis, *Journal Containing the Most Important Items of My Life and Ministry*, 154–55.

43. Daniel Tyler, Journals 1853–56, Daniel Tyler Papers, Mss. SC 481, Folder 2, L. Tom Perry Special Collections, Harold B. Lee Library, Brigham Young University, Provo, UT.

44. Francis, *Journal Containing the Most Important Items of My Life and Ministry*, 158–59.

45. Homer, "Italian Mission."

46. Brigham Young, *Journal of Discourses* 2:141, http://www.journalofdiscourses .org/ (accessed July 12, 2012).

47. Ibid., 2:143.

48. Ibid., 2:141.

49. Brigham Young and Daniel H. Wells to George A. Smith, October 15, 1872, in George A. Smith, Lorenzo Snow, Paul A. Schettler, and Eliza R. Snow, *Correspondence of Palestine Tourists* (Salt Lake City: Deseret News Steam Printing, 1875), 1–2.

50. Eliza Snow to editor, *Woman's Exponent*, December 29, 1872, in ibid., 100–101.

51. Eliza Snow to editor, *Woman's Exponent*, February 14, 1873, in ibid., 178; italics in original.

52. Ibid., 174.

53. Lorenzo Snow to editors, *Salt Lake Herald*, January 29, 1873, in ibid., 164.

54. George A. Smith to Brigham Young, February 8, 1873, in ibid., 166.

55. Eliza Snow to Mrs. Jane S. Richards, January 1, 1873, in ibid., 106–7.

56. Lorenzo Snow to editor, *Deseret News*, March 6, 1873, in ibid., 239.

57. Eliza Snow, March 6, 1873, in ibid., 242–43. She never published this poem in a newspaper, but it was included in the published book.

58. George A. Smith to Brigham Young, February 8, 1873, in ibid., 167.

59. Mark Twain, *Roughing It* (New York: Harper and Row, 1962), 92.

60. Ibid.

61. James F. Rusling, *Across America: or the Great West and the Pacific Coast* (New York: Sheldon, 1874), 160.

62. Ibid., 199.

63. Ibid., 201–2.

64. Ibid., 192.

65. J[ohn] H[anson] Beadle, *The Undeveloped West: or, Five Years in the Territories* (Philadelphia: National Publishing, 1873), 39; italics in original.

66. Ibid., 685–86.

67. Ibid., 142.

68. Quoted in Julian Puncefote to A.F.O. Liddell, September 4, 1879, in Mormon Emigration Records, 1879, Mss. 4150, L. Tom Perry Special Collections, Harold B. Lee Library, Brigham Young University, Provo, UT.

69. J. Vaughan, Police Magistrate, to A.F.O. Liddell, September 13, 1879, in ibid.

70. Secretary Crop, Under Secretary of State, to M. J. Hoppin, United States Chargé d'Affaires, September 1879, in ibid.

71. Alder, *German Speaking Immigration to Utah*, 27.

72. Ibid., 31.

73. Mormonism has been spreading rapidly in non-white countries, and now many Mormons are from non-white racial and ethnic groups. Yet the image of Mormons as whites remains powerful enough that the church specifically addresses the issue in the "Frequently Asked Questions" section of its website: http://mormon.org/faq/#Race (accessed December 15, 2011).

ENFORCING THE WHITE MAN'S WEST THROUGH VIOLENCE IN TEXAS, CALIFORNIA, AND BEYOND

Anglo-Americans relied on violence to take possession of the West. Upon completing that conquest, they also used it to smother challenges to their ascendant economic and political hegemony and, in the words of historian Richard Maxwell Brown, to "preserve their favored position in the social economic and political order." While Brown did not focus on whiteness in his discussion of vigilante violence, clearly it provided the underlying basis on which "their favored position" had been constructed. Seemingly law-abiding citizens therefore could at times embrace lynchings, vigilantism, and mob violence to allegedly protect societal values and a status quo implicitly based on ideas of white racial superiority and privilege.[1] Violence therefore provided the most powerful tool for marginalizing non-white peoples and protecting the white man's West.

Violence as part of the western experience has long been recognized as integral to the settlement and development of the region.[2] Indeed, it saturated every aspect of the conquest of the West, including the defeat of Indian peoples at the hands of the military. To be sure, non-Anglos, including American Indians and Hispanic outlaws, employed violence, resisting American expansion and

DOI: 10.5876/9781607323969.c008

trying to retain control of their lands and territory. Yet these rearguard actions proved too little to defeat the domination of white Americans and the social and economic order their arrival presaged. As western communities grew, violence remained critical to creating and enforcing the dominance of whites over non-whites, marking both spatial and psychological boundaries in the process. From Texas to Washington State, Anglo-Americans employed violence to smother challenges to their control; and vigilante movements, in various times and places, targeted American Indian peoples, African Americans, Hispanics, the Chinese, and in rare instances even European ethnic groups. Anti-Chinese violence, for example, left Chinese men dead in riots in Denver, Colorado, and Rock Springs, Wyoming, in the 1880s.[3] Anglo-American residents of Tacoma, in the fall of 1885, forcibly evicted their entire Chinese population, driving them into the cold rain.[4] In Idaho, thirty-one Chinese miners perished in an ambush by Anglo assailants. Yet the Chinese endured in all these places, often successfully finding a better life for themselves, even though there could be little doubt of the subservient place they occupied in American society.[5] In Bisbee, Arizona, on the morning of July 12, 1915, armed vigilantes wearing white armbands rounded up Hispanics, Eastern Europeans, and supporters of the radical labor union the Industrial Workers of the World, loaded them onto railroad boxcars, and dumped them in the desert of western New Mexico. Their only crime was their status, deemed less than truly white like their Anglo neighbors.[6]

As these episodes suggest, violence against non-whites materialized throughout the West, but the tone and scope of such violence were first set in two places: California and Texas. This should not come as a surprise. Both places figured prominently in the early stages of the settlement of the trans-Mississippi West, and both contained fairly dense populations of American Indian peoples and Hispanic residents, both of whom had a long history in the region. In addition, Chinese immigrants presented another challenge in California, and in Texas African Americans struggled against slavery and, later, segregation. In places, American Indian peoples faced nearly complete eradication, and Hispanics, including the old elite, saw their power and influence circumscribed through political and economic chicanery and the violent imposition of a kind of de facto segregation.

The violent conquest and transformation of Texas began in the 1830s. For white southerners like David Crockett and Sam Houston, both down-on-their-luck former politicians, Texas beckoned with the promise of restored prosperity and the hope for a new beginning. Glowing accounts predictably painted the Mexican state as an expansive Garden of Eden, with rich soil and a long growing season. Yet Texas remained a land of potential, under-populated and underdeveloped. Fortunately, for ambitious Anglo-Americans this state of arrested development could be attributed to the supposedly inferior and indolent Mexicans. Injecting a little Anglo-American vigor in the state would no doubt work wonders. Armed with this swagger and the belief in Mexican inferiority, white Americans began pouring into Texas (often dragging African Americans slaves with them). These newcomers soon led calls for a revolution against Mexico.

The Reverend A. B. Lawrence of New Orleans, in the introduction to an 1840 guidebook on Texas, praised the successful Texas revolution for freeing the new nation from "that besotted and priest-ridden nation [Mexico]." The overthrow of religious backwardness and tyranny by Anglo-Texans, he claimed, promised to develop a once marginal territory into a new and prosperous nation: "The prospects of Texas in [the] future are as fair as a fertile soil, a genial climate and healthful regions can render a country."[7] Thus the westward march of Anglo-Saxons would continue, sweeping away savagery and indolence and making Texas literally bloom, or such seemed the promise of an allegedly vigorous Anglo society.

While Anglo-Texans unself-consciously considered themselves superior, in truth the imposition of white supremacy faced the multiracial and multiethnic reality of Texas. Violence would be needed to eliminate the Indian presence, force Tejanos (Hispanic Texans) into a subservient status, and ensure the subordination of African Americans as slaves before 1865 and as inferior citizens after that date.

There can be little doubt that life along the Texas frontier was violent. The Texas Republic had been born through violence, but Texians (as they still called themselves) found themselves surrounded by enemies. To the south, Mexico threatened constant invasion, irritated by a treaty that had clearly been negotiated under duress, and to the west the powerful Comanche and Kiowa empire controlled the Texas plains. These threats caused Texans to create an official volunteer army, but a variety of paramilitary groups also emerged, most notably the Texas Rangers. In the words of historian Gary Clayton Anderson, Texans embraced a "'culture of war' or a persisting belief that violence against people was necessary for nation building."[8] Texans

FIGURE 8.1. Texas Rangers with dead bandits, October 8, 1915. The famed Texas Rangers straddled more than the US-Mexico border. They also patrolled borders of race and ethnicity, protecting Anglo-American values from challenges by Hispanics, Indians, and African Americans. At no point did the challenge become greater than in the years of the Mexican Revolution, when the border became a very violent place. Their legacy as either gallant and fearless heroes or the tools of white supremacy continues to be contested today. *Courtesy*, Robert Runyon Photograph Collection, Center for American History, University of Texas at Austin.

therefore turned to violence to solve the challenges posed by the presence of Indians and Tejanos in the republic/state.

Anderson argues that Texans relied on violence to conquer and dispossess American Indian peoples through a process he believes amounted to ethnic cleansing. If Indians would not abandon Texas peacefully, then violent conquest could be the only outcome, and for nearly fifty years (far longer than anywhere else in the West) attacks and counterattacks between Anglos and Indians gradually forced Indian peoples out of Texas.

As an independent nation from 1836 to 1845, the Texas government, at least on paper, controlled the lands to the west. Unlike other western territories, the independent nation could set the course of its Indian policy without interference from easterners or the federal government, giving Texas lawmakers a free hand to deal with the presence of Indians in their republic. In general, they envisioned a Texas without reservations and Indians. However, despite the scribbled lines on a map, in reality Indian peoples controlled most of Texas; as settlers pushed up the Trinity, Colorado, and Brazos Rivers, they invariably came into conflict with Indians like the Caddos and Wichitas and, beyond them, the plains tribes. Even after annexation, the state (unique among western states) maintained control of its public domain. Thus the federal government, which typically conquered the land and negotiated with Indian peoples through the treaty process, played little role in mediating in Texas until after the Civil War. During the 1850s the federal government did establish two small reservations on the upper Brazos, but vocal Texans demanded the removal or extermination of these Indians.

John R. Baylor, a politically ambitious newspaper owner, led the charge to destroy the reservations in Texas. His paper, provocatively titled *The Whiteman*, advocated the destruction of the reservations and the extermination of Indians who resisted. By 1858 an increasing number of Texans agreed with the vitriolic newspaperman. Baylor organized petition campaigns in frontier towns like Weatherford, Jacksboro, and Gainesville to ask authorities to close the reservations. Soon, several hundred Indian haters—including influential pioneers and former rangers like George Erath—and rough ne'er-do-wells gravitated to Baylor's cause. Not content to fight solely with words, he formed a vigilante group, which adopted the legitimate-sounding name "Jacksboro Rangers." These "rangers" cowed local law enforcement and began a campaign of terror against reservation Indians. The attacks began in the spring of 1859 when a group of Baylor's men took up positions outside the reservation, eventually killing and scalping an Indian letter-carrier. Robert Neighbors, a respected Indian agent and advocate of Indian rights, decried the attack and demanded that a US marshal arrest the perpetrator, one Patrick Murphy. Despite the support of federal troops and armed Indians, the marshal's attempt to arrest Murphy in Jacksboro failed, and the marshal left with little more than his life. *The Whiteman* soon published the rangers' justification for their actions. Their manifesto declared, "We regard the killing of Indians of whatever tribe to be morally right."[9] Baylor and his rangers now advocated open genocide of all Indian peoples—including the peaceful Caddos—and the establishment of a Texas without an Indian presence.

On May 23, Baylor's mob assaulted a reservation village and murdered an elderly Indian couple. The reservation erupted in violence. Enraged Indians attacked Baylor's drunken mob. Federal troops, commanded by Captain Joseph Plummer, joined in on the side of the Indians. Baylor's men, their alcohol-fortified courage failing them, soon turned and ran. Fewer than 50 Indians and a handful of federal troops had sent Baylor and his roughly 300 men scurrying away. While Baylor had clearly lost the battle, he did win the war when federal officials relocated the Indian residents to Indian Territory in July. Bereft and penniless, over a thousand eastern Comanches, Caddos, Wichitas, Shawnees, Delawares, and Tonkawas left the Brazos agency and their homes behind.[10] A few months later, Patrick Murphy and an accomplice murdered Agent Neighbors in broad daylight on Fort Belknap's muddy main street. Terrified of drawing Murphy's ire, townspeople left his body where it fell until nightfall.[11] Violence had proven its effectiveness, eliminating both a reservation and its staunchest defender.

Ironically, the actions of the Jacksboro Rangers actually made the frontier less secure. The removal of reservation Indians and the buffer they provided, along with the start of the Civil War, presented the Comanches and Kiowas with an opportunity to push back against invading whites and attack Anglo settlements. With many of the best rangers fighting for the Confederacy, the frontier became an even more dangerous place for settlers. Moreover, the lack of control provided a refuge for those seeking to avoid conscription in either the Union or the Confederate Army and an opportunity for rustlers and outlaws, including Baylor's rangers. Indeed, much of the violence blamed on Indians may well have been the work of these groups. Blaming outlaws for violence, however, did not play well politically; nor did it help keep Texans out of the killing fields of the Civil War. Governor Francis Lubbock (elected in the fall of 1861) used the perceived threat of Indian attacks to form "frontier regiments," which could not be sent out of state to fight—despite demands from Confederate officers and officials to do so. Many of these regiments proved ineffective and incompetent, as a small battle between Kickapoo Indians and Texans near modern-day San Angelo demonstrated. The well-armed Kickapoos, migrating to Mexico to escape drought and violence on the plains, routed the Texans and sent them fleeing for their lives.[12]

Yet the lawlessness, violence, and possibility of Indian attacks (real or imagined) so greatly terrified settlers that in places, the line of settlement retreated eastward more than 100 miles, and northwestern counties like Wise and Jack became untenable for settlers. Governor James Throckmorton (elected in

1866 but replaced following the Reconstruction Act of 1867) claimed that 162 Texans had been killed by Indian attacks with another 43 taken captive between May 1865 and July 1867. Caving to pressure from angry Texans like Throckmorton, federal troops adopted some of the techniques of the ranger groups, and the US Department of War reestablished and expanded a line of forts along the frontier, many of which had been abandoned during the war. The string of refurbished or new forts included Forts Richardson, Griffin, Concho, McKavett, Clark, and Duncan and, farther west, Forts Stockton, Davis, and Bliss.[13] While too far apart to prevent attacks, the forts would eventually provide jumping-off points for successful campaigns against plains Indians.

The encroachment of settlers and the decline of the bison threatened the independence of Comanche and Kiowa peoples on the southern plains. By the late 1860s a younger, angrier, and more violent generation of warriors arose, including Quanah Parker. These younger warriors had heard plenty of promises from federal Indian agents, but promises could not restore bison or feed hungry people. The resulting raids in 1868 were some of the most violent on record, a sure sign of the anger and desperation of some Kiowas and Comanches.[14]

As attacks continued, President Ulysses S. Grant found his administration under pressure to act, including from Texas's new Republican governor, Edmund J. Davis. Following a near miss at the hands of a Kiowa war party, General William Tecumseh Sherman (head of the US Army's Division of the Missouri, which essentially covered the West) felt compelled to act. Embarrassed and angered by the episode, Sherman came to agree with Texans' belief that the plains Indians needed to be destroyed, but only if the political situation changed.

He soon got his chance. An attack by a band of Kiowa on the Lee family, living along the Clear Fork of the Brazos, left the parents and a young child dead. Two daughters and a son were taken captive. This attack helped end efforts to arrive at a peaceful compromise and gave Sherman free reign to loose the dogs of war.

An empire that had flourished for a century, resisting the advances of Spaniards, Mexicans, and Texans alike, now faced an impossible prospect: resisting the advance of a powerful industrial nation that had essentially enveloped it. Up until this point, Americans' lack of interest in the Great Plains (the Great American Desert, as Pike and Long declared), the internal conflict of the Civil War, and Grant's peace policy had largely kept soldiers out of Comanche territory. That suddenly changed, and the Comanches and Kiowas now faced a powerful new foe. The United States Army, though still learning how to fight plains Indian peoples, nevertheless had imposing advantages in technology, resources, and communication. In the words of historian Pekka Hämäläinen, "The U.S. Army that moved into Comanchería was an adversary unlike any Comanches had encountered."[15]

The ensuing "Red River War," combined with drought and the decline of the bison, crippled the tribes of the southern plains. Invoking a total war strategy similar to the one employed against the South in the Civil War (not surprising since both Sheridan and Sherman had helped the Union Army develop the strategy), troops began to press closer and closer into Comanche territory and, when they located villages, to attack everyone. In the fall of 1871, Sherman sent Colonel Ranald Mackenzie and the Fourth Cavalry and two companies of the Eleventh Infantry deep into the Llano Estacado, the heart of the Comanche empire.[16] The following spring, Mackenzie with 300 soldiers located and attacked a village of Kwahada-Kotsoteka Comanches, killing 24 warriors and taking 124 women and children captive, as well as 3,000 horses.

Finally, on September 28, 1874, Mackenzie and his men attacked a village in Palo Duro Canyon. At the first sign of the soldiers, the Comanches, Cheyennes, and Kiowas in the village fled. Rather than pursue them, Mackenzie instead ordered the tepees, the food, and over a thousand horses destroyed. Deprived of their most important resource by the droves of buffalo hunters, hounded and hunted throughout their territory, and facing the prospect of starvation, the most militant of the Comanche bands and their allies had no choice but to surrender. Within a year, even Quanah Parker's band would give up and accept life in Indian Territory.[17] The conclusion of the Red River War spelled the end of a powerful Indian presence in Texas, just as residents and state officials wanted. The vast sea of grass would remain solely for white settlers. Texans embraced a Texas without reservations and largely without Indians. It had been a bloody half-century, with victims on both sides, but in the end Texans won. Prolonged violence had accomplished its goal of dispossessing the Indians and making all of Texas a white man's country.

Unlike Indians, Tejanos would endure. Nevertheless, Anglo-Texans wanted to ensure that the vast majority of Tejanos, who ostensibly had rights to citizenship and equal participation, remained in an inferior and subservient position. Violence and legal manipulation therefore played a role in marginalizing Texas's Tejano population.

With the exception of a smattering of sailors like Richard Henry Dana in California, Texas provided the first opportunity for Anglo-Americans to encounter the peoples of the former Spanish empire. These newcomers, in the words of historian Arnoldo De León, "saw very few redemptive attributes in the Tejanos; and aside from patronizing compliments about hospitality, courtesy and other amenities, their remarks and opinions tended toward disparagement."[18] Anglo-Texans denounced Tejanos for their often mixed-race ancestry, their dark skin, the primitive conditions in which they lived, their alleged lack of ambition and work ethic, and their supposed savage cruelty and sexual depravity. Earlier in the nation's history, African Americans and American Indians had been accused of possessing many of these same negative attributes. Indeed, upon encountering a new dark-skinned population, Anglos attempted to force Tejanos into familiar categories of non-whites and to marginalize them as a racial "other."[19] These native Texas Mexicans became "foreigners in their native land," fewer in number, handicapped by a language barrier, and increasingly despised by the incoming population of Anglos.[20] By denying whiteness to the vast majority of Tejanos, Anglo-Texans could feel justified, even relieved, in placing them in a subservient position. The problem, however, lay in the Tejanos' unwillingness to stay in that position. The tool most often employed to affect their subservience would be violence.

Tejano men in particular became the target of violence. Texans accused these men of being loyal to Mexico rather than Texas and of opposing slavery. Anglo-Texans sometimes attacked them simply because Tejanos owned things the newcomers wanted. This violence originated at the dawn of Texas independence—despite the assistance and leadership of Tejanos like Juan Seguín during the revolution.

On many occasions Anglo-Texans had driven Tejanos from their homes on the flimsiest of pretexts, but the fear of Texas Hispanics aiding in a slave rebellion in Colorado County in the fall of 1856 aroused a particularly violent response. Slaves in the county, authorities suspected, were working with local Tejanos to organize and lead a slave revolt. In the dark of night, slaves on several plantations would rise up and murder all Anglo men and children, sparing only the women to use for their own nefarious purposes. Following this bloody assault, the fugitives and their Tejano allies would fight their way to Mexico. In response to this feared insurrection, local authorities arrested all Hispanic Texans in the area and gave them five days to leave the county. The black leaders of the plot faced a sterner punishment: 3 were hanged, over 200 were whipped, and 2 were beaten to death.[21] The fervor over the plot exposed Anglo fears of violence, distrust, and rape that underlay ordinary existence. Slaves and Tejanos, both supposedly violent and sexually depraved, might live in close proximity, but they could never really be trusted.

Suspicion of the Tejano population in the state endured throughout the nineteenth century and well into the twentieth century, and the task of dealing with the perceived threat of their treachery and deceit fell to the Texas Rangers. While Anglos have long celebrated the Rangers as larger-than-life heroes, Tejanos and Mexicans had a very different view, seeing the group as staunch defenders of white supremacy who indiscriminately lashed out at innocent people because of the color of their skin.[22] The early, all-volunteer rangers certainly ran the gamut, from brave and heroic to those who did little more than parade around in boots and a hat and finally to those, like Baylor's men, who hid behind the legitimacy of the "ranger" idea but acted little better than common outlaws.

In the turbulent 1870s, the state revived and professionalized the Texas Rangers, transforming them into the statewide law enforcement arm of the Texas government. Like all law enforcement entities, the Texas Rangers strove to protect their communities and those communities' values. Given that white supremacy was a community value, it is not surprising, then, that the Texas Rangers fought in defense of it. In an era of heightened racial tension, an era redolent with violence, the Rangers walked a fine line between legitimate law enforcement and vigilantism. Fears of Mexican raiders and the "terrifying image whites conjured up of cruel Mexicans" justified Ranger attacks on and intimidation of Tejanos, especially in the Rio Grande valley.[23] Certainly, many incidents of Ranger violence against Hispanics occurred, as illustrated in numerous crackdowns. Once every generation or so, Rangers lashed out violently against Tejano and Mexican residents of the border, attacking both suspected criminals and civilians—the line between guilty and innocent often became too fine for the Rangers to distinguish.

In 1859 Rangers targeted Juan Cortina and his supporters. The trouble began when Cortina wounded an Anglo sheriff in Brownsville after the sheriff called him a derogatory name, but underlying tensions transformed the incident into a larger social movement. Cortina and his growing number of supporters denounced the theft and violence directed against them and demanded real rights and justice. Anglos, however, saw Cortina and his followers as outlaws and ungrateful degenerates who deserved stern punishment. Suspicion continued through the Civil War years (many Tejanos faced accusations of disloyalty to the Confederacy, and some paid with their lives). The following decade, the Rio Grande border became a killing field over the rights to unbranded, maverick cattle. Anglo ranchers claimed the cattle for themselves and accused Tejanos of rustling the animals and moving them into Mexico.

One of the most violent and bizarre episodes occurred near El Paso, Texas, in the 1870s and involved, of all things, the control of salt. For decades Paseños—Mexicans and Mexican Americans living on either side of the Rio Grande near modern El Paso/Juarez—had harvested salt from the Guadalupe Salt Lakes to use in cooking and preserving food and as an item of barter. Anglo entrepreneurs, however, harbored grander and more profitable visions for the lakes. Vast amounts of salt aided in the smelting of silver, and great silver strikes dotted the West in the 1870s. Seeing a way to profit from this growing market, Austin banker George B. Zimpelman and his son-in-law Charles Howard asserted a legal claim to the lake in 1877—ignoring older claims and habits of area residents. Zimpelman and Howard demanded that Paseños pay for the salt they took from the lakes. Sides formed quickly along ethnic and class lines, with Anglo business interests and their supporters on one side and Hispanic residents on the other. The Texas Rangers and the local sheriff, Charles Kerber, supported Anglo claims to the area, while local Paseños took to the field to defend their rights. These peasant villagers proved more than able to defend themselves, having battled Apache Indians for decades and more recently fought against Confederate efforts to steal their produce and livestock.[24]

The dispute over salt grew and mingled with local politics. Finally, in 1877 Charles Howard was captured and nearly murdered by an angry Paseños mob. Escaping with his life, he vowed revenge on those he felt had caused the humiliating episode, most notably his political rival Louis Cardis, an Italian immigrant and competing businessman who drew support from local Hispanic residents. On October 10, Howard apparently murdered Cardis in a local store (he claimed the killing was self-defense).[25] In the wake of the killing, Anglo residents pleaded for protection from "an ignorant, prejudiced, and blood-thirsty Mexican mob."[26] The US military, however, stayed out of the grow-ing violence, prompting Howard to call for the intervention of the Texas Rangers. Finally, Texas governor Richard Hubbard responded and decided to send Texas Ranger John B. Jones to investigate the situation. Jones met with Paseños leaders but secretly began organizing a company composed mostly of Anglo-Texas Rangers, which he placed under the command of Lieutenant J. B. Tays. With Tays in charge, Jones left for Austin. Tays struggled to find enough Anglos to fill a twenty-man Ranger company and soon turned to recruiting a few Paseños he deemed trustworthy. In the end, according to his-torian Paul Cool, Tays's "detachment was a mixed bag of young and old, of Anglos and 'law-and-order' Paseños, of community pillars and man-killers."[27]

In December 1877 Howard, who had fled the area, returned. Protected by the Rangers and his friend Sheriff Kerber, he set out to stop the harvesting of salt on the lakes he considered his property. His party arrived in the town of San Elizaro on December 12, 1877. Accompanied by the Rangers, he strode into the stronghold of local resistance and demanded the arrest of those responsible for stealing "his" salt. Instead of complying with his demands, locals attacked Howard and his protectors. Under a cloud of gunfire, the men retreated to some nearby buildings and a siege began. Following nearly a week of the siege, the embattled band surrendered on December 17. After surrendering, Howard and two other men were summarily executed by the enraged rebels. The surviving but now unarmed and humiliated Rangers left town with their horses and nothing to show for their efforts.[28]

The deaths of the three Anglos at the hands of the mob brought an immediate response, with soldiers coming from several posts as well as an increased Ranger presence. Sheriff Kerber asked for other volunteers, and soon twenty-seven rough characters led by Grant County deputy sheriff Dan Tucker and John Kinney (the latter a rather notorious outlaw who would later feature in the Lincoln County War) came in from Silver City, New Mexico. Many of these men came in search of a paycheck and the opportunity to plunder. Tays and his Rangers, Sheriff Kerber, and an unknown number of other men began to terrorize the Hispanics of the area, raping, plundering, and murdering those residents unfortunate enough to cross their path. The arrival of federal troops finally calmed the violence, but tensions and anger endured for years.[29]

The bloody "salt wars," in which Tejanos stood up for their rights against those who sought to deprive them of their traditional resources, only to be crushed in an orgy of violence, was but one example of similar riots. A decade later a similar riot occurred in Alpine, Texas, another at Rio Grande City in 1888, and two riots in the city of Laredo in 1886 and 1899.

The Mexican Revolution, if anything, increased tensions and distrust between Anglos and Mexican Americans, as demonstrated in the 1915 "bandit war." This explosion of violence emerged from long-simmering tensions and the "Plan de San Diego," a conspiracy, perhaps supported by Mexican president Venustiano Carranza, to start a war along the US-Mexico border. The ostensible goal was to recapture territory lost in the Mexican-American War of 1846–48 and restore dignity to Tejanos who had long suffered under Anglo rule. Carranza apparently used this plan to hurt his enemy, Francisco "Pancho" Villa, in the northern border area. Most troubling for Anglo-Texans was the provision that called for the murder of any Anglo man over age sixteen. Essentially, the plan advocated an all-out race war in South Texas, and, regardless of how impractical, it exposed the distrust between Tejanos and Mexicans on one side and Anglos on the other. While the date of this fictitious uprising (February 20) came and went, the situation remained tense.[30]

Violence finally erupted in July 1915, as an armed force of Mexicans crossed the Rio Grande onto American soil. Texas Rangers, supported by volunteers and two dozen US cavalry troops, patrolled Cameron and Hidalgo Counties in search of the "bandits." On July 9 a foreman on the massive King Ranch killed one of the alleged gunmen. Three days later, at a dance near Brownsville, two Cameron County police officers, both Tejano, were gunned down, and on July 12 a band of gunmen robbed Nils Peterson's store near Lyford, Texas. On July 20 eighteen-year-old Bryan K. "Red" Boley died after being shot twice by an unknown Hispanic assailant. Paranoia grew to panic in the wake of Boley's murder, with Texas governor James Ferguson demanding an increase in federal troops—a request the government largely ignored, believing the governor had exaggerated the severity of the situation. With no other alternative, Ferguson used emergency funds to create a new Ranger company, Company D, and put Henry Lee Ransom—a lawman with a long record of suspicious assaults and shootings in his past—in command. Over the course of the next several weeks, murders and robberies continued, culminating in a battle at the King Ranch's Norias sub-headquarters on August 8, 1915. Outnumbered at least four to one, a handful of soldiers, members of law enforcement, and ranch hands fought off at least sixty of the militants. While it appeared inevitable that the defenders would eventually be overwhelmed, the death of the bandits' leader siphoned off the attackers' courage and ended the assault. Now realizing the severity of the situation, the federal government finally sent army reinforcements to help patrol the border, while Rangers launched search-and-destroy missions against suspected guerrillas as well as forcing Mexican refugees back across the river.[31]

Given the level of violence and tension along the border, the Rangers acted to the best of their abilities to protect property and lives, but racist attitudes and their zeal to punish the bandits invariably led to incidents that took their toll on innocent people. For example, following the attack on an elderly rancher, James B. McAllen, Rangers sought the assailants. Unable to locate those responsible, they instead shot two Tejano farmers who had reluctantly provided assistance to the Mexican gunmen. The worst extra-legal violence occurred between September 24 and 27, when fourteen Mexican and Tejano corpses turned up, alleged victims of the Rangers. In October, however, the "bandit war" ended when relations between the United States and Mexico improved after President Woodrow Wilson threw his support behind Carranza.[32]

In the years since the "bandit war," blame has fallen on the Rangers. To be fair, the Rangers responded to an unprecedented level of violence and the fear of an armed insurrection with measures intended to protect civilians. Moreover, every death of a Tejano or Mexican national has been attributed to the Rangers, obscuring the fact that other groups of Anglo vigilantes and law enforcement took the field and certainly bore some of the responsibility for the murders of innocent people.[33] Nevertheless, by targeting Hispanic residents of the border, in this case at least, the Rangers reified the views of their detractors as violent defenders of white supremacy.

At a fundamental level, the Rangers' actions in these various encounters reflected their society, a society that placed Indians, African Americans, and Hispanics in inferior positions. Keeping these groups in their place not surprisingly fell to law enforcement, especially the Texas Rangers; they could be either heroic or evil, depending on one's perspective. At the very least, since many of the people the Rangers apprehended were of Mexican descent, a deep and long-simmering distrust of the Rangers has endured.[34]

Like Tejanos and American Indians, African Americans also became the targets of violence, especially in East Texas. Prior to the Civil War, the important economic position slaves occupied meant they faced little organized violence (undoubtedly they faced a great deal of personal violence, both physical and psychological, as a way of keeping them in line). Certainly, rumors of slave insurrection were often met with massive retaliation, as the 1856 insurrection in Colorado County demonstrated. After the Civil War, however, the situation changed dramatically, and newly freed African Americans faced decades of horrific violence intended to deprive them of their hard-won rights and newfound status.

This violence originated from two main causes. First, Texas Democrats hoped to smother the Republican Party in the state, and open wounds between Union troops (occupying the South after the war) and Confederates still festered. African Americans and a small number of white Unionists played an important role in supporting the Republicans and their reconstruction efforts. Second, violence offered white supremacists a tool they could employ to keep African Americans in a subordinate status. Texas still needed its African American population, but keeping them in their place could preserve white supremacy. These goals and the use of violence to achieve them went well beyond Texas, encompassing all of the former Confederacy in the decade after the Civil War, but reconstruction and anti-reconstruction "redemption" efforts played somewhat differently in the Lone Star State.[35]

As in the rest of the South, Texas experienced the emergence of groups like the Ku Klux Klan. In the words of historian Kenneth W. Howell, "It is certain that the Klan and other terrorist groups were responsible for the murder and mayhem that plagued the state. Despite the best efforts of the Republican government in Texas, these groups continued to wreak havoc on blacks and white Unionists."[36] East Texas in particular became a killing ground as the Klan and other groups swept through the area, intimidating and killing anyone who opposed them. Texas also became home to a large number of white Democrats who had left the Deep South in search of a new start. These newcomers helped ensure that the Democratic Party would have no difficulty in reasserting control over Texas, which it accomplished by 1873. However, blacks comprised the majority of the population in many of the cotton counties in East Texas, and, if they were allowed to vote unmolested, these areas would remain Republican. Violence therefore endured in these counties long after the statewide "redemption" of the Democratic Party.[37]

Texas, however, differed from other former Confederate states in many important aspects, for it straddled the boundary between South and West, one bowlegged boot in each region. During the turbulent years of Reconstruction, Texans still faced the possibility of Indian attacks on frontier settlements. The relatively unpoliced frontier and international border with Mexico also gave outlaws and other opportunists plenty of room to operate. A few thousand federal troops could not patrol such a vast territory. Further, to the best of their abilities, African Americans, American Indians, and Tejanos fought against repression in the state, making the era of Reconstruction, in the words of Arnoldo De León, "the most violent in Texas history. During this time, Central Texas was embroiled in a wide variety of violent episodes growing out of troubles from the Civil War and Reconstruction, outlaw activity, vigilantism, community feuds, agrarian radicalism, and political agitation . . . It was in this era that the colored thread of multiracial society posed the greatest challenge to white racial order."[38] Smothering that challenge and thus preserving white supremacy and therefore the white man's West became paramount.

Certainly, anti-black violence reached its worst manifestations in East Texas, the section of the state with the highest population of African Americans, but the attitudes forged in the Cotton Belt made their way to the Texas frontier. To lessen confrontations between Anglo-Texans and black soldiers, the US Army stationed these "buffalo soldiers" at frontier outposts like Fort Concho, near San Angelo, Texas, and Fort McKavett, near Menard, Texas. Buffalo soldiers, in fact, occupied forts throughout the West, but they nevertheless faced the most animosity from Texans, who viewed them as racially inferior symbols of the occupying federal government and the hated Republican Party.

Repeatedly throughout the 1870s, black soldiers died at the hands of white frontiersman. In 1870 Private Boston Henry died in a confrontation with John Jackson, a white man living near Fort McKavett. As Jackson fled the scene, he shot and killed Corporal Albert Marshall and Private Charles Murray. Eventually apprehended, Jackson faced trial for the trio of murders, but the white jury quickly acquitted him of any wrongdoing. Two years later, two more soldiers died in an ambush near Rio Grande City, Texas. A grand jury indicted nine men, with one brought to trial. This lone defendant was also acquitted by the jury.[39]

Two of the worst and most dangerous episodes of violence between soldiers and Anglo-Texans occurred in San Angelo in 1878 and 1881. A group of rough cowboys and buffalo hunters tore a black sergeant's stripes off his uniform in a local watering hole. In retaliation for this humiliation, angry black soldiers entered the saloon, and both sides quickly opened fire. During the battle, one white hunter died. Nine troopers faced prosecution and one, William Mace, received the death penalty.

Three years later, on February 3, 1881, a local sheepherder named Tom McCarthy murdered a black trooper in a San Angelo saloon. Soldiers soon apprehended the assailant and turned him over to the sheriff. Sheriff Jim Spears set McCarthy free, pending an examination trial. Enraged by this and numerous other slights, the soldiers posted a handbill in the town declaring: "We, the soldiers of the U.S. Army, do hereby warn the first and last time all citizens and cowboys, etc., of San Angelo and vicinity to recognize our right of way as just and peaceable men. If we do not receive justice and fair play, which we must have, some one will suffer—if not the guilty the innocent. 'It has gone too far, justice or death.' "[40]

A group of soldiers crossed the Concho River and entered the town, searching for McCarthy. Colonel Benjamin Grierson, the commanding officer of Fort Concho (and a Union war hero), sent a detachment to bring back his angry men, promising them that McCarthy would stand trial.

McCarthy was, in fact, held without bond the following morning, and tensions may well have abated at that point had not an unfortunate case of mistaken identity occurred. Tom McCarthy, it turned out, had a twin brother named Dave. Dave picked the wrong day to visit San Angelo. Someone spotted him and assumed that Tom had been released. When news of this sighting reached the soldiers, a large number grabbed their weapons and headed into town. Although no one died in the ensuing riot, the irate soldiers fired at least 150 rounds into area businesses. The troops dispersed when Grierson ordered bugle calls and drum rolls to indicate he planned to send a much larger group of soldiers to restore order.[41]

Meanwhile, Captain Bryan Marsh, commanding a detachment of Texas Rangers, warned Colonel Grierson that any soldier, black or white, caught leaving the fort and entering San Angelo would be shot.[42] Grierson, more to keep the peace than out of fear of facing fewer than two dozen rangers, temporarily confined his men to their barracks, and tensions cooled. McCarthy, after being indicted and transferred to Austin for trial, was absolved of any wrongdoing. These incidents proved that no white man would be convicted of killing a black soldier, an injustice that no doubt lingered in the minds of black troopers.

Tensions between white Texans and black soldiers seemed to cool through-out the 1880s and 1890s, perhaps because of the end of Reconstruction and the rigid imposition of Jim Crow. The years of relative calm, however, came to an end with the nineteenth century as long-simmering tensions between civilians (both Anglo and Hispanic) and black soldiers resurfaced. In March 1899, in the south Texas city Laredo, officer José Cuellar severely beat a black soldier for associating with a Hispanic woman, causing soldiers thereafter to travel in groups and carry weapons. That fall another officer, Willie Stoner, attempted to arrest a soldier for carrying a butcher knife but was prevented from doing so by the soldier's friends. Later that evening a group of per-haps 40 soldiers ambushed Stoner and beat him. Some local residents, both Anglo and Hispanic, demanded the removal of the soldiers.[43] On August 13, 1906, a group of armed whites opened fire on soldiers from the Twenty-fifth Infantry in Brownsville, Texas, in retaliation for the attempted rape of a white woman by a black soldier. Only one man perished in the gun bat-tle, but, following a decision by President Theodore Roosevelt, 167 troopers were kicked out of the army for not revealing the identity of the alleged rapist. Eleven years later, in the East Texas city of Houston, a riot between black soldiers and white law enforcement left 20 people dead, including 15 whites (5 of whom were policemen), 1 Tejano, and 4 black soldiers. One hundred and eighteen soldiers faced court-martial for the incident. Nearly 30 received the death penalty, another 53 others received life terms, 7 were acquitted, and the remainder received sentences of varying lengths. Justice in Texas proved anything but colorblind, and not even a uniform could pro-tect someone from the effects of violence.[44]

Whiteness provided an intellectual justification for the treatment of all these groups, and, indeed, even poor Anglo sharecroppers faced opprobrium as somehow less than fully white. In the early twentieth century some wealthy Anglo-Texans pondered sterilization for poor whites. Edward Everett Davis, a researcher active in the 1920s and 1930s, condemned cotton agriculture for attracting blacks, Mexicans, and inferior whites to Texas. His novel *White Scourge* posited that both cotton and inferior whites were a "white scourge" on the state's culture and society. The historian Neil Foley, playing off the title of Davis's novel, suggests that the real scourge was the idea of whiteness itself, an idea that conveyed and justified privilege and power to a select few.[45]

Anglo-Americans, the vast majority of whom entered Texas from the slave-holding South, encountered a multiethnic and racial society in Texas and, not surprisingly, set out to impose a color line between themselves and "non-white peoples." In the end, they attained nearly complete control over the state. Jim Crow laws kept African Americans in a subservient position, and a kind of de facto segregation kept Tejanos down as well. American Indians, whose presence had long shaped Texas, were forced north to Indian Territory, leaving behind only place names and ghosts. Anglo-Texans' control of the political system aided in this conquest, but violence ultimately allowed for the imposition of whiteness in Texas, and because of it Texas truly became a white man's country.

Like Texas, California seemed destined to figure prominently in the future of the United States, and, like the Lone Star State, it had a preexisting and prob-lematic population of American Indians and Hispanic peoples. Unlike Texas, however, the transformation of California into a place dominated by Anglo-Americans occurred at a meteoric pace. The hopes and appetites unleashed by James Marshall's discovery of gold in the winter of 1848 at John Sutter's sawmill created a situation in which violence would be used against anyone standing in the way of a hundred thousand prospectors' dreams. Given that California had only recently passed into American control, the area's con-siderable population of Californios (Hispanic Californians) and American Indians now found themselves in these prospectors' way—their land claims, their traditions, their legal rights, and, in the case of Indian peoples, their lives were of little interest to these newcomers. In the frenzied atmosphere of desire and greed unleashed by golden dreams and with rudimentary legal institutions to check the worst of human nature, it is not surprising that many Anglo-Americans relied on violence to secure their piece of California.

The terrible story of the fate of California's Indian population is well-known to most students of western American history.[46] Vilified as "unciv-ilized savages" who served no purpose and represented only an obstacle to progress and riches, California Indians faced devastating disease outbreaks, enslavement, political disfranchisement, forced exile on the margins of soci-ety, and a state-sponsored policy that sanctioned hunting them as little more than vermin.[47] Anti-Indian racism, obviously, was far older than the United

States, but Anglo-Americans singled out California's Indians with a level of scorn and disgust almost unprecedented in American history.

Many Indian peoples in the area survived traditionally by digging roots, a subsistence strategy that demonstrated to Anglo observers their overall laziness and supposed savagery and gave rise to the derogatory nickname "diggers" to describe these people—a name that described their activity and degeneracy and certainly hinted at another commonly used term for African Americans.[48] Indeed, "diggers" and "niggers" shared a common blackness that marked them as inferior in white eyes. Anglo-American observers decried their filthy appearance; their dark, almost black complexions; and their supposedly animal-like behavior—blackness, of course, represented the polar opposite of whiteness and was even less desirable than the noble "red" of the supposedly more attractive Indian peoples.[49] Hinton Rowan Helper, in his 1855 book *Land of Gold*, typically characterized the digger Indians as "filthy and abominable," concluding that "a worse set of vagabonds cannot be found bearing the human form."[50] Men, he continued, did little work, and the gathering of grasshoppers and roots fell to the women—a gender division that again demonstrated supposed Indian inferiority. California Indians, devouring insects and scraping for roots with sticks, in short, did not mesh with the romantic, noble savages of the Great Plains, who, despite their savagery, hunted and fought on horseback—the world would hardly miss such useless creatures, or at least that seemed the inescapable conclusion from observations like Helper's. Nor could California Indian peoples, who lived in very small bands, mount the spectacular resistance plains Indians peoples attempted, although they did try to fight back as best they could.

The arrival of Americans to the California goldfields and the overall conquest of the area proved catastrophic to indigenous peoples. The pre-contact Indian population of California totaled approximately 300,000, but by 1848 that population had declined, mostly from disease, to 150,000. The Gold Rush of the 1850s brought a population apocalypse as the remaining Indian population plummeted by over 80 percent, to around 30,000. Disease, dispossession, and homicide lay behind the demographic collapse.[51]

In the early years of the Gold Rush, settlers desired Indian labor as an antidote to the chronic labor shortage that plagued the newly acquired land. Indians had, in fact, long labored for Mexican economic and religious elites, and, indeed, until the massive influx of people following the discovery of gold, Indians offered one of the only large labor pools in California—a fact not lost on men like John Sutter. Sutter, for example, employed Indians to perform a variety of tasks, including harvesting his wheat crop, in the years before and after the discovery of gold. While Sutter paid them in currency and goods, he also relied on violence to maintain the loyalty and subservience of his Indian workforce. He occasionally whipped, jailed, and even executed Indians who disobeyed his orders.[52] Sutter's abuse of Indians foreshadowed the coming problems of the Gold Rush.

The dismal treatment of Indians received official sanction with the California legislature's passage in 1850 of An Act for the Government and Protection of Indians, an Orwellian title for an act that essentially allowed whites to coerce "unemployed" Indians into laboring for only food and clothing. Since few Indians fit the category of "employed" in the conventional sense, essentially, any Indian could be pressed into service. Many found themselves working for little or no food, and Indian children in particular became victims of kidnappers who sold them as slaves. In Northern California during the first two years of the rush, some miners forced hundreds of Indians to labor in the placer diggings. Newer miners, jealous of the extra labor Indians provided, systemically murdered them in an effort to drive this labor force off the diggings, a strategy that ultimately proved effective.[53] Being forced to labor as slaves by some miners, only to be attacked by other miners, illustrated the wretched and hopeless condition of these Indian laborers.

By the early 1850s California Indians found themselves increasingly pushed to the margins of society, and their traditional subsistence strategies became untenable as mining destroyed salmon runs, feral pigs consumed the acorns many Indians relied upon, cattle replaced wild game, and miners tore up the land. Stealing livestock therefore became one of the only ways to stave off starvation, but inevitably it brought swift and powerful retaliation. When Indians killed livestock, whites responded with raids that usually killed Indians.[54] California's Indians, Hinton Rowan Helper predicted, "must melt away before the white man like snow before a spring sun. They are too indolent to work, too cowardly to fight."[55] Indeed, Helper continued, once their labor was no longer necessary, whites would have no use for them, and, inevitably, their penchant for stealing would lead to their extermination. "Some of these miserable people," he blithely explained, "have been cruelly butchered by the whites for indulging their propensity to make free with other people's property." Rather than condemn murder as a punishment for minor transgressions, Hinton laughed off the cruelty as a side-effect of progress and blamed the victims for their own murders. Inevitably, he concluded, California's Indians would be crushed under the "advancing wheels" of civilization.[56] Indeed, Helper's prediction had already started to come to pass.

While overmatched and scattered federal forces mostly tried to keep the peace, the majority of conflicts with Indians involved volunteer vigilante groups and state-sponsored militias. On October 25, 1850, California's first governor, Peter Burnett (who recall also championed black exclusion in both Oregon and California), authorized El Dorado County sheriff William Rogers to call up "two hundred able bodied Militia" to locate and punish Indians who had been preying on cattle in the area. Over the next several weeks, Rogers and his men waged a series of attacks on Indians (most likely Miwoks) and claimed to have killed more than a dozen. The expedition, however, proved too expensive, and Burnett, on the advice of Brigadier General William M. Winn, commander of the state militia, ended the expedition.[57] The governor remained convinced that Indians posed a threat to Californians. In his message to the state legislature in January 1851, Burnett explained that settlers could not tolerate Indian raids on their livestock because the raids invariably hurt them financially. Since Indian raids would never stop, "A war of extermination will continue to be waged between the races until the Indian race becomes extinct," the governor argued.[58] Despite the fact that he resigned as governor soon after, Burnett's call for genocide did not go unheeded.[59]

From the late 1840s through the 1860s, California's Indian peoples became the target of indiscriminate and widespread attacks at the hands of white vigilantes. One of the first major attacks occurred in 1849 at Clear Lake. A group of Pomos, who had been virtually enslaved by two whites, Andrew Kelsey and Charles Stone, struck out against their tormenters and murdered them. In retaliation, a group of 75 volunteers attacked a Pomo village, killing nearly all its inhabitants. In 1853 whites from Crescent City fell upon a Tolowa village and again spared no one.[60] These attacks marked only the beginning of a longer war of extermination.

Some of the most egregious attacks occurred in Humboldt and Mendocino Counties in northwest California. The New York *Century* published an article in May 1860, which was reprinted in the San Francisco *Bulletin*, on a series of attacks on Indian villages in Humboldt County. The paper noted, "The [white] perpetrators seem to have acted with a deliberate design to extermi-nate the Indian race. Their butchery was confined to women and children, the men being absent at the time."[61] A December 1860 attack by local vigi-lantes killed more than two dozen Indians. The *Bulletin* devoted a great deal of coverage to the slaughter of 200 Indians in February 1860 in Humboldt County. In response to the paper's condemnation of the attack, Humboldt County sheriff Barrant Van Ness argued that the attack was justified given the losses stockmen had endured in addition to the death of rancher James Elleson, ostensibly at the hands of Indians. Finding federal soldiers unwilling or incapable of stopping Indian depredations, Ness explained, stockmen had no choice but to form a militia force. "Now," he explained, "they are heavy tax-payers, and they are losing all they possess. So, they get desperate, and perhaps are prompted to deeds of desperation."[62]

Major Gabriel J. Raines of the US Army filed a report with the assistant adjutant general denouncing the attack as unprovoked. Visiting the site of the massacre, he "beheld a spectacle of horror, of unexampled description— babes, with brains oozing out of their skulls, cut and hacked with axes, and squaws exhibiting the most frightful wounds in death which imagination can paint—and this done . . . without cause . . . as I have not heard of any of them [white settlers] losing life or cattle by the Indians. Certainly not these Indians, for they lived on an Island and nobody accuses them."[63] The events of the "Mendocino war" attracted the attention of the California legislature, which set up a Special Joint Committee to investigate the attacks. The committee's report concluded, "Accounts are daily coming in . . . of the sickening atrocities and wholesale slaughters of great numbers of defense-less Indians in that region of the country."[64] The legislature did nothing to stop these attacks.

At least 8,000 California Indians met a gruesome fate at the hands of various bands of white vigilantes and militias in the first two decades of California statehood.[65] As the historian Richard White has observed, while extermination of Indian peoples was never the official policy of the United States, on occasion Anglo-Americans "could put [genocide] into practice," and indeed in California they largely succeeded.[66]

Those Indian peoples who survived disease, starvation, and murder found themselves forced onto California's cultural and geographic margins. Efforts to set aside reservations for Indians began as early as 1851 with the arrival of a three-person federal commission. Three federal officials—Redick McKee, George Barbour, and Oliver Wozencraft—negotiated a series of treaties with California Indians, setting aside over 6.5 million acres on eighteen reservations, but at the request of California's congressional delegation the treaties went unratified.[67]

Leaving millions of acres in the hands of Indians would never be palatable to land-hungry Anglo-Californians, and almost immediately the treaties ran into trouble as state officials turned against the treaty process. The California state legislature voted against the treaties and asked the state's congressional delegation to lobby against their ratification. Following the defeat, another effort was undertaken to create five reservations, each of which was not to exceed 25,000 acres. By 1869 only three reservations had been created: Tule Lake (which replaced the reserve at Tejon Pass), Round Valley, and Hoopa Valley.[68] The vast majority of the state's Indian population existed without any form of federal protection, surviving as best they could in a hostile world.[69] In the coming decades they endured this legal twilight, scrounging for work and food on the margins of society.[70] The dominant white population had made it abundantly clear that Indians had no place in California's white society.

Hispanics, though not as severely mistreated as the Indian population, nevertheless faced widespread discrimination and hostility in California. At first the Gold Rush seemed a potential windfall for the Californios, Mexicans, and Chileans who found themselves in a perfect position to benefit from these discoveries, given their close proximity and the relative ease with which they could make the journey to California, especially when compared with the arduous transit Anglo-Americans in the eastern United States faced. However, these various Hispanic miners quickly found themselves battling against Anglo miners and leaders who sought to force them off their claims and place them in an inferior status. According to historian Susan Johnson, "Anglo-American opposition to Mexicans in the mines took three basic forms: individual incidents of harassment; mining district 'laws' that excluded Mexicans and other non-US citizens from particular areas; and a statewide foreign miner's tax, approved in 1850, that charged foreign miners twenty dollars a month to work the placers."[71] In a blatant violation of the terms of the Treaty of Guadalupe Hidalgo, which specified that former citizens of Mexico would be extended citizenship in the United States, Californios had to pay the foreign miner's tax, despite having lived in California for their entire lives, while most European and Australian miners did not pay the tax.[72] The message rang clear: California's gold belonged to whites only.

Hispanic and Chinese miners, subjected to the foreign miner's tax, also found themselves the targets of violence intended to chase them away from the goldfields completely. By the early 1850s Anglo miners in Calaveras and nearby counties began to clear out Hispanic settlements, claiming that they provided shelter and support to bandits like the famed Joaquin Murrieta. An armed vigilante group attacked the largely Hispanic "Yackee Camp" (named after the Yaqui Indians who first established it). They promptly lynched one Mexican man, whom they believed to be a bandit, before moving on to the nearby Cherokee Camp, where they lynched and shot two more Mexican men. As one miner explained, Hispanics were not welcome in the goldfields, and it was the duty of every American to take the Mexican's "horse, his arms" and tell him to leave the area. A meeting in the town of Double Springs ended with the resolution to make it "the duty of every American citizen . . . to exterminate the Mexican race from the county."[73] Such attacks solidified Anglo control over the goldfields and presaged the loss of land and control for Hispanics in California as they drowned in a deluge of new immigrants from the East who had no interest in preserving their tenure on the land.

Ostensibly citizens, Californios could vote, hold public office, testify in court, and own land. Yet Anglo-Americans soon recognized that sharp class divisions split the society of Mexican California. The ranchero elite occupied the top position of society, owning vast tracts of land. Claiming a white, Spanish ancestry, they comprised the *gente de razon* (people of reason). Smaller rancheros, farmers, artisans, and skilled laborers occupied a tiny middle class, and the bottom of Mexican California's class system belonged to Indian laborers and mestizos (mixed Hispanic and Indian peoples). Many of these laborers functioned as slaves in all but name, and allegedly their lack of intelligence and fondness for menial labor made them *gente sin razon* (people without reason), who depended on the ranchero elite to protect them in similar fashion to the supposedly patriarchal arrangement between southern white landowners and African American slaves.[74] Racial differences therefore helped construct and reinforce the class system of old California. Not surprisingly, Anglos judged Indians and mestizos by their supposed blackness.[75] Significantly, their darker skins and inferior social status made them easy targets for violence, while the "whiter" and wealthier ranchero elites were largely spared violent attacks on their property or persons—although not always. The wealthy Berreyesa family, for example, lost their grant and saw three family members lynched by Anglos.[76] The rancheros rarely faced such violence, but they would nevertheless see their lands wrested from them by newcomers.

Since citizenship in the United States also remained tethered to notions of race, Californios, especially the elite ranchero families, bragged of a European, and thus a "white," ancestry. Claiming whiteness enabled elite Californios to better integrate into the new social order unleashed by the Gold Rush and California statehood. Anglo-Americans, however, never entirely accepted this assertion and argued that even the elite families of California society were inferior. Writers like Richard Henry Dana praised the beauty of Spanish women and their fair complexions while nevertheless denouncing them for a supposed lack of morals. Californio men as well supposedly lacked the vigor and ambition of Anglo-Americans, in the view of Dana and writers like Alfred Robinson in *Life in California*.[77] This lack of ambition and vigor justified Anglo conquest of the region, but the white identity of the elite also made Californio women acceptable marriage partners for ambitious Anglo men. These marriages could prove advantageous for both sides. Anglo men, thanks to their new wives, married into families with often extensive land-holdings, instantly making them wealthy and powerful. Mexican families often benefited from the political and business acumen of their new Anglo in-laws. Sociologist Tomás Almaguer observes that having an Anglo son-in-law helped when dealing with "unscrupulous lawyers, merchants, and others who preyed on the ignorance of the Californios."[78] A son-in-law could turn on his new family, however, taking control of the estate.

If greedy sons-in-law did not take the estates, many other avaricious new-comers were seeking to wrest control of valuable land from the Californio elite. Many of these families faced years of costly legal battles to maintain control of their land grants, despite the Land Law of 1851 in which Congress acknowledged the validity of those grants. In many instances the Californio rancheros won their cases but ended up losing control of their grants to bank-ers and even the attorneys they hired to defend them in court. In addition, squatters killed their cattle, destroyed their orchards, and lived on their land. Horace Carpentier, for example, swindled the Peralta family out of their

19,000-acre grant on San Francisco Bay, erecting the city of Oakland on his newly acquired land.[79] Within a generation of Anglos' arrival, most of the once powerful and proud ranchero elite no longer owned anything of value except their names. Overwhelmed by new immigrants, they joined other Californios and immigrants from Mexico as a shrinking minority of the population. In Los Angeles, Californios comprised over 82 percent of the population in 1850, but by 1880, confined to barrios, they had slipped to only 19 percent of the city's population.[80] Statewide, a similar situation prevailed. As early as 1850, as the first waves of Gold Rush immigration washed over California, Hispanics (both Californios and immigrants from elsewhere) accounted for only 11 percent of the state's total population. By 1900 they accounted for less than 2 percent of the population and trailed the American Indian and Chinese populations. Moreover, the bulk of the population congregated in Southern California, and the fairly equal sex ratio (roughly the same number of men as women) made them even less of a threat to Anglo-American male occupations than the Chinese.[81] Violence, deceit, and the sheer number of newcomers conspired to steal California from Californio control.

Anglo-Americans, relying on violence and the legal system, successfully wrested control of California from Indians and Hispanics. Simultaneous with efforts to defeat Indians and strip Hispanics of their land and status, Anglo-Americans perceived a new threat coming from across the ocean: the Chinese. Whites would again employ violence and legal manipulation to control what they feared had become a new Chinese threat.

The Chinese, like most immigrants, crossed the ocean to find opportunity. China had been torn apart by numerous factors, including European imperialism and the opium trade, famines, and warlordism. Few young Chinese men—especially the millions comprising the peasant classes—could expect any marked improvement in their fortunes. The discovery of gold in California and a steamer ticket across the Pacific, however, offered hope of a better life. Chinese migrants, most hailing from Guangdong Province, typically purchased tickets from unscrupulous credit brokers, who charged outrageous interest rates or demanded a share of the profits they made in the "Gold Mountain," but, given these young men's poverty, most accepted the bargain. Upon reaching California's shores, Chinese workers invariably took out more loans from Chinese merchants to pay for passage to the goldfields in the Sierras. In the words of Richard White, these "were free laborers [not coolies or slaves] who carried their own small mountains of debt to the Golden Mountain."[82] Mortgaged to hope, these Chinese migrants often had to pay off the cost of their passage before they could make money for themselves.[83]

Stepping off the boat on the shores of California brought these Chinese immigrants to a new world where they encountered a society dominated by Anglo-Americans. This society, according to the historian Najia Aarim-Heriot, "was an inegalitarian, multiracial society . . . [in which] competition for scarce resources, and an unequal distribution of power had shaped a two-tiered racial hierarchy, which in turn had shored up the establishment of white supremacy."[84] In other words, white Americans had grown to believe that they alone controlled the nation, with Indian peoples, African Americans, and Hispanics on the wrong side of the color barrier and therefore confined to subservient and inferior positions in society. Whiteness made these groups an "other" and provided a precedent for circumscribing the position of the Chinese. The categorization of non-white instantly made the Chinese foreign outsiders, and Anglo-Americans feared their continued presence in the United States would only "lead to greater [racial] heterogeneity and latent racial strife," according to Aarim-Heriot.[85]

Much of the fear over the presence of the Chinese stemmed from their economic potential. Indians, Californios, and African Americans lacked the numbers to effectively challenge white supremacy in the state, but with a seemingly endless supply of people coming from the world's most populated nation, the Chinese posed a threat. Economically, the Chinese offered the potential labor source California had long lacked—one editor went so far as to compare the role of Chinese labor in the state to that of African labor in the South—but critics, especially those sympathetic to working-class whites, warned that too many Chinese immigrants would provide unfair competition and drive whites out of work. Working men and labor union activists came to fear the Chinese because of their alleged docility, their clannishness, and their apparent willingness to work for low wages. In the words of the historian Elliott West, the Chinese represented "free labor's ultimate nightmare: a race of automatons used by monopolists and labor bashers to undercut wages or cast out honest workers altogether."[86] Critics argued that their docility and lack of independence provided proof that the Chinese could not exist in the United States, since their very presence hurt free, working whites and threatened democracy itself. Other traits as well marked the Chinese as incompatible with American society, at least in the minds of their detractors. They, again according to West, "were America's most anomalous people. In language, dress, foodways, religion, and customs they seemed beyond the pale, and with their vast predominance of men, they lacked what all other groups, however different, had in common: the family as their central social unit."[87] Initially, this "vast predominance of men" developed from the nature of their immigration, but opponents of Chinese immigration soon realized the potential benefits of an all-male immigration and in fact encouraged it.

Chinese immigrants envisioned themselves as sojourners, coming to America for a brief period to make money on the Gold Mountain before returning to their homeland. The "sojourner myth" helped Chinese gold seekers break free of the "Sinocentric" belief that China stood at the center of the world, and thus no good Chinese man would ever leave his homeland. A sojourner might leave but would one day return. Facing mistreatment and told of their incompatibility with American civilization, the Chinese also held onto the sojourner myth to ease the sense of isolation caused by being strangers in a strange land; subsequently, most acted as foreigners with no intention to permanently set down roots.[88] The ubiquity of the sojourner myth largely ensured that the vast majority of Chinese immigrants remained male; moreover, married women traditionally served their in-laws and would not leave them behind to accompany a husband to California.[89] Moral Chinese women, in short, did not wander far from home, and good Chinese men did not stay away any longer than necessary.

The great gender imbalance (and Anglo-American taboos on race mixing) meant that Chinese men could find few sex partners in the Gold Mountain. Invariably, this led to the rise of Chinese female prostitution. Indeed, the vast majority of Chinese women in California worked as prostitutes. The 1860 census showed that of a total population of 681 Chinese women in San Francisco, 583 served as prostitutes. Excluding girls under twelve and women living with a male head of household, this meant that 96 percent of the Chinese women who worked for wages worked as prostitutes.[90] Being a Chinese woman in America, for all intents and purposes, meant being a prostitute—and that at least was the impression etched into the minds of whites. Prostitution, along with the equally scandalous vice of opium smoking, played into negative representations of the Chinese and supported the arguments of those opposed to Chinese immigration.[91] Taken as a whole, therefore, critics made a persuasive case that the Chinese did not belong in America and, as sojourners, did not want to stay permanently anyway.

The absence of women was certainly a result of Chinese cultural beliefs, but encouraging their continued absence became official government policy with the passage of the little-known 1875 federal Page Law. The brainchild of California congressman Horace F. Page, the legislation did not interfere with the immigration of Chinese men (who, after all, provided an important labor source for industries like the railroads) and instead focused on the immigration of Chinese women. Government officials, under the law, now possessed the power to prevent any Chinese woman from immigrating to the United States if they suspected her of being a prostitute or participating in any "lewd" or "immoral" activity. Whether intentionally or not, immigration officials effectively used their powers to prevent any woman, even married women, from entering the United States. This prohibition ensured that the temporary and overwhelmingly male character of Chinese immigration would continue, allowing corporations to hire men for low wages and house them in bunkhouses and other substandard arrangements that families would not tolerate. Further, without a population of women and children to support, the state would not need to offer educational facilities or other services. Finally, by denying the arrival of women, Chinese immigrants could not establish viable communities and could not have children who would, thanks to the recent ratification of the Fourteenth Amendment, be citizens at birth. Companies could therefore exploit Chinese labor, and ordinary Americans could rest assured that when employers no longer required their labor, these immigrants would return to China.[92]

Lacking citizenship and therefore legal rights, the Chinese became easy targets of violence, especially in the placer mining areas of the state. White miners had long used violence, intimidation, and the legal system to ensure their control of the best locations. As Aarim-Heriot notes, such tools essentially made "whiteness the test of access to the mines and to California at large."[93] The Chinese, like African Americans and Hispanics before them, were denied access to the best goldfields, and violence played a key role in protecting this white dominance. Forbidden from working the best areas, the Chinese occupied marginal diggings and areas that whites had already mined and abandoned as unprofitable—often purchasing seemingly worthless claims from white owners for inflated prices.[94] One Amador County newspaper noted that a group of Chinese miners successfully worked a creek that flowed through the town of Jackson. It was an area that had been "worked over at least a dozen times." Yet the Chinese miners made "from $2.50 to $8 per day" each.[95] Such results, though not typical, occurred throughout the goldfields, and Chinese miners continued to work the placer diggings as late as 1858, long after most white miners had given up on placer mining.

Often, however, Anglo-American miners drove the Chinese out of the placer diggings altogether. The first widespread violence against the Chinese presence in the mines occurred in May 1852 in the town of Columbia in Tuolumne County (where a few years earlier French, Mexican, and Chilean miners had vociferously opposed the imposition of the foreign miners tax). White miners in the town banded together to pass several resolutions barring the presence of Pacific Islanders and Chinese in the district around Columbia while attacking the monied interests ("shipowners, capitalists, and merchants") who imported these "burlesques on humanity" to turn a profit at the expense of free, working white men. Most ominously, they also resolved to form a vigilance committee to ensure that Chinese miners could not contest their placer diggings. The *Alta California* denounced these miners as "entirely without precedent or parallel in their hatred and hostility for the Chinese."[96] As the paper and the other defenders of the Chinese would soon learn, more than a few Anglo-Americans agreed with the people of Columbia.

In the same year, along the American River, sixty white miners attacked Chinese miners digging at Mormon Bar. As they ransacked the camp and beat the Chinese, a brass band played music, a riot apparently more enjoyable with musical accompaniment. Later, white miners in El Dorado County turned back any wagons or stagecoaches carrying Chinese passengers. Nearby, at Weber Creek, an angry mob burned the Chinese camp. The year 1852, therefore, set the tone for the way the Chinese would be treated in the California goldfields.[97]

Out of this came the imposition of a new foreign miners tax. Unlike the earlier 1850 tax, which had levied a substantial twenty-dollar-per-month tax, the new tax amounted to a more reasonable three dollars per month. This tax, though blatantly discriminatory, did not deter the Chinese. On at least two occasions, angry Chinese miners refused to pay the tax and attacked the tax collectors. On both occasions the tax collector survived, but at least one Chinese man perished. Most Chinese miners, however, paid the tax and went about their business. Anglo miners, for their part, complained that the real purpose of the tax had been to scare foreigners away from gold mining altogether, thus leaving whites firmly in control of the diggings, but the new tax, they felt, did not sufficiently punish the Chinese and thus did not force them out of gold mining as hoped. Instead, the tax remained, providing much-needed revenue for the young state of California.[98]

Chinese miners remained ever vigilant to the possibility of whites turning against them and forcing them out. Thus they relied on smaller mining equipment, preferring, for example, the portable gold rocker to the immobile but larger and thus more profitable sluice boxes white miners employed. These portable tools enabled them to flee a district very rapidly and set up a new site just as quickly. Seemingly less disturbing of surrounding soil and much less efficient and profitable than the sluice boxes, the gold rocker came to be seen as a sign of Chinese inferiority. White miners feminized the Chinese miners, laughing at their small tools "which they handled like so many women," scratching at the soil so feebly.[99]

Californian (indeed American more generally) attitudes toward these incompatible others left them on the outside. Controlling this immigration, circumscribing their places in society once they came here, and finally closing the nation to the Chinese entirely became goals of a growing and vociferous anti-Chinese movement. The first salvo against Chinese immigration had been the Page Act, but for foes of Chinese immigration, that act did not go nearly far enough. The 1882 Chinese Exclusion Act provided a legislative "solution" to Chinese immigration, barring nearly all Chinese people from entering the United States. Even after the passage of the act, violence—both small- and large-scale—remained, as riots in Seattle, Denver, and Rock Springs, Wyoming, illustrated.[100] This violence imposed lines of control that enforced the unbridgeable "otherness" of this most anomalous group of people.

Taken together, Texas and California demonstrate how violence reshaped the West and protected the privileges of whiteness. The virtual extermination of Indians from both states, coupled with the denial of political rights to Hispanics and Chinese—and in the case of Texas the imposition of slavery and, later, segregation—ensured that the rule of whites would remain unchallenged. Violence therefore proved a vital tool in the creation of the white man's West.

NOTES

1. Richard Maxwell Brown, *Strain of Violence: Historical Studies of American Violence and Vigilantism* (New York: Oxford University Press, 1975), 4–5.

2. Library bookshelves groan under the weight of all the books written about violence in the West, but a few of the most important studies include ibid.; Richard Maxwell Brown, *No Duty to Retreat: Violence and Values in American History and Society* (Norman: University of Oklahoma Press, 1991); Richard Slotkin, *The Fatal Environment: The Myth of the Frontier in the Age of Industrialization, 1800–1890* (Norman: University of Oklahoma Press, 1985).

3. See Shi Xu, "Images of the Chinese in the Rocky Mountain Region, 1855–1882," PhD dissertation, Brigham Young University, Provo, UT, 1996, 90–114.

4. Jean Pfaelzer, *Driven Out: The Forgotten War against Chinese Americans* (New York: Random House, 2007), xv–xvi.

5. The historian Liping Zhu argues that Chinese immigrants to the goldfields of the Boise Basin enjoyed economic success with relatively little violence or discrimination. See Liping Zhu, *A Chinaman's Chance: The Chinese on the Rocky Mountain Mining Frontier* (Niwot: University Press of Colorado, 1997), 4.

6. The full story of this interesting episode is told in Katherine Benton-Cohen, *Borderline Americans: Racial Divisions in the Arizona Borderlands* (Cambridge, MA: Harvard University Press, 2009).

7. Rev. A. B. Lawrence, "Introduction," in an Emigrant (pseudonym), *Texas in 1840, or the Emigrant's Guide to the New Republic* (New York: Arno, 1973), xvii, xxii

8. Gary Clayton Anderson, *The Conquest of Texas: Ethnic Cleansing in the Promised Land, 1820–1875* (Norman: University of Oklahoma Press, 2005), 5.

9. Quoted in ibid., 319.

10. Ibid., 320–22.

11. Ibid., 312–20.

12. Ibid., 318–40.

13. Robert A. Calvert and Arnoldo De León, *The History of Texas* (Arlington Heights, IL: Harlan Davidson, 1990), 157–58.

14. Anderson, *Conquest of Texas*, 340–50.

15. Pekka Hämäläinen, *The Comanche Empire* (New Haven, CT: Yale University Press, 2008), 333.

16. Ibid., 334.

17. Anderson, *Conquest of Texas*, 355–56; Hämäläinen, *Comanche Empire*, 335–41.

18. Arnoldo De León, *They Called Them Greasers: Anglo Attitudes toward Mexicans in Texas, 1821–1900* (Austin: University of Texas Press, 1983), x.

19. Ibid., 6–12.

20. Calvert and De León, *History of Texas*, 86.

21. De León, *They Called Them Greasers*, 53.

22. Two of the more laudatory works on the Texas Rangers are the classic by Walter Prescott Webb, *The Texas Rangers: A Century of Frontier Defense* (Boston: Houghton Mifflin, 1935); and Mike Cox, *The Texas Rangers: Wearing the Cinco Peso, 1821–1900* (New York: Forge, 2008). Two of the more recent critical works are Miguel Levario, *Militarizing the Border: When Mexicans Became the Enemy* (College Station: Texas A&M Press, 2012); and Arnoldo De León, ed., *War along the Border: The Mexican Revolution and Tejano Communities* (College Station: Texas A&M Press, 2012).

23. De León, *They Called Them Greasers*, 88.

24. Paul Cool, *Salt Warriors: Insurgency on the Rio Grande* (College Station: Texas A&M University Press, 2008), 2–3, 27–32.

25. Ibid., 114–17, 126–28.

26. Quoted in ibid., 131.

27. Ibid., 138–46.

28. Ibid., 188–200.

29. Ibid., 223.

30. Ibid., 210–21.

31. Ibid., 278.

32. Ibid., 278–91.

33. Ibid., 290.

34. Robert M. Utley, *Lone Star Justice: The First Century of the Texas Rangers* (New York: Oxford University Press, 2002), 290–93, discusses Hispanic attitudes toward the Rangers as well as differing historical interpretations of them.

35. On violence in the Reconstruction South, see George C. Rable, *But There Was No Peace: The Role of Violence in the Politics of Reconstruction* (Athens: University of Georgia Press, 2007); Allen Trelease, *White Terror: The Ku Klux Klan Conspiracy and Southern Reconstruction* (New York: Harper and Row, 1971).

36. Kenneth W. Howell, ed., *Still the Arena of Civil War: Violence and Turmoil in Reconstruction Texas, 1865–1874* (Denton: University of North Texas Press, 2012), 11–12.

37. Ibid., 16–17.

38. De León, *They Called Them Greasers*, 87.

39. Quintard Taylor, *In Search of the Racial Frontier: African Americans in the American West, 1528–1990* (New York: W. W. Norton, 1998), 175–77.

40. William H. Leckie, *The Buffalo Soldiers: A Narrative of the Black Cavalry in the West* (Norman: University of Oklahoma Press, 2003), 239.

41. Ibid., 239–40.

42. Cox, *Texas Rangers*, 315–16.

43. James N. Leiker, *Racial Borders: Black Soldiers along the Rio Grande* (College Station: Texas A&M University Press, 2002), 122–23.

44. Taylor, *In Search of the Racial Frontier*, 176–81.

45. Neil Foley, *The White Scourge: Mexicans, Blacks, and Poor Whites in Texas Cotton Culture* (Berkeley: University of California Press, 1997), 6–7.

46. See, for example, Clifford E. Trafzer and Joel R. Hyer, eds., *Exterminate Them! Written Accounts of the Murder, Rape, and Enslavement of Native Americans during the California Goldrush, 1848–1868* (East Lansing: Michigan State University Press, 1999); Robert F. Heizer, ed., *The Destruction of California Indians* (Lincoln: University of Nebraska Press, 1993); Albert L. Hurtado, *Indian Survival on the California Frontier* (New Haven, CT: Yale University Press, 1988).

47. Tomás Almaguer, *Racial Fault Lines: The Historical Origins of White Supremacy in California* (Berkeley: University of California Press, 1994), 4.

48. The best discussion of the origin and use of the term *Nigger* is in Randall Kennedy, *Nigger: The Strange Career of a Troublesome Word* (New York: Vintage, 2002).

49. Almaguer, *Racial Fault Lines*, 111–13.

50. Hinton Rowan Helper, *Land of Gold: Reality versus Fiction* (Baltimore: Henry Taylor, 1855), 268.

51. Hurtado, *Indian Survival*, 1.

52. Ibid., 57–59.

53. Richard White, *It's Your Misfortune and None of My Own: A New History of the American West* (Norman: University of Oklahoma Press, 1991), 339.

54. Ibid., 340.

55. Helper, *Land of Gold*, 272.

56. Ibid., 273.

57. Hurtado, *Indian Survival on the California Frontier*, 132–33.

58. Quoted in ibid., 135.

59. Not surprisingly, Burnett made no mention of this in his memoir, *Recollections and Opinions of an Old Pioneer* (New York: D. Appleton, 1880).

60. Almaguer, *Racial Fault Lines*, 122–25.

61. Quoted in Heizer, *Destruction of the California Indians*, 254.

62. Quoted in ibid., 255–58.

63. Quoted in ibid., 259.

64. Quoted in ibid., 126.

65. Ibid., 130.

66. White, *It's Your Misfortune*, 340.

67. Hurtado, *Indian Survival*, 137–38.

68. Ibid., 138–48.

69. Ibid., 141–48.

70. Charles Fletcher Lummis made one such group, the Warner's Ranch Indians, his pet project, helping establish a small reservation for them in Southern California. See Mark Thompson, *American Character: The Curious Life of Charles Fletcher Lummis and the Rediscovery of the Southwest* (New York: Arcade, 2001), 213–43.

71. Susan Lee Johnson, *Roaring Camp: The Social World of the California Gold Rush* (New York: W. W. Norton, 2000), 31–32.

72. White, *It's Your Misfortune*, 238.

73. Johnson, *Roaring Camp*, 36–37.

74. Almaguer, *Racial Fault Lines*, 47–48, 55.

75. Ibid., 55, 113.

76. White, *It's Your Misfortune*, 238; Almaguer, *Racial Fault Lines*, 65–68.

77. Almaguer, *Racial Fault Lines*, 52. See also chapter 2, this volume, for similar views of Hispanic men and women, especially those of Richard Henry Dana.

78. Ibid., 59.

79. White, *It's Your Misfortune*, 238.

80. Ibid., 240.

81. Almaguer, *Racial Fault Lines*, 70–71.

82. White, *It's Your Misfortune*, 193–94.

83. Almaguer, *Racial Fault Lines*, 154–55.

84. Najia Aarim-Heriot, *Chinese Immigrants, African Americans, and Racial Anxiety in the United States, 1848–82* (Urbana: University of Illinois Press, 2003), 7.

85. Ibid., 10.

86. Elliott West, "Reconstructing Race," in West, *The Essential West* (Norman: University of Oklahoma Press, 2012), 116.

87. Ibid.

88. Yanwen Xia, "The Sojourner Myth and Chinese Immigrants in the United States," PhD dissertation, Bowling Green State University, Bowling Green, OH, 1993, 1–4.

89. Benson Tong, *Unsubmissive Women: Chinese Prostitutes in Nineteenth-Century San Francisco* (Norman: University of Oklahoma Press, 1994), xvi.

90. Ibid., 94.

91. On the role of opium in shaping the immigration debate, see Diana L. Ahmad, *The Opium Debate and Chinese Exclusion Laws in the Nineteenth-Century American West* (Reno: University of Nevada Press, 2007.

92. George Anthony Peffer, *If They Don't Bring Their Women Here: Chinese Female Immigration before Exclusion* (Urbana: University of Illinois Press, 1999), 3–8.

93. Aarim-Heriot, *Chinese Immigrants*, 29.

94. Ibid., 36.

95. Quoted in Johnson, *Roaring Camp*, 243–44.

96. Ibid., 246.

97. Pfaelzer, *Driven Out*, 10–11.

98. Johnson, *Roaring Camp*, 248–49.

99. Quoted in ibid., 246.

100. White, *It's Your Misfortune*, 341–42.

CONCLUSION

The Limits and Limitations of Whiteness

Being white mattered in the West. Whiteness conferred status and gave people easier access to positions of power and privilege. Although the US Congress extended citizenship to some non-whites—Hispanics after the Mexican-American War and African Americans after the Civil War—it was still something not every group could achieve. Furthermore, in practice, Hispanics and African Americans were often denied equal treatment in society. Immigration had always been tied to whiteness, and by the first decades of the twentieth century the nation increasingly tried to stem the tide of immigration using race and ethnicity. Being considered white therefore gained one acceptance into American society.

The year 1924 was a signal year for American immigration history as the 43rd Congress set about outlining the limits of citizenship. In April the US Senate voted in favor of the bill that would redefine immigration into the United States and therefore the country's racial and ethnic makeup.[1] The Johnson-Reed Act (more commonly known as the 1924 Immigration Act) would alter the course of immigration for a generation. The law officially

DOI: 10.5876/9781607323969.c009

barred Japanese immigration and therefore all Asian immigration (which had largely stopped under the so-called Gentleman's Agreement in 1907). The act also established quotas of 2 percent of the number of foreign-born citizens of each European nationality. By 1927 the law called for a total quota of 150,000 immigrants who would be divided up in the same ratios as the national origins of white citizens in the United States.[2] This meant the admission of far fewer Southern and Eastern Europeans and many more Northern Europeans than were currently entering the nation. The result would be the preservation of a "desirable" Northern European racial stock for the nation.

Tatos O. Cartozian, a Portland, Oregon, rug merchant, knew this well. Cartozian, like many other immigrants, came to America in search of opportunity. He worked hard and became successful, and his years of struggling paid off when the government granted him US citizenship in 1923. It was a story repeated time and again in early-twentieth-century America, so common, in fact, that the rags-to-respectability story of immigrants became woven into the narrative of what it meant to be an American. Anti-immigrant hostility, however, had been steadily building in the first decades of the twentieth century. Racial restrictions on Asians, which began with the passage of the Page Law in 1875, became models for restricting immigration based on similar ethnic and racial standards.[3] Eugenicists like Charles Benedict Davenport and Madison Grant warned that the indigestible tide of immigration would smother the Anglo-American stock that had made America great. In the spring of 1924, as Congress debated the question of immigration and the possibility of immigration restrictions based on race and ethnicity, Cartozian found himself in federal court in Portland. He had committed no crime, but the government hoped to strip him of his citizenship on the grounds that he "did not come from the white race."[4]

Cartozian, of Armenian ancestry, found himself in the odd position of proving his whiteness. Attorneys for the United States argued that the framers of the US Constitution had been clear that citizenship could only be extended to "free white persons." The courts, in an earlier case involving an East Indian man, had concluded that Indians, as Asians, could be barred entry into and denied citizenship in the United States. Cartozian, a Christian Armenian, came from the historical borderland between Asia and Europe. Authorities therefore found it difficult to determine his race. His defense team, in an effort to prove his racial background, collected depositions from some of America's leading ethnologists: Paul Rohrbach, Roland B. Dixon, and Franz Boas. Each concluded that Armenians shared a European ancestry with ethnic groups permitted citizenship. The government countered, arguing that being white could best be determined by whether the "man on the street" considered a person white. The average American, the government's attorneys argued, would not consider an East Indian, Filipino, or Armenian to be white; the Founding Fathers, passing the first naturalization law in 1790, would have reached a similar conclusion.[5]

Cartozian explained to the Portland *Morning Oregonian*'s correspondent that he had never been discriminated against and that his brothers belonged to the Masons, a group that allowed only whites to become members. "The Armenians," he asserted, "are generally law-abiding people. They have been a Christian nation for more than 16 centuries. Those of them who are in the United States mingle on terms of equality with native Americans and frequently intermarry with them. We are loyal to the American government and value highly our American citizenship."[6]

In May 1924 the trial began. John S. Coke, the US district attorney prosecuting the case, introduced extracts from scientists and ethnologists that proved, he claimed, Armenians' Asiatic origins. Next he read extracts from the speeches of the Founding Fathers designed to show that they would not have considered Armenians to be white. The defense countered with testimony from several prominent Armenians, including Mrs. Otis Floyd Lampson, and members of numerous civic and benevolent orders that required all members to be white. Mrs. Lampson, an Armenian Christian, had immigrated to the United States to escape the Turkish genocide of 1919 and had taught in several private girls' schools. After turning down a position at Vassar, she decided to study medicine. While in medical school, she met and married her husband, a prominent Seattle surgeon. Many Armenians, she asserted, had blue eyes and light skin, clear indications of their whiteness.[7]

Earlier cases had not cleared up the issue of which groups could be classified as white. Between 1878 and 1952 (when Congress finally ended the practice of basing naturalization laws on race and ethnicity), fifty-two federal cases on the issue of immigrant racial identity made their way through US courts.[8] The courts heard seventeen of these cases between 1909 and 1916, a period of super-heated nativism. Of the seventeen cases, six involved Syrians, four East Indians, three Filipinos, one Armenian, one Japanese, and two German

Japanese. The courts, using the "man-on-the-street" approach, meaning that the legal standard of belonging to the white race depended on commonly held views of what being white meant, concluded that three of the Syrians were white while the other three were not; three of the four East Indians won, and the Armenian defendant also won. Results like these demonstrated that authorities faced complex problems in ascertaining whiteness.[9] As Ian Haney López asserts, the man-on-the-street standard in essence exposed the inherent social construction of race and the importance of law in circumscribing the limits of whiteness.[10] By the early 1920s, however, courts were continually contracting the geographic boundaries of whiteness, drawing a line around Europe. In *United States v. Thind* (1923) the court ruled that East Indians were not white.[11] However, in July 1925, a year after hearing the case, Judge Wolverton agreed with the defense and ruled that Tatos Cartozian was indeed white.[12]

As Cartozian defended his citizenship, a would-be prophet busied himself establishing his vision of a utopian society outside San Jose, California. William E. Riker dubbed his perfect society "Holy City." Riker founded his colony in 1919 on the idea of strict racial separation. Indeed, strict racial separation of whites from other races was one of the few consistent views Riker held. In a pamphlet for one of his unsuccessful bids for governor he declared, "California is a white man's home." Singling out Asians as the source of California's problems in the 1930s, he continued, "Their polluting undermining system of business must eternally stop in Our White Man's Home and besides this, they must keep their polluting hands off our White Race Women; they belong only to us White Race People." "Negroes and Orientals," he declared during his first gubernatorial campaign in 1937, should remain as "servants in our White Man's home and country."[13] Riker's Holy City never prospered, though at its peak at least 100 people lived there. He promised that people who stopped at Holy City would learn about the "world's perfect government," but in practice his society amounted to little more than a dictatorship, with Riker owning all of the land and property and making all political decisions, which he no doubt felt was perfect. The commune, located along a busy highway, soon grew into a roadside attraction that offered—in addition to Riker's version of political and religious enlightenment—an alcoholic soda pop stand, special healing spring water, a newspaper, a radio station, and a peep show of "ideal" women.

Once the desperation of the Great Depression gave way to World War II, Riker's idiosyncratic philosophy came into conflict with changing realities. He had been an outspoken supporter of Adolph Hitler, writing several letters of encouragement to der Führer during the 1930s. In 1942 the government charged him with sedition. Although the case ended in his acquittal, Riker never recovered and Holy City limped into the postwar years, its tourism base vanishing after the state rerouted the highway away from his utopian society / roadside attraction—a move he saw as a deliberate attempt to undermine the colony's economic survival.[14]

Cartozian and Riker could not have been more different. Cartozian simply wanted to be accepted as an American. Riker sought to limit the rights and privileges of citizenship (and salvation) to whites only, and his vision would remain on the fringe. Both men, however, understood the importance of whiteness in determining one's lot in life. States, railroads, and local boosters tirelessly promoted whiteness, encouraging the "right kind" of settlers, but despite their best efforts whiteness would never be the determining factor in the settlement of the region.[15] In addition, the region would never become the Anglo-American refuge those like Riker wanted. Yet both men existed within the larger society, a society that had been uncertain of what it would look like. Indeed, while whiteness never dominated the region, it did play a prominent role in determining the West's characteristics.

Racial considerations fed into Americans' perceptions of the trans-Mississippi West. Initially, many Americans saw the new Territory of Louisiana, acquired in 1803, as a possible dumping ground for Indians and African Americans, given its distance and isolation from the heart of the republic. Prominent Americans, including President Thomas Jefferson, entertained the idea of creating new territories populated entirely by free blacks or American Indians. Thus America might consist of a pure white eastern core with a frontier composed of civilized Indian tribes and free blacks who had been removed beyond the Mississippi River. "Civilized" Indians could be given more time to become like whites, and anomalous free blacks could be allowed to live as they chose and still be separated from whites. Perhaps, in fact, slavery itself could be ended and all blacks could go west to a black territory.

Beyond these territories of relocated eastern Indians and free blacks, the lands would remain the haunt of supposedly savage Indian groups. While

FIGURE 9.1. Tatos Cartozian with his daughters, April 14, 1924. Cartozian, an Armenian immigrant and businessman, went to court to defend his whiteness. His was but one of several cases fought over the boundaries of whiteness in the first decades of the twentieth century. *Courtesy, Oregonian* Collection, Oregon Historical Society, Portland; used with permission.

the federal government never attempted to create a territory for freed blacks, it undertook Indian removal during the Jackson administration in the 1830s. The nation wanted nothing more from eastern Indians than their land, but the labor of blacks had to be retained. Indian Territory did come into being, but the larger vision of an America geographically segregated by race never materialized. Even Indian Territory would not remain remote for long. In little more than a decade, Americans had acquired Texas, California, and the rest of the Southwest. Indian Territory, designed to be forever on the edge of the country, instead became the geographic center of a continental nation.

Further, the nation did not solve its racial dilemmas. Expansion, in fact, created new racial tensions and brought to the fore the issue of slavery and its expansion. This new West, however, differed markedly in environment from anything in the previous Anglo experience. Much of it was hot and dry, and, according to the leading scientific minds of the day, environment was the chief determinate of racial development. Anglo-Americans, as descendants of Northern Europeans, considered themselves the fittest, strongest race on the planet. This alleged fitness came as a result of the ancient struggle against Old Man Winter. This contest transformed them into strong, resourceful, hardworking people, the attributes needed for ongoing American and European domination of the globe. It seemed to follow that the native peoples of the West would be grossly inferior given the region's better weather. Americans considered the Indians savages, living off of whatever nature chose to give them. According to white commentators, the native Hispanics of the Southwest—residing in villages scattered from Texas to California—displayed the characteristics of racial degeneration that scientists like Samuel Stanhope Smith believed would result from settling in temperate climates. These descendants of once vigorous and proud Spanish conquistadors had grown weak and lazy from living too long in an environment that precluded struggle. Over time, almost every American observer of the nineteenth century claimed, Hispanics had degenerated into weakness, laziness, stupidity, deceitfulness, and superstition.

Americans who settled these lands might end up in a similar predicament. The scientists of the polygenic school tried to alleviate some of these fears, arguing that God created whites separately from the world's other races and therefore they would fare better, but not even these reassuring assessments could totally put to rest the fear that whites would degenerate racially if they settled in the West.

In the last third of the nineteenth century, as settlement continued apace, western proponents attacked assertions that settlement would lead to racial degeneration. The writer and magazine editor Charles Fletcher Lummis argued that California and the Southwest would not undermine white racial vigor. Instead, he countered, whites would advance to a state of development unprecedented in the history of the world simply because they did not have to struggle to survive. Their work ethic and ingenuity could instead be put in service of continued technological and material development. At the same time, he argued, it would also be healthy to occasionally rest and enjoy the blessings of a land of sunshine, the title, incidentally, of Lummis's magazine and chief vehicle for his crusade to elevate the status of the Southwest.

Another turn-of-the-century Californian took a slightly different tack. Joseph Pomeroy Widney argued that the roots of Engle-Americans (as he called white Americans) stretched back thousands of years to the nomadic tribes of the Asian steppe. There, in the grasslands of Central Asia, whites first developed. Over time, some of the descendants of the ancient Aryan horsemen moved into the colder, wetter environs of Northern Europe, but they carried, as a kind of race memory, those centuries of riding along the Asian plains. When they arrived in eastern North America, the Engle-Americans found a landscape that mirrored Europe's. Not surprisingly, therefore, they flourished. Two centuries after the Pilgrims landed on Cape Cod, Engle-Americans once again entered a new climate, leaving the East behind and heading west. According to Widney, this movement did not require Americans to adapt to an alien environment, since they carried their ancestors' experiences in their souls. Their arrival represented a return to the landscape of their genesis, this time to the Great Plains and the American West. Racial degeneration would not occur because the dry West resembled the Aryans' ancestral homeland—the Asian steppe. Both Widney and Lummis, therefore, actively tried to justify the settlement of the West and lay to rest the notion that the region was racially dangerous for whites.

Widney, Lummis, the California promoter Charles Nordhoff, and William Jackson Palmer, the president of the Denver and Rio Grande Western Railroad, also asserted the inherent superiority of the West's population compared with that of the East. Rankling at the characterization of the West—the youngest region of the country—as backward and underdeveloped, late-nineteenth-century westerners argued that the East better exhibited the undesirable characteristics of a true frontier. In eastern cities such as New York and Boston, immigrants from Southern and Eastern Europe annually poured through Castle Garden and, later, Ellis Island. These generally poor immigrants, westerners asserted, crowded into filthy, disease-ridden, lawless slums. Overwhelmed by these inferior hordes, Anglos struggled in vain to maintain their control of the levers of government and society, since, despite being not really white, these newcomers could nevertheless participate as equals in American democracy. In comparison, only the best, most talented, and wealthiest of these immigrants could escape the trap of tenements, slums, and political machines; these few migrated west, where they became desirable settlers alongside the region's dominant Anglo-Americans.

The cities and towns of the West, populated by the best old-stock Americans and a sprinkling of more recent immigrants, displayed a superior level of civilization and development, westerners claimed.

To be sure, the West had Indians, Hispanics, Chinese, and some African Americans, but none of these groups threatened Anglo-American dominance. American Indian peoples had been defeated and relegated to reservations located far from the region's growing cities and towns. Hispanics, though allowed citizenship, had little real power in most western states and territories. White Americans denied the Chinese citizenship, and legislation controlled their numbers, ensuring a small and largely powerless group. Finally, African Americans, as a result of their low numbers, wielded no collective power. Westerners celebrated the distinctiveness and romance the occasional Chinatown, adobe house, or Indian village gave to their region and lived without fear of losing their political and social domination.

Westerners like Lummis and Montana's Frank Bird Linderman even attempted to preserve the culture of these groups. Lummis and a number of Californians, including the author Helen Hunt Jackson, forged a romantic image of Southern California from the ruins of its Spanish past. Linderman saw a great deal of nobility in American Indians and sought to help protect their cultural traditions. An ardent opponent of the new immigrants, Linderman assailed the immigrant-heavy mining town of Butte as a blight on the social landscape, crusading for immigration restrictions. Indians, in his view, should be afforded a place in twentieth-century America, but not immigrants. Power played a key role in this debate. The comparatively powerless racial and ethnic groups of the West did not present the challenge to Anglo-American domination that European immigrants did in the East. The West evolved, therefore, into a kind of white racial paradise—or so Linderman, Lummis, and others claimed.

Although the white man's West was largely an intellectual construction, the brainchild of western defenders and developers, their claims reflected a partial reality. To be sure, historical, cultural, and economic processes worked to create the racial characteristics of the West, and they were too powerful for any group to control. The Southwest, for example, owed its high percentage of Hispanics to the old Spanish empire, with Texas and the territory acquired by the Treaty of Guadalupe Hidalgo accounting for virtually the entire Hispanic population of the country. It was this past that made the area so different and appealing to people like Lummis and Jackson. This presence persisted long after the region's conquest by the United States.

Yet when boosters and developers could exert power over the construction of place, they did so. For example, the railroads and their land offices created entire communities populated by desirable farmers, influencing in no small measure the settlement of the northern Great Plains. Granted enormous tracts of public land with little discernible population and therefore anemic demand for their services, the railroads enthusiastically encouraged settlers to come to their lands, embarking on elaborate and expensive advertising campaigns. The first railroad to actively recruit settlers to the lands along its line was the Illinois Central Railroad (IC), which began construction in the 1850s. Receiving the first land grant given to the railroads by the US government, the IC recruited Germans and Scandinavians to relocate. Soon, thousands of settlers converged on the area, giving it a distinctively Northern European and therefore white cast. These settlers eagerly left their European nations behind, propelled by a scarcity of land and prohibitive prices, and settled in Illinois. The IC preferred Germans and Scandinavians to the other major group then immigrating to the United States: the Irish. IC executives, like many Americans, considered the Irish too boisterous and unreliable but believed the Germans were hardworking, sober, and centered on family life. Thus the line encouraged Germans and tried to discourage the arrival of many Irish settlers.

Beginning in the 1870s, the transcontinental railroads faced the same problem as the Illinois Central but on a much larger scale. Their land grants in many cases amounted to millions of acres spread out across the West. Much of this land, especially on the northern plains, was still in the hands of Indians like the fearsome Lakota as the lines commenced construction. The government entrusted the US Army with the mission of breaking Indian resistance, thereby enabling widespread settlement, but the fact remained that the railroads would not have a market for their services in most cases until settlers could be installed on the open land. These settlers would then use the railroads to ship their produce to market and, in turn, rely on the lines to bring manufactured goods to them. The supply would, in effect, precede the demand.

Where, railroad executives wondered, could settlers be found? Several possibilities presented themselves. They needed experienced, hardworking farmers willing to leave behind their homelands and strike out for a new country. Several European groups seemed likely candidates, but African

Americans fit the bill as well. By the late 1870s, as the lines actively recruited settlers, thousands of African Americans abandoned the increasingly hostile and segregated South and struck out for the West. Despite having little capital or experience in dryland farming, the "Exodusters" nonetheless settled towns in Oklahoma, California, Colorado, and, most famously, Kansas. Yet despite the clear desire for African Americans to head west, the railroads did nothing to appeal to them, and in the case of the Kansas Pacific some actually went to great lengths to discourage them. Only in the case of the Louisville, New Orleans and Texas Railroad did a line encourage blacks to settle on railroad land, and this, significantly, on land in the Mississippi Delta. To be sure, African Americans lacked the capital to afford to travel in luxury on railroad lines or to buy large tracts of railroad-owned farmland, but the railroads did allow reduced passage over their lines for white settlers and even extended credit to them when necessary. The transcontinental lines overlooked an eager, close group of settlers and instead sought out European settlers, spending hundreds of thousands of dollars in the process. In doing so, they helped transform the West into a predominately white country.

The Northern Pacific Railroad opened offices in London and other Northern European cities, encouraging settlers from these nations. Immigration agents especially preferred the Mennonites, German-speaking pacifists who had emigrated to Russia. Accustomed to similar conditions on the Russian steppe, these experienced wheat farmers would likely thrive on the Great Plains, and numerous railroads—including the Northern Pacific—courted them, sending representatives to meet with them in person. As a consequence, Germans, Englishmen, Norwegians, Swedes, and Russian Mennonites overwhelmingly populated Minnesota, the Dakotas, and other northern states. This settlement pattern did not result by accident but rather from a deliberate effort on the part of railroad executives. The practice of preferring Northern Europeans over the Irish and completely ignoring African Americans does not appear to have resulted from much explicit racism. Rather, the lines believed that Northern Europeans made the best farmers, but by choosing to advertise to them, the railroads nonetheless created a region dominated by whites, a dominance that lingers in the region to this day.

Similarly, the Mormon stronghold of Utah became synonymous with a Northern European population. Utah's population in no small measure resulted from Mormon efforts at proselytizing. Mormon theology until the

1970s stressed that Africans and African Americans had inherited the "curse of Cain," making them unworthy of conversion. Elsewhere around the world, as a result of cultural and language differences, missionaries found themselves unable to reach out to peoples in Southern Europe, Asia, and the Middle East. Only successful efforts in the Pacific proved an exception, an accomplishment that surprised the missionaries themselves. These converts, however, remained in their homelands instead of coming to Utah. Missionaries had much more success in Northern Europe, in part because language did not prove as great a barrier—especially in the British Isles— and because the long tradition of Protestantism created an environment in which new religious ideas could compete. Mormon efforts in Southern Europe, led by the Italian mission, foundered because language and culture proved insurmountable. A heavily Northern European population resulted from these successes and failures. Whiteness therefore indelibly marked the Mormons of Utah.

Westerners also tried to enforce legal racial restrictions, which denied non-whites the right to settle in the region, and thus ensure a white population. As the debate over slavery and its expansion reached a critical mass, Oregon and California attempted to bar both slavery and African Americans. Both would successfully prevent slavery but fail at preventing African Americans from living in their territory. Neither state, however, saw a large influx of African Americans before World War II, so the population remained overwhelmingly white. Westerners had more success in limiting the number of Asians in the region. Legislation, like the Chinese Exclusion Act, and vigilante violence successfully led to the development of a small Asian population. Chinese and Japanese immigrants, however, persevered and fought to carve out a niche for themselves in the United States. Neither American Indians nor Hispanics disappeared, either; indeed, in recent decades both have reasserted their presence in the West. The racial and ethnic background of the West owed much to forces far beyond the racial and ethnic considerations of those who sought to create the white man's West. Economic opportunity in particular pulled people from all corners of the world to the West. The population of Mormon Utah also reflected religious and cultural concerns. All of these forces greatly influenced who came west and why. Yet the pursuit of whiteness was not entirely fruitless. The desire to fashion a region where whites would remain powerful and non-whites would be relegated to the status of servants or romantic anachronisms never entirely died. Indeed, while all these groups persisted and contributed to the culture of the West, there can be little doubt that political power and control lay in the hands of Anglo-Americans.

Today, the modern West is a racially diverse and more egalitarian society. If there were any doubts about the profound changes occurring in the West, the 2010 census must surely have settled the debate. While the states of the northern Great Plains and Rockies remain overwhelmingly white (North Dakota's non-Hispanic white population accounts for 89% of the state's total population; its southern neighbor's percentage is 84; Wyoming is at 85%; Idaho is 83% non-Hispanic white), the rest of the West is changing. Today, non-Hispanic whites constitute less than half of the population in California (40%), New Mexico (40%), and Texas (45%). Slim white majorities hang on in Nevada (54%) and Arizona (57%).[16] Perhaps these numbers account for some of the acrimony over Arizona's Senate Bill 1070. Anglo-Arizonans hold a slim majority over the state's growing Hispanic population, but it is a majority in peril. In addition—unlike multiracial California, with its huge populations of whites, Hispanics, Asians, and African Americans—Arizona is much more a contest between Anglos and Hispanics (of the state's 6.3 million people, 4.6 million are white, which includes Hispanics in the census).

California in the 1990s provides an interesting parallel to what is happening in Arizona. After decades of unprecedented growth and opportunity, the California economy sunk into recession beginning in 1989. The split between the rich and the lower classes grew. Over 70 percent of the state's new arrivals were Hispanics, while the state also witnessed growth among Asians and African Americans. Whites, meanwhile, began to leave the state in droves, in part to get away from these newcomers. Between 1990 and 1994, 386,000 people (the vast majority of them white Californians) abandoned the Pacific Coast and moved to the interior (and whiter) West.[17]

California also provided a forerunner to Arizona's recent efforts to target undocumented immigrants with the successful passage of Proposition 187 in 1994. Prop 187 began as the "Save Our State" campaign in the largely non-Hispanic white suburbs of Los Angeles and Orange County. The ballot initiative gained widespread support from increasingly fearful non-Hispanic whites and made the ballot in the 1994 election. As the *Los Angeles Times* noted, "The movement tapped into unease with more than a decade of massive immigration, mostly from Latin America and Asia. Newcomers caused a seismic shift in the state's demographic makeup." Proponents of the amendment to California's constitution asserted that the law would help save the cash-strapped state by not allowing undocumented immigrants access to welfare programs and education, and it required law enforcement to question suspects about their legal status and report undocumented people to the federal Immigration and Naturalization Service. These provisions of Prop 187, critics contended, amounted to little more than covert racism. A strong majority of 60 percent of California voters approved the initiative in the fall election, but the law soon found itself the subject of legal action and was ruled unconstitutional by US district judge Mariana R. Pfaelzer in 1998. Finally, it died when the administration of Governor Gray Davis, a Democrat who had opposed the proposition, decided not to appeal her ruling. Judge Pfaelzer ruled that most of the provisions of Prop 187 were unconstitutional on the basis of the federal government having the authority to regulate immigration.[18] The role of the federal government to regulate immigration also influenced the fate of AZ SB 1070. While the US Supreme Court, in *Arizona v. United States* (2012), overturned much of the law, the court left the provision that allowed law enforcement to check the immigration status of people stopped for traffic violations intact.[19] Both laws, however, reflected the concern of Arizona's and California's Anglo populations that massive Hispanic immigration diluted their power and control. That immigration and the demographic changes it birthed are continuing unabated throughout the West.

Nationally, the 2010 census noted that the non-Hispanic white population grew at a much smaller rate than all other racial and ethnic groups, slipping from 75 percent of the total US population in 2000 to 72 percent in 2010. Further, three-fourths of the growth in the white population was of Hispanic whites, and in fifteen states non-Hispanic whites declined in population, including California, which saw a 5.4 percent decrease. The census numbers quantified what most people know intuitively: Hispanics are becoming a larger and larger part of the nation's population, especially in the Southwest, and Anglo-American control of the region, forged over a century and a half, is slipping away.[20]

However, whiteness is still shaping the West, if in limited ways. The interior West, for example, accounted for seven of the top ten whitest cities of over 100,000 people in the nation in 2010. Arvada, Colorado, a suburb of Denver, was second in the nation with a 94 percent white population, and all ten cities had populations that were more than 90 percent white.[21] Certainly, the dream of a region dedicated to the preservation of one racial group never came to pass—it was always an impossibility given the innate diversity of the region in the nineteenth century—but perhaps here in the interior West's small towns and affluent suburbs it will make its last stand, slipping into irrelevance as an anachronism from a different age. The 2010 census numbers and the focus of immigration, "anchor babies," and birthright citizens in the 2016 presidential campaign, however, suggest that the West is still wrestling with old visions of its past and new visions for its future.[22] Despite all the changes, from the rhetoric of white supremacist groups to the angry vitriol of some in the anti-immigration movement, echoes of the white man's West still reverberate

Notes

1. "Immigration Bill Passes Senate by Vote of 62 to 6," *New York Times*, April 19, 1924.

2. John Higham, *Strangers in the Land: Patterns of American Nativism, 1860–1925* (New Brunswick, NJ: Rutgers University Press, 1955), 324.

3. See George Anthony Peffer, *If They Don't Bring Their Women Here: Chinese Female Immigration before Exclusion* (Urbana: University of Illinois Press, 1999).

4. "Racial Questions Involved in Trial," *Morning Oregonian* [Portland], April 8, 1920. My thanks to Joshua Binus, a graduate student at Portland State University, for telling me about the Cartozian case.

5. Ibid.

6. Ibid.

7. "Armenian Fight Begun in Court," *Morning Oregonian* [Portland], May 8, 1924.

8. Ian Haney López, *White by Law: The Legal Construction of Race* (New York: New York University Press, 1996), 4.

9. Elliott Robert Barkan, *From All Points: America's Immigrant West, 1870s–1952* (Bloomington: Indiana University Press, 2007), 136.

10. López, *White by Law*, 9.

11. Ibid., 221–25.

12. *United States v. Cartozian*, 6 F.2d 919 (1925).

13. Pamphlet reproduced in Paul Kagan, *New World Utopias: A Photographic History of the Search for Community* (New York: Penguin, 1975), 102.

14. Ibid., 102–17.

15. David M. Wrobel, *Promised Lands: Promotion, Memory, and the Creation of the American West* (Lawrence: University Press of Kansas, 2002), 173–76.

16. I derived these numbers by dividing a state's total population from its "White alone, not Hispanic or Latino" category in table 4 of "The White Population: 2010:

2010 Census Briefs," United States Census Bureau, http://www.census.gov/prod/
cen2010/briefs/c2010br-05.pdf (accessed July 12, 2012). The western and midwestern
states are as follows, from the highest to lowest percentage of non-Hispanic whites:

State	Non-Hispanic Whites as Percentage of Total Population	State	Non-Hispanic Whites as Percentage of Total Population
North Dakota	89	Washington	72
Montana	87	Colorado	70
Wyoming	85	Oklahoma	68
South Dakota	84	Arizona	57
Idaho	83	Nevada	54
Nebraska	82	Texas	45
Utah	80	New Mexico	40
Oregon	78	California	40
Kansas	78		

17. Walter Nugent, *Into the West: The Story of Its People* (New York: Alfred A. Knopf, 1999), 362–69; William E. Riebsame, ed., *Atlas of the New West: Portrait of a Changing Region* (New York: W. W. Norton, 1997), 95–96. The perceived decline of the American dream in California has been chronicled in two books by Mike Davis: *City of Quartz: Excavating the Future in Los Angeles* (New York: Vintage, 1992) and *Ecology of Fear: Los Angeles and the Imagination of Disaster* (New York: Vintage, 1998).

18. "Davis Won't Appeal Prop. 187 Ruling, Ending Court Battles," *Los Angeles Times*, July 29, 1999.

19. Robert Barnes, "Supreme Court Upholds Key Part of Arizona Law for Now, Strikes down Other Provisions," *Washington Post*, June 25, 2012.

20. US Census Bureau, "The White Population: 2010: 2010 Census Briefs," 6, table four, table 6.

21. Ibid. Arvada, Colorado, was number two on the list. The number-one city was Hialeah, Florida, but 95 percent of its population was white Hispanics, according to the census, whereas the populations of the rest of the top ten were non-Hispanic whites. Fort Collins joined Arvada from Colorado; Boise and Spokane represented the Northwest; Fargo, North Dakota, made the list, as did Billings, Montana; and the affluent white suburb Scottsdale, Arizona, came in eighth.

22. Jose A. DelReal, "Jeb Bush: People Should 'Chill Out' on the 'Anchor Baby' Controversy," *Washington Post*, August 24, 2015, accessed September 21, 2015, www.washingtonpost.com/news/post-politics/wp/2015/08/24/jeb-bush-people-should-chill-out-on-the-anchor-baby-controversy/.

BIBLIOGRAPHY

Archival Collections

William A. Bell Collection. Mss. 49. Colorado Historical Society, Denver.

William F. Carter Papers. Mss. 3092. L. Tom Perry Special Collections, Harold B. Lee Library, Brigham Young University, Provo, UT.

Samuel Francis Papers. Mss. 3268. L. Tom Perry Special Collections, Harold B. Lee Library, Brigham Young University, Provo, UT.

Governor's Office, John St. John. Correspondence Received–Subject File, Kansas Historical Society, Topeka. http://.../www.kansasmemory.org/item /210296/page/1.

Frank Bird Linderman Collection. Mss. 7. K. Ross Toole Archive, Mansfield Library, University of Montana, Missoula.

Frank Bird Linderman Collection. Museum of the Plains Indian, Browning, MT, microfilm.

Charles Fletcher Lummis Papers. Braun Research Library, Southwest Museum, Autry National Center, Los Angeles, CA.

Mormon Emigration Records, 1879. Mss. 4150. L. Tom Perry Special
    Collections, Harold B. Lee Library, Brigham Young University, Provo, UT.
Northern Pacific Railway Company Land Department Records. Minnesota
    Historical Society, St. Paul, microfilm.
Daniel Tyler Papers. Mss. SC 481. L. Tom Perry Special Collections, Harold B.
    Lee Library, Brigham Young University, Provo, UT.
Brigham Young Papers. Mss. B 93. Utah State Historical Society, Salt Lake City.

PERIODICALS AND NEWSPAPERS

Bee-Hive (London, UK)
Congressional Globe
Everybody's
Harper's New Monthly Magazine
Jefferson (MO) Inquirer
Journal of Discourses
Land and Emigration (London, UK)
Land of Sunshine/Out West
Los Angeles Times
McClure's (New York)
Millennial Star (Mormon publication)
Morning Oregonian (Portland)
The Nation
New York Times
Rocky Mountain News (Denver, CO)
San Angelo (TX) Standard Times
Scribner's (New York)
Washington Post
Weekly Oregonian
Western Historical Quarterly
World's Work

OTHER SOURCES

Aarim-Heriot, Najia. *Chinese Immigrants, African Americans and Racial Anxiety in the
    United States, 1848–1882.* Urbana: University of Illinois Press, 2003.

Adams, David Wallace. *Education for Extinction: American Indians and the Boarding School Experience, 1875–1928*. Lawrence: University Press of Kansas, 1995.

Adams, Kevin. *Class and Race in the Frontier Army*. Norman: University of Oklahoma Press, 2009.

Adams, Samuel Hopkins. "Tuberculosis: The Real Race Suicide." *McClure's Magazine* 24 (January 1905): 234–49.

Agassiz, Louis. "The Diversity of Origin of the Human Races." *Christian Examiner* 49 (1850): 110–45.

Ahmad, Diana L. *The Opium Debate and Chinese Exclusion Laws in the Nineteenth-Century American West*. Reno: University of Nevada Press, 2007.

Alba, Richard D. *Ethnic Identity: The Transformation of White America*. New Haven, CT: Yale University Press, 1990.

Alder, Douglas Dexter. "German Speaking Immigration to Utah, 1850–1950." MA thesis, University of Utah, Salt Lake City, 1959.

Almaguer, Tómas. *Racial Fault Lines: The Historical Origins of White Supremacy in California*. Berkeley: University of California Press, 1994.

Anderson, Gary Clayton. *The Conquest of Texas: Ethnic Cleansing in the Promised Land, 1820–1875*. Norman: University of Oklahoma Press, 2005.

Anonymous. *Tyrannical Libertymen: A Discourse upon Negro Slavery in the United States*. Hanover, NH: Eagle Office, 1795.

Arnesen, Eric. "Whiteness and the Historians' Imagination." *International Labor and Working-Class History* 60 (Fall 2001).

Aryan Nations website. http://aryan-nations.org. Accessed December 20, 2011.

Athearn, Robert G. *In Search of Canaan: Black Migration to Kansas, 1879–1880*. Lawrence: Regents Press of Kansas, 1978.

Athearn, Robert G. *The Mythic West in Twentieth Century America*. Lawrence: University Press of Kansas, 1989.

Athearn, Robert G. *Rebel of the Rockies: A History of the Denver and Rio Grande Western Railroad*. Yale Western Americana Series. New Haven, CT: Yale University Press, 1962.

Athearn, Robert G. *Union Pacific Country*. Lincoln: University of Nebraska Press, 1982.

Bakken, Gordon Morris, and Brenda Farrington, eds. *Racial Encounters in the Multi-Cultural West*. New York: Garland, 2000.

Banning, Evelyn I. *Helen Hunt Jackson*. New York: Vanguard, 1973.

Barkan, Elliott Robert. *From All Points: America's Immigrant West, 1870s–1952*. Bloomington: Indiana University Press, 2007.

Bayor, Ronald H., ed. *The Columbia Documentary History of Race and Ethnicity in America*. New York: Columbia University Press, 2004.

Beadle, J[ohn] H[anson]. *The Undeveloped West: or, Five Years in the Territories*. Philadelphia: National Publishing, 1873. Reprint, New York: Arno, 1973.

Bell, William A. *New Tracks in North America: A Journal of Travel and Adventure Whilst Engaged in the Survey for a Southern Railroad to the Pacific Ocean during 1867–68.* London: Chapman and Hall, 1869.

Bell, William A. *A Paper on the Colonies of Colorado in Their Relation to English Enterprise and Settlement.* London: Chapman and Hall, 1874.

Benton-Cohen, Katherine. *Borderline Americans: Racial Divisions in the Arizona Borderlands.* Cambridge, MA: Harvard University Press, 2009.

Berlin, Ira. *Many Thousands Gone: The First Two Centuries of Slavery in North America.* Cambridge, MA: Belknap, 1998.

Berwanger, Eugene H. *The Frontier against Slavery: Western Anti-Negro Prejudice and the Slavery Extension Controversy.* Urbana: University of Illinois Press, 1967.

Bieder, Robert E. *Science Encounters the Indian, 1820–1880: The Early Years of American Ethnology.* Norman: University of Oklahoma Press, 1986.

Bingham, Edwin R. *Charles F. Lummis: Editor of the Southwest.* San Marino, CA: Huntington Library Press, 1955.

Bird, Isabella L. *A Lady's Life in the Rocky Mountains.* Norman: University of Oklahoma Press, 1960.

Bowler, Peter J. *Evolution: The History of an Idea.* Berkeley: University of California Press, 1989.

Boxer, Elise. "'To Become White and Delightsome': American Indians and Mormon Identity." PhD dissertation, Arizona State University, Tempe, 2009.

Bradley, Glenn Danford. *The Story of the Santa Fe.* Boston: Badger, 1920.

Branagan, Thomas. *Serious Remonstrances: Addressed to the Citizens of the Northern States, and Their Representatives.* Philadelphia: Thomas T. Stiles, 1805.

Brantlinger, Patrick. *Dark Vanishings: Discourse on the Extinction of Primitive Races, 1800–1930.* Ithaca, NY: Cornell University Press, 2003.

Bringhurst, Newell G. *Saints, Slaves, and Blacks: The Changing Place of Black People within Mormonism.* Westport, CT: Greenwood, 1981.

Britsch, R. Lanier. *Unto the Islands of the Sea: A History of the Latter-day Saints in the Pacific.* Salt Lake City: Deseret Book, 1986.

Brown, Richard Maxwell. *No Duty to Retreat: Violence and Values in American History and Society.* Norman: University of Oklahoma Press, 1991.

Brown, Richard Maxwell. *Strain of Violence: Historical Studies of American Violence and Vigilantism.* New York: Oxford University Press, 1975.

Browne, J. Ross. *Report of the Debates in the Convention of California on the Formation of the State Constitution in September and October, 1849.* Washington, DC: John T. Towers, 1850.

Burnett, Peter H. *Recollections and Opinions of an Old Pioneer.* New York: D. Appleton, 1880.

California State Constitution. 1849. http://www.archives.cdn.sos.ca.gov/1849/full-text.htm. Accessed July 12, 2012.

Calvert, Robert A., and Arnoldo De León. *The History of Texas.* Arlington Heights, IL: Harlan Davidson, 1990.

Carlson, Paul H., and Tom Crum. *Myth, Memory, and Massacre: The Pease River Capture of Cynthia Ann Parker.* Lubbock: Texas Tech University Press, 2010.

Carroll, Mark M. *Homesteads Ungovernable: Families, Sex, Race, and the Law in Frontier Texas, 1823–1860.* Austin: University of Texas Press, 2001.

Castle, William Ernest, John Merle Coulter, Charles Benedict Davenport, Edward Murray East, and William Lawrence, eds. *Heredity and Eugenics.* Chicago: University of Chicago Press, 1912.

Chambers, Thomas A. *Drinking the Waters: Creating an American Leisure Class at Nineteenth-Century Mineral Springs.* Washington, DC: Smithsonian Institution Press, 2002.

Chicago, Rock Island, and Pacific Railroad. *The Great West.* Chicago: Rollings, 1880.

Church of Jesus Christ of Latter-day Saints website. http://mormon.org. Accessed December 15, 2011.

Coates, Peter. *American Perceptions of Immigrant and Invasive Species: Strangers on the Land.* Berkeley: University of California Press, 2006.

Cole, Stephanie, and Alison Parker, eds. *Beyond Black and White: Race, Ethnicity, and Gender in the U.S. South and Southwest.* College Station: Texas A&M University Press, 2004.

Coleman, Annie Gilbert. *Ski Style.* Lawrence: University Press of Kansas, 2004.

Colton, Walter. *Three Years in California.* New York: S. A. Rollo, 1859.

Cool, Paul. *Salt Warriors: Insurgency on the Rio Grande.* College Station: Texas A&M University Press, 2008.

Courtwright, David T. *Violent Land: Single Men and Social Disorder from the Frontier to the Inner City.* Cambridge, MA: Harvard University Press, 1996.

Cox, Mike. *The Texas Rangers: Wearing the Cinco Peso, 1821–1900.* New York: Forge, 2008.

Crockett, Norman L. *The Black Towns.* Lawrence: Regents Press of Kansas, 1979.

Cross, Coy F. *Go West Young Man! Horace Greeley's Vision for America.* Albuquerque: University of New Mexico Press, 1995.

Dain, Bruce. *A Hideous Monster of the Mind: American Race Theory in the Early Republic.* Cambridge, MA: Harvard University Press, 2002.

Dana, Richard Henry, Jr. *Two Years before the Mast and Other Voyages.* Ed. Thomas Philbrick. New York: Library of America, 2005.

Daniel, Thomas. *The Captain of Death: The Story of Tuberculosis.* Rochester, NY: University of Rochester Press, 1999.

Daniels, Roger. *Coming to America: A History of Immigration and Ethnicity in American Life.* New York: Harper Perennial, 1990.

Davis, Mike. *City of Quartz: Excavating the Future in Los Angeles.* New York: Vintage, 1992.

Davis, Mike. *Ecology of Fear: Los Angeles and the Imagination of Disaster.* New York: Vintage, 1998.

De León, Arnoldo. *Racial Frontiers: Africans, Chinese, and Mexicans in Western America, 1848–1890.* Albuquerque: University of New Mexico Press, 2002.

De León, Arnoldo. *They Called Them Greasers: Anglo Attitudes toward Mexicans in Texas, 1821–1900*. Austin: University of Texas Press, 1983.

De León, Arnoldo, ed. *War along the Border: The Mexican Revolution and Tejano Communities*. College Station: Texas A&M University Press, 2012.

Deloria, Philip. *Playing Indian*. New Haven, CT: Yale University Press, 1998.

Denver and Rio Grande Western Railway. *The Opinions of the Judge and the Colonel as to the Vast Resources of Colorado*. Denver: Denver and Rio Grande Western Railway, 1894.

Deverell, William. *Whitewashed Adobe: The Rise of Los Angeles and the Remaking of Its Mexican Past*. Berkeley: University of California Press, 2004.

Dippie, Brian. *The Vanishing American: White Attitudes and US Indian Policy*. Lawrence: University Press of Kansas, 1982.

Dirlik, Arif, ed. *Chinese on the American Frontier*. Lanham, MD: Rowman and Littlefield, 2001.

Dye, Victoria E. *All Aboard for Santa Fe: Railway Promotion of the Southwest, 1890s to 1930s*. Albuquerque: University of New Mexico Press, 2005.

Edwards, G. Thomas, and Carlos Schwantes, eds. *Experiences in a Promised Land: Essays in Pacific Northwest History*. Seattle: University of Washington Press, 1986.

Emigrant, an (pseudonym). *Texas in 1840, or the Emigrant's Guide to the New Republic*. New York: Arno, 1973.

Emmons, David M. *Beyond the American Pale: The Irish in the West, 1845–1910*. Norman: University of Oklahoma Press, 2010.

Emmons, David M. *Garden in the Grasslands: Boomer Literature of the Central Great Plains*. Lincoln: University of Nebraska Press, 1971.

Etulain, Richard. *Re-imagining the Modern American West: A Century of Fiction, History, and Art*. Tucson: University of Arizona Press, 1996.

Faragher, John Mack, ed. *Rereading Frederick Jackson Turner*. New York: Henry Holt, 1994.

Ferber, Abby L. *White Man Falling: Race, Gender, and White Supremacy*. Lanham, MD: Rowman and Littlefield, 1998.

Fields, Barbara J. "Ideology and Race in American History." In *Region, Race, and Reconstruction: Essays in Honor of C. Vann Woodward*, edited by J. Morgan Krousser and James M. McPherson, 143–77. New York: Oxford University Press, 1982.

Fisher, John S. *A Builder of the West: The Life of General William Jackson Palmer*. Caldwell, ID: Caxton, 1939.

Fisk, Turbese Lummis, and Keith Lummis. *Charles F. Lummis: The Man and His West*. Norman: University of Oklahoma Press, 1975.

Foley, Neil. *The White Scourge: Mexicans, Blacks, and Poor Whites in Texas Cotton Culture*. Berkeley: University of California Press, 1997.

Foner, Eric. *Free Soil, Free Labor, Free Men: The Ideology of the Republican Party before the Civil War*. New York: Oxford University Press, 1995.

Foos, Paul. *A Short, Offhand, Killing Affair: Soldiers and Social Conflict during the Mexican-American War*. Chapel Hill: University of North Carolina Press, 2002.

Foucault, Michel. *The History of Sexuality*, vol. 1: *An Introduction*. New York: Vintage Books, 1990.

Franklin, Benjamin. *The Papers of Benjamin Franklin*, vol. 4. Ed. Leonard Labaree. New Haven, C T: Yale University Press, 1961.

Frazier, Ian. *Great Plains*. New York: Penguin Books, 1989.

Fredrickson, George M. *The Black Image in the White Mind: The Debate on Afro-American Character and Destiny, 1817–1914*. New York: Harper and Row, 1971.

Frémont, John C., and Samuel M. Smucker. *The Life of Colonel John Charles Fremont*. New York: Miller, Orton, and Mulligan, 1856.

Frost, Linda. *Never One Nation: Freaks, Savages, and Whiteness in U.S. Popular Culture, 1850–1877*. Minneapolis: University of Minnesota Press, 2005.

Garvin, Roy. "Benjamin, or 'Pap,' Singleton and His Followers." *Journal of Negro History* 33, no. 1 (January 1948): 7–23. http://dx.doi.org/10.2307/2714984.

Gates, Paul Wallace. *The Illinois Central Railroad and Its Colonization Work*. Cambridge, MA: Harvard University Press, 1934. http://dx.doi.org/10.4159/harvard.9780674281615.

Gilpin, William. *Mission of the North American People: Geographical, Social, and Political*. Philadelphia: J. B. Lippincott, 1874.

Glass, Bentley, Owsei Temkin, and William L. Strauss Jr., eds. *Forerunners of Darwin: 1745–1859*. Baltimore: Johns Hopkins University Press, 1959.

Goetzmann, William H. *Exploration and Empire: The Explorer and the Scientist in the Winning of the American West*. New York: Alfred A. Knopf, 1966.

Gordon, Linda. *The Great Arizona Orphan Abduction*. Cambridge, MA: Harvard University Press, 1999.

Gorren, Aline. *Anglo-Saxons and Others*. New York: Charles Scribner's Sons, 1900.

Gossett, Thomas F. *Race: The History of an Idea in America*. Dallas: Southern Methodist University Press, 1963.

Gould, Stephen J. *The Mismeasure of Man*. New York: W. W. Norton, 1981.

Grant, Madison. *The Passing of the Great Race*. New York: Charles Scribner's Sons, 1918.

Graves, Joseph L., Jr. *The Emperor's New Clothes: Biological Theories of Race at the Millennium*. New Brunswick, NJ: Rutgers University Press, 2001.

Gregg, Josiah. *Commerce of the Prairies*. Ed. Max L. Moorhead. Norman: University of Oklahoma Press, 1954.

Gross, Ariela J. *What Blood Won't Tell: A History of Race on Trial in America*. Cambridge, MA: Harvard University Press, 2008.

Gutierrez, David. *Walls and Mirrors: Mexican Americans, Mexican Immigrants and the Politics of Ethnicity*. Berkeley: University of California Press, 1995.

Hahn, Steven. *A Nation under Our Feet: Black Political Struggles in the Rural South from Slavery to the Great Migration*. Cambridge, MA: Belknap, 2003.

Hämäläinen, Pekka. *The Comanche Empire.* New Haven, CT: Yale University Press, 2008.

Hannaford, Ivan. *Race: History of an Idea in the West.* Baltimore: Johns Hopkins University Press, 1996.

Harris, Cheryl. "Whiteness as Property." *Harvard Law Review* 106, no. 8 (June 1993): 1707–91. http://dx.doi.org/10.2307/1341787.

Hayden, Ferdinand V., ed. *The Great West: Its Attractions and Resources.* Bloomington, IL: Charles R. Brodix, 1880.

Hedges, James Blaine. "The Colonization Work of the Northern Pacific Railroad." *Mississippi Valley Historical Review* 13, no. 3 (December 1926): 311–42. http://dx.doi.org/10.2307/1893110.

Hedges, James Blaine. "Promotion and Immigration to the Pacific Northwest by the Railroads." *Mississippi Valley Historical Review* 15, no. 2 (September 1928): 183–203. http://dx.doi.org/10.2307/1895644.

Heizer, Robert F., ed. *The Destruction of California Indians.* Lincoln: University of Nebraska Press, 1993.

Heizer, Robert F., ed. *They Were Only Diggers: A Collection of Articles from California Newspapers, 1851–1866, on Indian and White Relations.* Ramona, CA: Ballena, 1974.

Hibbard, George B. *Land Department of the Northern Pacific Railroad Company: Bureau of Immigration for Soldiers and Sailors.* N.p.: Northern Pacific Railroad, 1873.

Hietala, Thomas R. *Manifest Design: Anxious Aggrandizement in Late Jacksonian America.* Ithaca, NY: Cornell University Press, 1985.

Higham, John. *Strangers in the Land: Patterns of American Nativism, 1860–1925.* New Brunswick, NJ: Rutgers University Press, 1955.

Hill, Mike, ed. *Whiteness: A Critical Reader.* New York: New York University Press, 1997.

Hinsley, Curtis M., Jr. *Savages and Scientists: The Smithsonian Institution and the Development of American Anthropology, 1846–1910.* Washington, DC: Smithsonian Institution Press, 1981.

Hofstadter, Richard. *Social Darwinism in American Thought.* New York: George Braziller, 1959.

Holt, Michael F. *The Fate of Their Country: Politicians, Slavery Extension, and the Coming of the Civil War.* New York: Hill and Wang, 2004.

Homer, Michael. "The Italian Mission, 1850–1867." *Sunstone* 7, no. 3 (May-June 1982): 16–21.

Horsman, Reginald. *Josiah Nott of Mobile: Southerner, Physician, and Racial Theorist.* Baton Rouge: Louisiana State University Press, 1987.

Horsman, Reginald. *Race and Manifest Destiny: The Origins of American Racial Anglo-Saxonism.* Cambridge, MA: Harvard University Press, 1981.

Howell, Kenneth W., ed. *Still the Arena of Civil War: Violence and Turmoil in Reconstruction Texas, 1865–1874.* Denton: University of North Texas Press, 2012.

Hoxie, Frederick. *A Final Promise: The Campaign to Assimilate the Indians.* Lincoln: University of Nebraska Press, 1994.

Hurtado, Albert L. *Indian Survival on the California Frontier*. New Haven, CT: Yale University Press, 1988.

Hyer, Joel R. *We Are Not Savages: Native Americans in Southern California and the Pala Reservation, 1840–1920*. East Lansing: Michigan State University Press, 2001.

Ignatiev, Noel. *How the Irish Became White*. New York: Routledge, 1995.

Irving, Washington. *Three Western Narratives*. New York: Library of America, 2004.

Irving, Washington. *The Western Journals of Washington Irving*. Ed. John Francis McDermott. Norman: University of Oklahoma Press, 1944.

Iseminger, Gordon L. "*Land and Emigration*: A Northern Pacific Railroad Company Newspaper." *North Dakota Quarterly* 48, no. 2 (Summer 1981): 70–92.

Jackson, Andrew. "Annual Messages, 1830–33." In *A Compilation of the Messages and Papers of the Presidents*, ed. James D. Richardson, 10:1082–86. US Congress. New York, 1896.

Jackson, Helen Hunt. *Glimpses of Three Coasts*. Boston: Roberts Brothers, 1886.

Jackson, Helen Hunt. *Westward to a High Mountain: The Colorado Writings of Helen Hunt Jackson*. Ed. Mark I. West. Denver: Colorado Historical Society, 1994.

Jacobson, Matthew Frye. *Whiteness of a Different Color: European Immigrants and the Alchemy of Race*. Cambridge, MA: Harvard University Press, 1998.

Jaehn, Tomas. *Germans in the Southwest, 1850–1920*. Albuquerque: University of New Mexico Press, 2005.

Jahoda, Gustav. *Images of Savages: Ancients [sic] Roots of Modern Prejudice in Western Culture*. New York: Routledge, 1999.

Jefferson, Thomas. *The Complete Jefferson, Containing His Major Writings, Published and Unpublished, Except His Letters*. Ed. Saul K. Padover. New York: Tudor, 1943.

Jefferson, Thomas. *The Writings of Thomas Jefferson*, vol. 19. Ed. Andrew A. Lipscomb and Albert Bergh. Washington, DC: Thomas Jefferson Memorial Association, 1905.

Jeffrey, Julie Roy. *Converting the West: A Biography of Narcissa Whitman*. Norman: University of Oklahoma Press, 1991.

Jeffrey, Julie Roy. *Frontier Women*. New York: Hill and Wang, 1998.

Johannsen, Robert W. *Frontier Politics and the Sectional Conflict: The Pacific Northwest on the Eve of the Civil War*. Seattle: University of Washington Press, 1955.

Johannsen, Robert W. *To the Halls of the Montezumas: The Mexican War in the American Imagination*. New York: Oxford University Press, 1985.

Johnson, Susan Lee. *Roaring Camp: The Social World of the California Gold Rush*. New York: W. W. Norton, 2000.

Jones, Billy Mack. *Health-Seekers in the Southwest, 1817–1900*. Norman: University of Oklahoma Press, 1967.

Jordan, David Starr. *The Blood of the Nation: A Study of the Decay of Races through the Survival of the Unfit*. Boston: American Unitarian Association, 1910.

Jordan, David Starr. *The Days of Man: Being Memories of a Naturalist, Teacher, and Minor Prophet of Democracy*. 2 vols. New York: World Book Company, 1922.

Jordan, Winthrop. *White over Black: American Attitudes toward the Negro, 1550–1812.* Chapel Hill: University of North Carolina Press, 1968.

Kagan, Paul. *New World Utopias: A Photographic History of the Search for Community.* New York: Penguin, 1975.

Kaufman, Herbert. "Southwestward Ho! America's New Trek to Still-Open Places." *Everybody's* 22, no. 6 (June 1910): 725–31.

Kennedy, Randall. *Nigger: The Strange Career of a Troublesome Word.* New York: Vintage, 2002.

Kidd, Colin. *British Identities before Nationalism: Ethnicity and Nationhood in the Atlantic World, 1600–1800.* New York: Cambridge University Press, 1999. http://dx.doi.org/10.1017/CBO9780511495861.

Kincheloe, Joe L., Shirley R. Steinberg, Nelson M. Rodriquez, and Ronald E. Channault, eds. *White Reign: Deploying Whiteness in America.* New York: St. Martin's, 1998.

Kingsley, Rose Georgina. *South by West, or, Winter in the Rocky Mountains and Spring in Mexico.* London: W. Isbister, 1874.

Kolchin, Peter. "Whiteness Studies: The New History of Race in America." *Journal of American History* 89, no. 1 (June 2002): 154–73. http://dx.doi.org/10.2307/2700788.

Kownslar, Allan O. *The European Texans.* College Station: Texas A&M University Press, 2004.

Kukla, Jon. *A Wilderness So Immense: The Louisiana Purchase and the Destiny of America.* New York: Alfred A. Knopf, 2003.

Lapp, Rudolph M. *Blacks in Gold Rush California.* New Haven, CT: Yale University Press, 1977.

Lears, T. Jackson. *No Place of Grace: Antimodernism and the Transformation of American Culture, 1880–1920.* New York: Pantheon, 1981.

Leckie, William H. *The Buffalo Soldiers: A Narrative of the Black Cavalry in the West.* Norman: University of Oklahoma Press, 2003.

Leiker, James N. *Racial Borders: Black Soldiers along the Rio Grande.* College Station: Texas A&M University Press, 2002.

Levario, Miguel. *Militarizing the Border: When Mexicans Became the Enemy.* College Station: Texas A&M University Press, 2012.

Lightner, David L. *Labor on the Illinois Central Railroad, 1852–1900: The Evolution of an Industrial Environment.* New York: Arno, 1977.

Limerick, Patricia Nelson. *The Legacy of Conquest: The Unbroken Past of the American West.* New York: W. W. Norton, 1987.

Linderman, Frank Bird. *Montana Adventure: The Recollections of Frank B. Linderman.* Ed. H. G. Merriam. Lincoln: University of Nebraska Press, 1968.

Linderman, Frank Bird. *Pretty-shield: Medicine Woman of the Crows.* Lincoln: University of Nebraska Press, 1972.

Linderman, Frank Bird. *Wolf and the Winds.* Norman: University of Oklahoma Press, 1986.

Lipsitz, George. *The Possessive Investment in Whiteness: How White People Profit from Identity Politics*. Philadelphia: Temple University Press, 2006.

Long, Stephen Harriman. *Account of an Expedition from Pittsburg to the Rocky Mountains*, vol. 2. London: Longman, Hurst, Rees, Orme and Brown, 1823.

López, Ian Haney. *White by Law: The Legal Construction of Race*. New York: New York University Press, 1996.

Lovoll, Odd S. *Norwegians on the Prairie: Ethnicity and the Development of the Country Town*. St. Paul: Minnesota Historical Society Press, 2006.

Ludlow, Daniel H., ed. *Encyclopedia of Mormonism*. 4 vols. New York: Macmillan, 1992.

Luebke, Frederick C., ed. *Ethnicity on the Great Plains*. Lincoln: University of Nebraska Press, 1980.

Luebke, Frederick C., ed. *European Immigrants in the American West: Community Histories*. Albuquerque: University of New Mexico Press, 1998.

Lummis, Charles [Fletcher]. *Letters from the Southwest*. Ed. James Byrkit. Tucson: University of Arizona Press, 1989.

Lummis, Charles Fletcher. *A Tramp across the Continent*. Lincoln: Bison Books, 1982.

Lummis, Charles Fletcher. Various articles in numerous issues of *Land of Sunshine*.

Magoffin, Susan Shelby. *Down the Santa Fé Trail and into Mexico: The Diary of Susan Shelby Magoffin*. Ed. Stella M. Drumm. New Haven, CT: Yale University Press, 1926.

Mahoney, Barbara. "Oregon Voices, Oregon Democracy: Asahel Bush, Slavery, and the Statehood Debate." *Oregon Historical Quarterly* 110, no. 2 (Summer 2009): 202–27.

Malcomson, Scott L. *One Drop of Blood: The American Misadventure of Race*. New York: Farrar, Straus, Giroux, 2000.

Malmborg, Oscar. "Letters of an Early Illinois Central Emigration Agent." *Swedish-American Historical Bulletin* 3, no. 2 (June 1930): 7–52.

Mauss, Armand L. *All Abraham's Children: Changing Mormon Conceptions of Race and Lineage*. Urbana: University of Illinois Press, 2003.

Meinig, Donald W. *The Shaping of America: A Geographical Perspective on 500 Years of History*, vol. 2: *Continental America, 1800–1867*. New Haven, CT: Yale University Press, 1993.

Melosi, Martin Van. *Pollution and Reform in American Cities, 1870–1930*. Austin: University of Texas Press, 1980.

Mexican-American Legal Defense and Educational Fund website. www.maldef.org. Accessed December 20, 2011.

Miller, Stuart Creighton. *The Unwelcome Immigrant: The American Image of the Chinese, 1785–1882*. Berkeley: University of California Press, 1969.

Milner, Clyde A., II. *A New Significance: Re-envisioning the History of the American West*. New York: Oxford University Press, 1996.

Money, Edward. *The Truth about America*. London: Sampson, Lowe, Marston, Searle and Rivington, 1886.

Montgomery, Charles. *The Spanish Redemption: Heritage, Power, and Loss on New Mexico's Upper Rio Grande*. Berkeley: University of California Press, 2002.

Morgan, Edmund S. *American Slavery, American Freedom: The Ordeal of Colonial Virginia*. New York: W. W. Norton, 1975.

Morrison, Michael A. *Slavery and the American West: The Eclipse of Manifest Destiny and the Coming of the Civil War*. Chapel Hill: University of North Carolina Press, 1997.

Morrison, Michael A., and James Brewer Stewart, eds. *Race and the Early Republic: Racial Consciousness and Nation-Building in the Early Republic*. New York: Rowman and Littlefield, 2002.

Morrison, Toni. *Playing in the Dark: Whiteness and the Literary Imagination*. New York: Vintage, 1992.

Muir, John. *Steep Trails*. Ed. William Frederic Badé. New York: Houghton Mifflin, 1918. http://dx.doi.org/10.5962/bhl.title.56187.

Murphy, Thomas W. "Imagining Lamanites: Native Americans and the Book of Mormon." PhD dissertation, University of Washington, Seattle, 2003.

Nash, Linda. *Inescapable Ecologies: A History of Environment, Disease, and Knowledge*. Berkeley: University of California Press, 2006.

Nash, Roderick. *Wilderness and the American Mind*. New Haven, CT: Yale University Press, 1967.

Nevels, Cynthia Skove. *Lynching to Belong: Claiming Whiteness through Racial Violence*. College Station: Texas A&M University Press, 2007.

Nordhoff, Charles. *California for Health, Pleasure, and Residence: A Book for Travellers and Settlers*, revised ed. New York: Harper Bros., 1882.

Nott, J[osiah] C[lark]. "The Mulatto or Hybrid—Probable Extermination of the Two Races if the Whites and Blacks Are Allowed to Intermarry." *American Journal of the Medical Sciences* 6, no. 11 (July 1843): 252–56. http://dx.doi.org/10.1097/00000441-184307000-00106.

Nott, J[osiah] C[lark], and Geo[rge] R. Gliddon. *Types of Mankind, or, Ethnological Researches, Based upon the Ancient Monuments, Paintings, Sculptures, and Crania of Races, and upon Their Natural, Geographical, Philological and Biblical History*. Philadelphia: Lippincott, Grambo, 1855.

Nugent, Walter. *Into the West: The Story of Its People*. New York: Alfred A. Knopf, 1999.

Odell, Ruth. *Helen Hunt Jackson*. New York: D. Appleton-Century, 1939.

Olmsted, Frederick Law. *A Journey through Texas, or, a Saddle-Trip on the Southwestern Frontier*. New York: Dix, Edwards, and Co., 1857.

Östman, Kim B. "Mormons, Civil Authorities and Lutheran Clergy in Finland, 1875–1889." *Scandinavian Journal of History* 35, no. 3 (September 2010): 268–89. http://dx.doi.org/10.1080/03468751003734909.

Painter, Nell Irvin. *Exodusters: Black Migration to Kansas after Reconstruction*. New York: Alfred A. Knopf, 1977.

Painter, Nell Irvin. *The History of White People*. New York: W. W. Norton, 2010.

Parkman, Francis. *The Oregon Trail: Sketches of Prairie and Rocky-Mountain Life*, 4th ed. Boston: Little, Brown, 1905.

Peffer, George Anthony. *If They Don't Bring Their Women Here: Chinese Female Immigration before Exclusion*. Urbana: University of Illinois Press, 1999.

Perdue, Theda, and Michael D. Green. *The Cherokee Removal: A Brief History with Documents*. New York: Bedford, St. Martins, 2005.

Petrowski, William Robinson. *The Kansas Pacific: A Study in Railroad Promotion*. New York: Arno, 1981.

Pfaelzer, Jean. *Driven Out: The Forgotten War against Chinese Americans*. New York: Random House, 2007.

Pike, Zebulon Montgomery. *The Expeditions of Zebulon Montgomery Pike, to Headwaters of the Mississippi River, through Louisiana Territory, and in New Spain, during the Years 1805–6–7*, vol. 2. Ed. Elliott Coues. New York: F. P. Harper, 1895.

Pomeroy, Earl. *In Search of the Golden West: The Tourist in Western America*. Lincoln: University of Nebraska Press, 1990.

Prucha, Francis Paul. *American Indian Policy in Crisis: Christian Reformers and the Indian, 1865–1900*. Norman: University of Oklahoma Press, 1977.

Prucha, Francis Paul. *American Indian Policy in the Formative Years: The Indian Trade and Intercourse Acts, 1790–1834*. Lincoln: University of Nebraska Press, 1970.

Prucha, Francis Paul. *The Great Father: The United States Government and the American Indians*. 2 vols. Lincoln: University of Nebraska Press, 1984.

Rable, George C. *But There Was No Peace: The Role of Violence in the Politics of Reconstruction*. Athens: University of Georgia Press, 2007.

Rae, John Bell. *The Development of Railway Land Subsidy Policy in the United States*. New York: Arno, 1979.

Remy, Jules. *A Journey to Great Salt Lake City*, vol. 2. London: W. Jeffs, 1861.

Riebsame, William E., ed. *Atlas of the New West: Portrait of a Changing Region*. New York: W. W. Norton, 1997.

Roediger, David R. *The Wages of Whiteness: Race and the Making of the American Working Class*. New York: Verso, 1991.

Roediger, David R. *Working toward Whiteness: How America's Immigrants Became White*. New York: Perseus Books, 2005.

Rohrbough, Malcolm J. *Days of Gold: The California Gold Rush and the American Nation*. Berkeley: University of California Press, 1994.

Ronda, James P. *Lewis and Clark among the Indians*. Lincoln: University of Nebraska Press, 1984.

Roosevelt, Theodore. *The Winning of the West: The Spread of the English-Speaking Peoples*. New York: G. P. Putnam's Sons, 1889.

Rothman, Hal K. *Devil's Bargains: Tourism in the Twentieth-Century American West*. Lawrence: University Press of Kansas, 1998.

Rusling, James F. *Across America: or the Great West and the Pacific Coast*. New York: Sheldon, 1874.

Russell, Thomas C., ed. "Shirley, Dame." September 13, 1851. In *The Shirley Letters from California Mines in 1851–52*, 4–5. San Francisco: Thomas C. Russell, 1922.

Sandmeyer, Elmer C. *The Anti-Chinese Movement in California*. Illinois Studies in the Social Sciences Series 24, no. 3. Urbana: University of Illinois Press, 1939.

Saxton, Alexander. *The Indispensable Enemy: Labor and the Anti-Chinese Movement in California*. Berkeley: University of California Press, 1971.

Schlatter, Elizabeth. *Aryan Cowboys: White Supremacists and the Search for a New Frontier, 1970–2000*. Austin: University of Texas Press, 2006.

Schwantes, Carlos. *Railroad Signatures across the Pacific Northwest*. Seattle: University of Washington Press, 1993.

Shaffer, Marguerite S. *See America First: Tourism and National Identity, 1880–1940*. Washington, DC: Smithsonian Institution Press, 2001.

Slotkin, Richard. *The Fatal Environment: The Myth of the Frontier in the Age of Industrialization, 1800–1890*. Norman: University of Oklahoma Press, 1985.

Slotkin, Richard. *Gunfighter Nation: The Myth of the Frontier in Twentieth-Century America*. Norman: University of Oklahoma Press, 1992.

Slotkin, Richard. *Regeneration through Violence: The Mythology of the American Frontier, 1600–1860*. Norman: University of Oklahoma Press, 1973.

Smedley, Audrey. *Race in North America: Origin and Evolution of a Worldview*. Boulder: Westview, 1993.

Smith, George A., Lorenzo Snow, Paul A. Schettler, and Eliza R. Snow. *Correspondence of Palestine Tourists*. Salt Lake City: Deseret News Steam Printing, 1875.

Smith, Henry Nash. *Virgin Land: The American West as Symbol and Myth*. Cambridge, MA: Harvard University Press, 1950.

Smith, Joseph. *The Book of Mormon: Another Testament of Jesus Christ*. Salt Lake City: Church of Jesus Christ of Latter-day Saints, 1981.

Smith, Samuel Stanhope. *Essay on the Variety of Complexion and Figure in the Human Species*. Ed. Winthrop Jordan. Cambridge, MA: Belknap Press of Harvard University Press, 1965. http://dx.doi.org/10.4159/harvard.9780674866331.

Smith, Sherry L. *Reimagining Indians: Native Americans through Anglo Eyes, 1880–1940*. New York: Oxford University Press, 2000.

Snow, Lorenzo. *The Italian Mission*. London: W. Aubrey, 1851.

Solly, Samuel Edwin. *Manitou, Colorado, USA: Its Mineral Waters and Climate*. St. Louis: J. McKittrick, 1875.

Sparks, Jared. *The Life of Gouverneur Morris*, vol. 3. Boston: Gray and Bowen, 1832.

Sprague, Marshall. *Newport in the Rockies: The Life and Good Times of Colorado Springs*. Denver: Sage Books, 1961.

Stanton, William. *The Leopard's Spots: Scientific Attitudes toward Race in America, 1815–59*. Chicago: University of Chicago Press, 1960.

Starr, Kevin. *Americans and the California Dream*. New York: Oxford University Press, 1973.

Starr, Kevin. *Inventing the Dream: California through the Progressive Era.* New York: Oxford University Press, 1985.

Starr, Kevin. *Material Dreams: Southern California through the 1920s.* New York: Oxford University Press, 1990.

Stern, Alexandra. *Eugenic Nation: Faults and Frontiers of Better Breeding in Modern America.* Berkeley: University of California Press, 2005.

Stover, John F. *History of the Illinois Central Railroad.* New York: Macmillan, 1975.

Strom, Claire. *Profiting from the Plains: The Great Northern Railway and Corporate Development of the American West.* Seattle: University of Washington Press, 2003.

Takaki, Ronald T. *Iron Cages: Race and Culture in Nineteenth-Century America.* New York: Alfred A. Knopf, 1979.

Taylor, Bayard. *At Home and Abroad, a Sketch-book of Life, Scenery and Men.* New York: G. P. Putnam, 1860.

Taylor, Bayard. *Eldorado; or Adventures in the Path of Empire.* New York: G. P. Putnam's Sons, 1861.

Taylor, Quintard. *In Search of the Racial Frontier: African Americans in the American West, 1528–1990.* New York: W. W. Norton, 1998.

Taylor, Quintard. "Slaves and Free Men: Blacks in the Oregon Country, 1840–1860." *Oregon Historical Quarterly* 83, no. 2 (Summer 1982): 153–70.

Thompson, Mark. *American Character: The Curious Life of Charles Fletcher Lummis and the Rediscovery of the Southwest.* New York: Arcade, 2001.

Tocqueville, Alexis de. *Democracy in America,* vol. 1. Trans. Henry Reeve, corrected by Francis Bowen, edited by Phillips Bradley. New York: Vintage Books, 1990.

Tong, Benson. *Unsubmissive Women: Chinese Prostitutes in Nineteenth-Century San Francisco.* Norman: University of Oklahoma Press, 1994.

Trachenberg, Alan. *Shades of Hiawatha: Staging Indians, Making Americans, 1880–1930.* New York: Hill and Wang, 2004.

Trafzer, Clifford E., and Joel R. Hyer, eds. *Exterminate Them! Written Accounts of the Murder, Rape, and Enslavement of Native Americans during the California Goldrush, 1848–1868.* East Lansing: Michigan State University Press, 1999.

"Treaty between the United States of America and the French Republic." Yale University Avalon Project. http://avalon.law.yale.edu/19th_century/louis1.asp. Accessed July 12, 2012.

Trelease, Allen. *White Terror: The Ku Klux Klan Conspiracy and Southern Reconstruction.* New York: Harper and Row, 1971.

Turner, Frederick Jackson. "The Significance of the Frontier in American History." In *Rereading Frederick Jackson Turner,* ed. John Mack Faragher, 31–60. New York: Henry Holt, 1994.

Twain, Mark. *Roughing It.* New York: Harper and Row, 1962.

United States Congress. "Homestead Act." Yale University Avalon Project. http://avalon.law.yale.edu/19th_century/homestead_act.asp. Accessed July 28, 2015.

University of Virginia Library. "Historical Census Browser." http://mapserver.lib. virginia.edu/index.html. Accessed July 12, 2012.

Utley, Robert M. *High Noon in Lincoln: Violence on the Western Frontier.* Albuquerque: University of New Mexico Press, 1987.

Utley, Robert M. *The Indian Frontier of the American West, 1846–1900.* Albuquerque: University of New Mexico Press, 1984.

Utley, Robert M. *Lone Star Justice: The First Century of the Texas Rangers.* New York: Oxford University Press, 2002.

Valenčius, Conevery Bolton. *The Health of the Country: How American Settlers Understood Themselves and Their Land.* New York: Perseus Books Group, 2002.

Valenza, Janet Mace. *Taking the Waters: Springs, Spas, and Fountains of Youth.* Austin: University of Texas Press, 2000.

Warner, J. J., Benjamin Hayes, and Joseph Pomeroy Widney. *An Historical Sketch of Los Angeles County, California: From the Spanish Occupancy, by the Founding of the Mission San Gabriel Archangel, September 8, 1771, to July 4, 1876.* Los Angeles: Louis Lewin, 1876.

Webb, Walter Prescott. *Great Plains.* Lincoln: University of Nebraska Press, 1981.

Webb, Walter Prescott. *The Texas Rangers: A Century of Frontier Defense.* Boston: Houghton Mifflin, 1935.

Weber, David J., ed. *Foreigners in Their Native Land: Historical Roots of the Mexican-Americans.* Albuquerque: University of New Mexico Press, 1973.

Weber, David J., ed. *New Spain's Far Northern Frontier: Essays on Spain in the American West.* Albuquerque: University of New Mexico Press, 1979.

West, Elliott. *The Essential West: Collected Essays.* Norman: University of Oklahoma Press, 2012.

West, Elliott. *The Last Indian War.* New York: Oxford University Press, 2009.

White, Richard. "The Current Weirdness in the West." *Western Historical Quarterly* 28, no. 1 (Spring 1996): 4–16.

White, Richard. *It's Your Misfortune and None of My Own: A New History of the American West.* Norman: University of Oklahoma Press, 1991.

White-Parks, Annette. *Sui Sin Far/Edith Maude Eaton: A Literary Biography.* Urbana: University of Illinois Press, 1995.

Widney, Joseph P[omeroy]. *The Race Life of the Aryan Peoples,* vol. 2: *The New World.* New York: Funk and Wagnalls, 1907.

Williams, George H. "The Free State Letter of Judge George H. Williams." *Oregon Historical Quarterly* 9, no. 3 (September 1908): 254–73.

Wray, Matt. *Not Quite White: White Trash and the Boundaries of Whiteness.* Durham, NC: Duke University Press, 2006. http://dx.doi.org/10.1215/9780822388593.

Wrobel, David M. *Promised Lands: Promotion, Memory, and the Creation of the American West.* Lawrence: University Press of Kansas, 2002.

Wrobel, David M., and Patricia T. Long, eds. *Seeing and Being Seen: Tourism in the American West.* Lawrence: University Press of Kansas, 2001.

Wrobel, David M., and Michael C. Steiner, eds. *Many Wests: Place, Culture, and Regional Identity*. Lawrence: University Press of Kansas, 1997.

Xia, Yanwen. "The Sojourner Myth and Chinese Immigrants in the United States." PhD dissertation, Bowling Green State University, Bowling Green, OH, 1993.

Xu, Shi. "Images of the Chinese in the Rocky Mountain Region, 1855–1882." PhD dissertation, Brigham Young University, Provo, UT, 1996.

Zhu, Liping. *A Chinaman's Chance: The Chinese on the Rocky Mountain Mining Frontier*. Niwot: University Press of Colorado, 1997.

Zo, Kil Young. *Chinese Emigration into the United States, 1850–1880*. New York: Arno, 1978.